THE CLASSIC O

TRANSLATIONS FROM THE ASIAN CLASSICS

THE CLASSIC OF THE WAY AND VIRTUE

A New Translation of the Tao-te ching *of Laozi*
as Interpreted by Wang Bi

Translated by Richard John Lynn

COLUMBIA UNIVERSITY PRESS ▲ NEW YORK

Columbia University Press
Publishers Since 1893
New York   Chichester, West Sussex
Translation copyright © 1999 Columbia University Press

Library of Congress Cataloging-in-Publication Data

Lao-tzu.
[Tao te ching. English]
The classic of the way and virtue : a new translation of the Tao
-te ching of Laozi as interpreted by Wang Bi / translated by Richard
John Lynn.
p.   cm. — (Translations from the Asian classics)
Includes bibliographical references and index.
ISBN 0–231–10580–0 (cloth)—0–231–10581–9 (pbk.)

I. Wang, Bi, 226–249.   II. Lynn, Richard John.   III. Title.
IV. Title: New translation of the Tao-te ching of Laozi as
interpreted by Wang Bi.   V. Series.
BL1900.L26E5   1999
299'.51482—dc21   98–44394

⊚

Casebound editions of Columbia University Press books are printed
on permanent and durable acid-free paper.
Printed in the United States of America
c 10 9 8 7 6 5 4 3 2 1
p 10 9 8 7 6 5 4 3 2

CONTENTS

This classic Chinese work is best known to Western readers in its Wade-Giles transliteration, the *Tao-te ching of Lao-tzu*. In this book the translator refers to the Chinese author and text in contemporary pinyin as the *Daode jing of Laozi*.

THE CLASSIC OF THE WAY AND VIRTUE

THE WORK

The *Sayings of the Old Master* (*Laozi*), or *Classic of the Way and Virtue* (*Daode jing*), consists of eighty-one short aphoristic sections, that, though self-contained, often refer to each other and as a whole present a consistent and integrated view of how the sage rules the world in accordance with the spontaneous way of the Natural (*ziran zhi dao*). Although the text is traditionally attributed to Li Er, a keeper of the archives of the state of Chu in southeast China, whose style name or family/personal name (*zi*) was Dan and who was supposedly a contemporary of Confucius (551–479 B.C.E.), it is likely that it dates from sometime during the fourth century B.C.E. and should be regarded as of anonymous, probably composite authorship. The *Daode jing* might reflect a tradition of thought founded by someone called the "Old Master," who might have lived as early as the time of Confucius, and this "Old Master" might be identified with Li Er or Li Dan. But there is no proving any of this.[1]

The *Laozi*, or *Daode jing*, is one of the two foundation texts of Daoist philosophy in China, the other being the *Zhuangzi* (Sayings of Master Zhuang), which preserves the tradition of thought associated with Zhuang Zhou (369–286 B.C.E.). The two texts have a very different emphasis, however: whereas the *Laozi* is primarily addressed to the ruler who would be a sage-king and is mainly concerned with achieving the good society through harmony with nature, the *Zhuangzi* is contemptuous of rulership—in theory or practice—and indifferent to social life in general and instead focuses almost exclusively on personal self-realization and the quest for happiness through the individual's integration with nature.

Yet although the naturalist ethos of the *Laozi* seems originally designed to provide advice to the prince, its message was also recognized as having important implications for the cultivation of personal life, and people regarded its advice to rulers as analogously applicable to understanding and solving the problems of individual human existence. This approach, of course, characterizes the way the *Laozi* was usually read—as a philosophical text—throughout the traditional era in China and how readers in the premodern Chinese cultural sphere of East Asia (Japan, Korea, and Vietnam) largely interpreted it to find wisdom and solace. It also accounts for the popularity and fascination of the *Laozi* in the modern West. This nonpolitical reading of the *Laozi*, however, seems to have been influenced by the sustained popularity of the *Zhuangzi*, which is an explicit philosophical guide to personal understanding and self-cultivation; that is, the *Laozi*, regardless of its original intent, came to be interpreted as the *Zhuangzi* was designed to be read. This happened probably as early as the third or fourth century C.E., when the *Laozi*, the *Zhuangzi*, and the *Classic of Changes* (*Yijing*) began to provide the textual basis for the resurgence of interest in Daoism and the so-called learning of the mysterious (*xuanxue*) movement. In this respect, it is worth noting that although Wang Bi's (226–49) reading of the *Laozi*—the subject of this book—is explicitly political and public, much in his approach implies private, nonpolitical considerations, and what is only implicit in Wang's approach becomes explicit and predominant in many later commentaries.

Daoism exists in China in two radically different forms: as a philosophical tradition and as a religion. In the latter, Laozi was deified as a cosmic sage about the middle of the second century C.E. and made the patron of religious Daoism, and the *Daode jing* was subsequently interpreted as a primary doctrinal text and read in terms of such things as cosmology, myth, magic, retribution for good and evil, immortality, and personal salvation. The founding and growth of Daoism as a religion is a fascinating subject fully warranting the increasing attention accorded it in recent years and crucial for understanding the dynamics of much premodern and modern Chinese civilization. But it does not figure in this study and translation of the *Laozi*, which is interpreted from the point of view of Wang Bi's commentary, for Wang's approach is firmly positioned within the philosophical Daoist tradition, and I can find nothing of religious Daoism in it.[2]

From any perspective—as political treatise, inspirational guide of personal philosophy, or holy book of religious teachings—the *Laozi* is undoubtedly one of the most important texts in the Chinese tradition. It is a canonical work that has repaid repeated and different readings throughout the centuries in East Asia and now in the modern West. This book presents only one of many possible interpretations, but it is, thanks to Wang Bi's brilliant and influential commentary, an important reading of lasting significance that can speak to the modern age as it has spoken to the many ages since it was composed more than seventeen centuries ago.

WANG BI

Wang Bi lived at a time of great social and political uncertainty and military strife, marked by rebellion, usurpation, civil war, invasion, and desperate economic conditions. It was the beginning of that time of disunity in China between the great Han (206 B.C.E.–220 C.E.) and Tang (618–906) dynasties—initially, the period of the Three Kingdoms (220–65); later, the Six Dynasties Era or Southern and Northern Dynasties Era (317–589)—a disunity that lasted nearly four centuries. During its existence, the Wei (220–65) had to share the territory of the once-unified empire with two rivals: the later Han state (221–64) in Sichuan, which occupied the southwest, and the state of Wu (222–80), which controlled the southeast. Even within its own polity, the Wei was far from secure, and its quick rise to power was marked by an equally swift fall.

Wang Bi was not only in the middle of all this political and military turmoil, he was also right at the center of major intellectual trends that had been developing for at least the previous four or five generations. Both because of his own experiences and the earlier history of his family, Wang Bi was acutely aware that he lived in dangerous times, and it is quite possible to read his commentary to the *Laozi*, on one level at least, as a strategy for survival. For this reason, before considering his own life, it is useful to take a look at Wang's family and its place in the history of the late Han and early Wei eras.

During this period, the Wangs were a prominent gentry clan in Gaoping county, Shanyang commandery, Shandong, just south of present-day Jining city.[3] The first historically significant member was Wang Gong, who rose to be defender-in-chief (*taiwei*) of the empire and one of the three dukes (*sangong*), the highest ranks in officialdom, and became the popular leader of the anti-eunuch court faction during the reign of Emperor Shun (126–44).[4] A few years earlier, when serving as governor of Runan commandery in Henan, Wang Gong recruited for office two local talents, Huang Xian (75–122) and Chen Fan (d. 168). Huang soon died, but he and Chen were among the pioneers of the pure critiques (*qingyi*) movement, which involved the censure of court and government officials by popular (often provincial) opinion,[5] and Chen later went on to become defender-in-chief and one of the most important figures in government and politics of the late Han era.[6] Many of the leaders of the *qingyi* movement came from Runan and the neighboring Yingchuan commandery, so Wang Gong's close connection with Chen and Huang established links between the Wang clan's home district in Shanyang and this important intellectual center in Runan and Yingchuan, as well as with the larger *qingyi* movement itself, links that lasted into the Wei era and to Wang Bi's own day. Wang Gong's own son Wang Chang was closely associated during his career with Chen Fan and the *qingyi* movement and established a reputation for courage and incorruptibility, serving with distinction as governor of several provincial commanderies and ending as minister of works (*sikong*). He was also one of the three dukes.[7]

The next generation produced Wang Qian, the peak of whose modest career was to serve as chief secretary to He Jin (d. 189), defender-in-chief, staunch opponent of the palace eunuchs, and grandfather of He Yan (190–249), with whom Wang Bi was to be so closely associated. Wang Qian had one son, Wang Can (177–217), usually considered the best of the Jian'an *qizi* (seven masters of the Jian'an era), the prominent group of late Han poets who, as officials and literary figures, enjoyed the patronage of Cao Cao (155–220), the usurper of Han rule and father of Cao Pi (187–226), first emperor of the

Wei dynasty.[8] It is likely that Wang Can was born and grew up in Luoyang, apparently spending much of his childhood in the company of an older cousin, Wang Kai, the grandfather of Wang Bi. When the court was removed to Chang'an in 190, however, the Wangs moved with it. Two years later, when civil order broke down in Chang'an, Wang Can and Wang Kai fled to Xiangyang in Hubei, seeking the protection of Liu Biao (144–208), then governor and de facto ruler of Jingzhou, which comprised most of central, south, and southwest China. Liu was a fellow native of Gaoping in Shanyang and years before had been a political disciple of their grandfather, Wang Chang. (Eventually, Liu Biao considered Wang Can as a son-in-law, but he rejected him because of his small stature, his unprepossessing appearance, and his casual and familiar manner; instead, he married his daughter to Wang Kai, supposedly because of his handsome appearance. Liu's daughter was the mother of Wang Ye and so was Wang Bi's maternal grandmother.)

After some years had passed, and Wang Can had become an important fixture in scholarly circles in Jingzhou, Liu Biao, who had done much to promote classical learning and attract scholars, ordered him to make a record of scholarly activity in Jingzhou, which resulted in Wang's *Jingzhou wenxue ji guan zhi* (Record of classical learning in Jingzhou: An official account).[9] From this work and other sources, it appears that the school of Jingzhou scholarship favored simplicity and naturalness and overall represented a rejection of the elaborate but superficial and unfocused philology of the preceding era. It is very possible that Wang Can's participation in the Jingzhou school of learning later influenced Wang Bi, whose own approach to exegesis and scholarship generally exhibits similar characteristics.[10]

Just after Liu Biao died, Cao Cao marched on Xiangyang and rewarded Wang Can with high office for having persuaded Liu Cong, Liu Biao's heir, to capitulate. When Cao Cao returned north to Chang'an, Wang Can and Wang Kai, accompanied by their families (Wang Can had also married in the meantime and had two sons). Although Wang Kai does not appear to have held office after the return to Chang'an, Wang Can became a close personal adviser to Cao Cao, especially on literary and ritual matters, and was appointed a palace attendant (*shizhong*).

An odd twist to the family history took place in 219, about two years after Wang Can's death, when his two sons were implicated in Wei Feng's abortive revolt and were executed. Cao Cao, then absent on campaign, charged Cao Pi with investigating the revolt, giving him full authority to judge the ringleaders and accomplices. When he heard that Wang Can's sons had been executed, however, he is reported to have said: "If I had been there, I would not have inflicted loss of posterity on Zhongxuan [Wang Can]."[11] Later, after Cao Pi had become Emperor Wen, he decreed that Wang Ye, son of Wang Kai, would become Wang Can's legitimate heir, thereby allowing Wang Can, whose official and literary accomplishments and service to the Caos had far surpassed those of his cousin, to recover his posterity.[12]

That Wang Ye became the heir of Wang Can had important ramifications for his son Wang Bi. From 190 to 192, when the Wangs were living in Chang'an and before the flight to Xiangyang, the young teenager Wang Can had been enthusiastically accepted as a disciple of the leading classical scholar and literatus of the day, Cai Yong (132–92), who was so taken with him that he promised him his library of almost a "myriad scrolls"—a cliché signifying a stupendous number of books—a promise, apparently that was kept:

> Cai Yong had almost a myriad scrolls of books, which, sometime during his last years, he had loaded in several carts and delivered to Wang Can. After Wang Can died, Wei Feng, member of the staff of the counselor-in-chief, plotted revolt, and the two sons of Wang Can were implicated in the plot. Once they had been executed, the books that Cai Yong had given to Wang Can all went to Wang Ye.[13]

As Wang Ye's son, Wang Bi must have had access to this enormous library a generation later.

Wang Ye actually had two sons, both of whose family/personal names (style names) clearly allude to the fact that responsibility for the family tradition of Wang Can was transferred to them: the older, Wang Hong, was given the style name Zhengzong, "Main Upholder of the Succession," and Wang Bi, the younger, was given the style name Fusi, "Assistant to the Inheritance."[14] Wang Bi's public/official name (*ming*) also reflects this subordinate status: Bi means "assist," a sense derived from the original meaning of "bow frame," a frame to help bows to maintain their proper shape. Even their father, Wang Ye, had a style name loaded with family responsibility—Zhangxu, "Senior Keeper of the Family Heritage"—which he probably took after Emperor Wen decreed that he should become Wang Can's heir. Wang Bi must have grown up in a family tradition focused on and permeated with the literary, scholarly, and official accomplishments of Wang Can.

Neither Wang Ye nor his older son, Wang Hong, are known as thinkers or writers, and both seem to have spent their lives in the practical pursuit of official careers. Wang Ye served as a secretarial court gentleman (*shang shulang*), a subordinate position within the imperial secretariat concerned with drafting edicts and other court documents; this was probably his highest rank and achieved late in life. The only other information known about him is that for a time, probably in his younger years, he served as a supervisor of receptionists (*yezhe puye*), that is, a manager of court attendants, a far less prestigious office. His son, however, achieved much higher office, for Wang Hong was appointed (dates unknown) metropolitan commandant (*sili xiaowei*), with the duty of supervising the entire officialdom of the capital, a rank equivalent to that of the director of the imperial secretariat. Other than this, nothing else is known about him.[15]

Despite the gaps, enough is known of the high official status and prestige the Wang family enjoyed in Wang Bi's own time and earlier to provide a context for understanding the development of his exegetical and philosophical writings, both of which exhibit a strong political slant that must have derived from his first-hand knowledge of his family's involvement in the government and politics of the late Han– early Wei period. Wang Bi was surely influenced by the memory of his kinsman Wang Can, whom he came to know through his writings. As I noted above, Wang Bi's simple, direct, and naturalistic approach to scholarship and exegesis was probably shaped by his knowledge of Wang Can's participation in the Jingzhou school of learning two generations earlier, and it is also likely that his tendency to take a political approach to understanding the *Laozi* was also influenced directly by his familiarity with some of Wang Can's essays, for example, the *An shen lun* (Treatise on keeping one's person safe):

To honor virtue, nothing makes more of a contribution than keeping one's person safe. To keep one's person safe, nothing is greater than making government secure; to make government secure, nothing is more important than freedom from self-interest; to achieve freedom from self-interest, nothing is more significant than minimizing desire. Thus it is that the noble man only makes a move after making his person safe, speaks only after calming his heart/mind, and takes action only after making his friendships firm.

Since this is so, one's movements decide whether good fortune or bad begins; one's speech controls whether honor or disgrace results; one's search for friends defines the starting point of either benefit or disaster; one's actions decide the difference between security and danger. Therefore, the noble man never makes reckless moves by ensuring that he moves only in accordance with the Dao; he never speaks in vain by ensuring that he speaks only in terms of the true principles of things; he never seeks wrong friendships by ensuring that they develop out of righteousness; he never acts inconsequentially by ensuring that his actions spring from rectitude.

In this way, one can avoid any encounter with misfortune and be blessed by the aid of Heaven.

Thus it is that when one's person is not safe, it is in peril; when one's speech is not compliant, it will result in conflict; when one's friendships are not examined carefully, one will be misled; when one's actions are not sincere, they will result in danger. If one harbors these four failings within, calamity and misery will be there to meet him without. Such meeting with misery and calamity surely arises from selfishness and flourishes because of the desires one has. One caught up in selfishness will never be able to fulfill his self-interest, and one who has desires cannot ever be delivered from them. Such are the ultimate principles of existence.[16]

The year in which Wang Bi was born, 226, was the last year in the reign of Cao Pi, Emperor Wen, and his short life of twenty-three years coincides with the reign of the two following Wei emperors, Cao Rui, Emperor Ming (227–39), and Cao Fang,

Emperor Qi (240–49). These years saw the imperial Cao family quickly lose power to another clan, the Sima, which was packing both civil and military offices with its own members. The Sima, led by Sima Yi (179–251), eventually carried out its own usurpation of power in 249, the year of Wang's death, and it held de facto state power, with the Wei emperors mere puppets, until 265, when Sima Yan (236–90) became the first emperor of the Jin dynasty (265–420). Before this, from 240 to 249, the imperial clansman Cao Shuang dominated the government, and it was under him that Wang Bi served at court. Sima Yi murdered Cao Shuang in 249, when he ordered the execution of most of Cao's coterie. Wang Bi was certainly identified with this coterie, but apparently he was not close enough to Cao to be perceived as a political threat. Thus he escaped execution, only to die of disease later in the year.

The primary source for information on Wang Bi's life and place in Chinese history is a biographical notice written by He Shao, a prolific essayist on the people and events of his times and the son of He Zeng (199–278), a high official under both the Wei and early Jin (265–317) courts. This notice on Wang Bi was preserved in Pei Songzhi's (372–451) commentary to the *Weizhi* (Chronicles of the Wei; also called the *Weishu* [History of the Wei era]) section of the *Sanguozhi* (Chronicles of the Three Kingdoms), where it is appended to the biography of Zhong Hui (225–64).[17]

Here follows He Shao's biographical notice in its entirety:

Wang Bi revealed his intelligence and wisdom even when still a child. By the time he was only about ten years of age, he had already developed a liking for the *Laozi*, which he understood thoroughly and could discuss with ease. His father was Wang Ye, a secretarial court gentleman.

At the time when Pei Hui was serving as director of the ministry of personnel (*libu lang*),[18] Wang Bi, who then had not yet been "capped" [i.e., had not yet reached the age of maturity at twenty *sui*, or nineteen years], went to pay him a visit. As soon as Pei saw him, he knew that this was an extraordinary person, so he asked him, "Nothingness [*wu*] is, in truth, what the myriad things depend on for existence, yet the Sage [Confucius] was unwilling to talk about it, while

Master Lao expounded upon it endlessly. Why is that?" Wang Bi replied, "The Sage embodied nothingness, so he also knew that it could not be explained in words. Thus he did not talk about it. Master Lao, by contrast, operated on the level of being [*you*]. This is why he constantly discussed nothingness; he had to, for what he said about it always fell short."[19] Shortly after that he also came to the attention of Fu Gu [209–55].[20]

At this time, He Yan was president of the ministry of personnel [*libu shangshu*], and he too thought Wang Bi most remarkable. Sighing in admiration, he said, "As Zhongni [Confucius] put it, 'Those born after us shall be held in awe.'[21] It is with such a person as this that one can discuss the relationship between Heaven and Mankind!" During the Zhengshi era [240–49], the position of director of the chancellery [*huangmen shilang*] became vacant a succession of times, and He Yan had managed to fill it with Jia Chong [217–82], Pei Xiu [224–71], and Zhu Zheng; now he also proposed Wang Bi for that office. However, it was then that Ding Mi and He Yan were vying for power [within the Cao Shuang clique], and, when Ding recommended Wang Li of Gao District to Cao Shuang, Cao appointed him to that position, in consequence of which he made Wang Bi a court gentleman [*tailang*]. When Wang Bi first took up his post and paid his ceremonial visit to Cao Shuang, he asked for a private interview. Cao dismissed his entourage, and Wang Bi discussed the Dao with him for an exceedingly long time, not ever touching on anything else, which made Cao laugh at him [since he would not discuss government in any terms other that the Dao of *Laozi*].[22]

It was at this time that Cao Shuang monopolized political power at court and formed a clique whose members recommended each other for office. Wang Bi, unconventional and brilliant, did not concern himself with high office and reputation. Shortly afterward, when Wang Li suddenly died of illness, Cao Shuang appointed Wang Chen to take Wang Li's place, so Wang Bi never did manage to obtain a place among Cao's inner circle. This made He Yan sigh with regret. Not only was Wang Bi now limited to superficial duties at court, even before that, it had not been his forte to accomplish anything of merit, something to which he paid less and less attention.

Liu Tao, a native of Huainan, was good at discussing the science of political strategies and alliances, for which he had quite a reputation at the time, but on every occasion when he debated these matters with Wang Bi, he was always defeated by him. The talent with which he was endowed by Heaven made Wang Bi an outstanding figure, and what it allowed him to achieve, no one could ever seize from him.

By nature gentle and reasonable, Wang enjoyed parties and feasts, was well versed in the technical aspects of music, and excelled at pitching arrows into the pot.[23] In his discussion of the Dao, he may not have been as good as He Yan was at forcing language to yield up meaning, but, in his handling of the Natural [*ziran*], his unique insights often excelled anything He Yan could come up with.[24] To some extent, he used the advantages with which he was blessed to make fun of other people, so he often incurred the enmity of the scholars and officials of his day. Wang Bi was, however, good friends with Zhong Hui, who was an established expert in disputation, thanks to his well-trained mental discipline, but he was always vanquished by Wang's high-flying élan.

It was He Yan's opinion that the sage is free of pleasure, anger, sadness, or happiness, and his discussion of this issue was meticulously argued. People such as Zhong Hui transmitted what he had to say, but Wang Bi took a different position from them and thought that what makes the sage superior to people in general is his intelligence [*shenming*] and what makes him the same as people in general is his having the five emotions [happiness, anger, sadness, pleasure, and desire]. It is because his intelligence is superior that he can embody gentleness and amiability and, in so doing, identify with nothingness. It is because he is the same as other people in having the five emotions that he is unable to respond to things free from either sadness or pleasure. Nevertheless, the emotions of the sage are such that he may respond to things but without becoming attached to them. Nowadays, because the sage is considered free of such attachment, one immediately thinks it can be said that he no longer responds to things. How very often this error occurs!

When Wang Bi wrote his commentary to the *Classic of Changes*, Xun Rong, a native of Yingchuan, found fault with Wang's *Dayan yi* [Meaning of the Great Expansion],[25] to which Wang responded in the same vein, drafting a note that teased him:

> "Even though one may have intelligence sufficient to delve into the most profound and subtle things, such a person will still be unable to distance himself from the nature he has thanks to his natural endowment [*ziran zhi xing*]. Whatever capacity Master Yan had,[26] it was something already realized beforehand in Confucius, yet when Confucius met him, he could not but feel pleasure, and, when Confucius buried him, he could not but feel sadness. Moreover, we often belittle this Confucius, considering that he was someone who never succeeded at pursuing principle [*li*] via the path of the emotions [*qing*]. But nowadays we have come to understand that it is impossible to strip away the Natural. Your capacity, sir, is already fixed within your breast, yet here we are parted only about half a month or so, and you feel the pain of separation as much as all that! Thus we know, when we compare Confucius to Master Yan, that he could not have surpassed him by very much!"

Wang Bi wrote a commentary to the *Laozi*, for which he provided a *General Introduction* [*zhilue*][27] marked by clear reasoning and systematic organization. He also wrote a *General Discussion of the Dao* [*Dao luelun*] and a commentary to the *Changes*, both of which frequently exhibit lofty and beautiful language.[28] Wang Ji [ca. 240–ca. 285] of Taiyuan was prone to disparage the *Laozi* and the *Zhuangzi*, yet he once said, "When I saw Wang Bi's commentary to the *Laozi*, there was much that I became enlightened about!"[29]

However, Wang Bi was shallow in his personal relationships and obtuse concerning how others felt. At first, he was good friends with Wang Li and Xun Rong, yet when Wang Li stole his chance to be director of the chancellery, he came to hate him, and he did not manage to finish up with Xun Rong on good terms either.

In the tenth year of the Zhengshi era [249] Cao Shuang was deposed, in consequence of which Wang Bi was dis-

missed from service at court. In the autumn of that year he
fell prey to a pestilence and died, then twenty-three years of
age. He had no son, so his line stopped with him. Concerning
his death, when Prince Jing of the Jin dynasty [the posthu-
mous title of Sima Shi (208–55)] heard the news, he sighed
and moaned over it for days on end; regret at his passing
was felt as keenly as this by those of the intelligentsia![30]

The favorable reputation that Wang enjoyed in his own day
as a thinker, exegete, and writer continued throughout the era of
the learning of the mysterious movement (sometimes referred
to as "Neo-Daoism" in Western scholarship), with, of course,
notable exceptions, the most serious of which is probably the
diatribe against him, He Yan, and others associated with the *xuanxue* phenomenon by Fan Ning (339–401), who, though a Buddhist in private life, was a strict Confucian advocate of ethical
formalism (*mingjiao*) in public life. Fan did all he could to restore
Confucian ritual and ethical standards to political and social
behavior and blamed what he considered to be their degeneration
on the pernicious influence of people like Wang Bi. He regarded
the rampant nihilism and libertinism of his own day as the result
of the *xuanxue* movement, which he hated and, in its original
formulation, never understood. The fact is that he knew it only
in the notorious form advocated by its followers, who did not
really understand it either but who used it simply as rationaliza-
tion for licentious and libertine behavior.[31] Nevertheless, if Wang
were still alive, I am sure he would have regarded Fan Ning, the
arch-moralist, as the perfect incarnation of the "person of inferior virtue."[32]

A far more balanced and sympathetic view of Wang Bi can
be found in Liu Xie's (ca. 465–522) great work of literary theory
and criticism, the *Wenxin diaolong* (The literary mind carves
dragons),[33] which makes two references to Wang Bi:

When the Wei first became a hegemony, as the art of government conjoined the teachings of the school of names and
that of the legalists, Fu Gu and Wang Can examined and
assessed names and principles, but, by the Zhengshi era, an
earnest wish had arisen to conserve the literary heritage,
and, thanks to such figures as He Yan, discourses on the

mysterious (*xuan*) began to flourish. It was then that Dan [Laozi] and Zhou [Zhuangzi] so came to prevail that they even contended with Master Ni [Confucius] for supremacy! When we carefully read the *Caixing* [On talent and individual nature] by Lanshi [Fu Gu], the *Qu dai* [On ridding oneself of boastfulness] by Zhongxuan [Wang Can], the *Analysis of Music* [*Sheng wu aile lun* (On the nonemotional character of music] by Shuye [Ji Kang (223–62)], the *On Origin in Mystery* [*Benwu lun* (On origin in nothingness)] by Taichu [Xiahou Xuan (209–54)], the two *General Remarks* by Fusi [Wang Bi] [*Zhouyi lueli* (General remarks on the *Changes of the Zhou*) and *Laozi weizhi lilue* (General remarks on the subtle and profound meaning of the *Laozi*)], and the two *Discourses* [*Wuwei lun* (On nonpurposeful action] and *Wuming lun* (On the nameless)] by Pingshu [He Yan], we discover that all express independent views based on original insight and argue with precision and tight organization. There is no doubt that these are outstanding examples of discourses.[34]

As for the commentary, its composition is a discourse broken into fragments, and, although the odds and ends of text that result differ [from that of the integral discourse], when the commentary is considered as a whole, it turns out to be much the same. But such works as Qin Yanjun's [Qin Gong (first century B.C.E.)] commentary to the *Canon of Yao* [in the *Classic of History*], in more than one hundred thousand characters, and Zhu Pu's [first century B.C.E.] exegesis on the *Classic of History*, in three hundred thousand words, have been the reason why profoundly learned scholars become exasperated with the commentary and are ashamed to apply themselves to section and sentence exegesis. As for such works as Master Mao's [Mao Heng] exegesis on the *Classic of Poetry*, [Kong] Anguo's [second century B.C.E.] commentary to the *Classic of History*, Master Zheng's [Zheng Xuan (127–200)] exegeses on the [three] *Rites*, and Wang Bi's commentary to the *Classic of Changes*, all these are concise but thoroughly lucid—worthy models indeed for exegetical writing![35]

Therefore Wang was both praised and condemned during the Wei, Jin, and Six Dynasties era, the third through the sixth centuries. The following passage exemplifies the controversy surrounding him:

> During the Zhengshi era of the Wei, people such as He Yan and Wang Bi followed the teachings of Laozi and Zhuangzi, honoring them as their patriarchs. They founded a doctrine that taught that Heaven, Earth, and the myriad things all had as their fundamental principle [*ben*] nondeliberate or nonpurposeful action [*wuwei*]. As for the "nothingness" [*wu*] involved, from the start of things to the completion of affairs, there is no undertaking in which it is not present. The yin and yang forces rely on it to create things [*huasheng*]; the myriad things rely on it to complete their physical existence [*cheng xing*]; worthies rely on it to complete their virtue [*de*]; and the antisocial rely on it to spare themselves from harm [*mian shen*]. Thus it is that nothingness functions in such a way that it is valuable without ever being honored. Wang Yan [256–311] thought very highly of this teaching [based on "nothingness"], but, as for Pei Wei [267–300], he regarded it as wrong and wrote a treatise ridiculing it, which Wang Yan, however, disposed of as freely as he pleased.[36]

"Nothing" or "nothingness" (*wu*, sometimes given as a compound word, *wuwu* or *wuyou*, meaning "that which has no physical or specific existence, no 'somethingness'"), is a key concept in the thought of Wang Bi. By it, he seems to mean the perfect absence of conscious design, deliberate effort, prejudice, or predilection. The presence, on the other hand, of conscious design, deliberate effort, prejudice, or predilection is signified by *you*, which literally means "something" but also can mean "being," in the abstract sense of the word, as well as the phenomenal existence of creatures, including humankind, everything in the plant world, physical phenomena in general, and events both natural and human. Wang identifies nothingness with the action or function (*yong*) of the Dao or the Natural (*ziran*). The Dao always "acts out of nothing" (*wu yi wei*) and thus never functions deliberately or with conscious design; that is, it never "acts out of something" (*you yi wei*).³⁷ As the true sage embodies nothing-ness and is one with the Dao, he never makes a false or wrong move. In the thought of Wang Bi, *wuwei* never means "no action" or the "absence of action"—inertia, quietude, and the like—but always "no conscious/deliberate action." Wang reads all the sec-tions of the *Laozi* in terms of this basic truth: Nothingness is the principal attribute of all that is natural. To act out of nothing and thus in accord with the Dao inevitably results in success, safety, contentment, and happiness. Somethingness always involves differentiation (*fen*). In nature, the differentiation of all the myriad things and all the myriad phenomena occurs spontane-ously and without conscious design. "Being" is an appropriate translation of *you* in this context. However, somethingness is also the principal attribute of all that is artificial. When creatures, including humans, act out of something and thus in violation of the Dao, failure, danger, dissatisfaction, and misery inevitably result.³⁸

Much more could be said here about nothingness and all its implications for Wang's interpretation of the *Laozi* as a whole, but, as Wang himself is best at explaining how he read the Daoist classic, I suggest the reader turn to his *Laozi zhilue* (Outline Intro-duction to the Laozi), which immediately follows the Translator's Note at the end of this section.³⁹

Wang Bi's place in the later tradition of Chinese thought is a subject beyond the scope of this introduction, so such fascinat-ing questions as how his thought helped to serve as a filter for the initial introduction of Buddhist ideas into China during the third and fourth centuries, what exactly the Song era (960–1279) Neo-Confucians borrowed from his thought in formulating their own philosophy of principle (*li*), substance (*ti*), and function (*yong*), and why they were so opposed to his equating the Dao with nothingness, among a host of others, must wait for another time.⁴⁰

WORKS BY WANG BI

To conclude this account of the life of Wang Bi, it is appropriate to provide a brief discussion of works that Wang Bi is known to have authored.

1. *Zhouyi zhu* (Commentary to the *Zhouyi* [Changes of the Zhou]). Extant. Numerous editions. A modern critical edition is contained in Lou Yulie, ed. *Wang Bi ji jiaoshi* (Critical edition of the works of Wang Bi with explanatory notes). A complete annotated translation appears in Richard J. Lynn, *The Classic of Changes: A New Translation of the* I Ching *As Interpreted by Wang Bi*. New York: Columbia University Press, 1994.

2. *Zhouyi lueli* (General introduction to the *Changes of the Zhou*). Extant. A modern critical edition is contained in Lou, *Wang Bi ji jiaoshi*. It appears that this work was occasionally listed in some premodern bibliographies and reference works under two other different titles: *Yibian* (The *Changes* explained) and *Zhouyi qiongwei lun* (On disclosing all the subtle meaning of the *Changes of the Zhou*). No texts seem to have survived with these titles, however, and nothing is known about their contents, although they might be different in whole or part from the *Zhouyi lueli*, so it seems likely that such references are to the same work.[41] A complete annotated translation appears in Lynn, *The Classic of Changes*.

3. *Laozi Daodejing zhu* (Commentary on the *Classic of the Way and Virtue* of Laozi). Extant. A modern critical edition is contained in Lou, *Wang Bi ji jiaoshi*. A complete annotated translation appears below.[42]

4. *Laozi zhilue* (Outline Introduction to the *Laozi*). Extant. A modern critical edition is contained in Lou, *Wang Bi ji jiaoshi*. This work is titled *Laozi weizhi lilue* (General remarks on the subtle meaning of the *Laozi*) as it appears in the Daoist canon (*Daozang* No. 1245). It is also referred to as *Dao luelun* (General discussion of the Dao) or *Daode luegui* (Summary remarks on the *Way and Virtue*) in various premodern bibliographies and other reference works.[43] A complete annotated translation appears below.

5. *Zhouyi dayan lun* (Discussion of the "Great Expansion" in the *Changes of the Zhou*). Lost. This work is referred to as the *Dayan yi* (Meaning of the Great Expansion) in He Shao's biographical notice on Wang Bi. The *Jingji zhi* (Treatise on bibliography) in the *Jiu Tang shu* (Old history of the Tang era) lists a *Zhouyi dayan lun* in one section (*juan*); the

Yiwen zhi (Treatise on bibliography) in the *Xin Tang shu* (New history of the Tang era) lists a *Dayan lun* (Discussion of the Great Expansion) in three sections.[44]

6. *Lunyu shiyi* (Resolving problems in interpreting the *Analects*). Lost but partially reconstructed. The treatise on bibliography in the *Suishu* (History of the Sui era) lists a work of this title in three sections, but the treatises on bibliography in the *Jiu Tang shu* and *Xin Tang shu* list it as a work in two sections. It appears to have been lost during the Song era. Ma Guohan (1794–1857) gathered together forty items (*jie*) of this work, gleaned from quotations in other sources, and published them in his vast compendium, the *Yuhan shan fang jiishu* (Reconstruction of lost works done in the Mountain Retreat Where Jade is Harbored). A reprint of Ma's reconstruction is contained in Lou. *Wang Bi ji jiaoshi*.[45]

7. *Wang Bi ji* (Collected works of Wang Bi). Lost. According to treatises in dynastic histories, Wang's collected works in five sections existed up to the Song era; no description of their contents survives.[46]

TRANSLATOR'S NOTE

The arrangement and formatting of this translation follow my earlier translation of Wang Bi's commentary to the *Zhouyi* (*Changes* of the Zhou): *The Classic of Changes: A New Translation of the* I Ching *As Interpreted by Wang Bi* (New York: Columbia University Press, 1994), so this work forms a companion volume and constitutes further exploration of Wang's thought and contribution to the Chinese hermeneutic tradition.

Two works were instrumental in the preparation of this translation: Hatano Tarō, *Rōshi Dōtokukyō kenkyū* (Researches on the *Classic of the Way and Virtue* of Laozi), and Lou Yulie, *Wang Bi ji jiaoshi* (Critical edition of the works of Wang Bi with explanatory notes). The bulk of Hatano's work, written entirely in *kanbun* (classical Chinese), consists of an *Ō chū kōsei* (Critical edition of the Wang commentary) (pp. 35–484), which includes hundreds of interpretive comments gleaned from earlier Chinese and Japanese scholarship, both premodern and modern, and new notes authored by Hatano himself. This part of the *Rōshi Dōto-*

kukyō kenkyū is a corrected and expanded version of work done earlier entitled *"Rōshi Ō chū kōsei"* (Critical edition of Wang's commentary on the *Laoꝫi*). Although much of the *Laoꝫi Daodejing ꝫhu* (Commentary on Laozi's *Daodejing*) in Lou's *Wang Bi jijiaoshi*, including the collation, the establishment of the critical edition, and interpretive notes, is derived from Professor Hatano's *Rōshi Ō chū kōsei* (I estimate perhaps as much as nine-tenths), Lou does not always agree with Hatano's conclusions and sometimes comes up with alternate or additional interpretations of his own. Because these have often proved helpful, I have tended to cite both works when dealing with textual or interpretive problems. I have also benefited from the useful critical and annotated edition of Wang's *Laoꝫi ꝫhilue* (Outline Introduction to the *Laoꝫi*) that Lou provides in his *Wang Bi jijiaoshi*. The modern Japanese annotated translations of the *Laoꝫi* prepared by Ogawa Tamaki in his *Rōshi* and by Fukunaga Mitsuji in his *Rōshi* have both proved very helpful at times in understanding the original text of the *Laoꝫi*, as has Robert G. Henricks, *Lao-Tꝫu Te-Tao Ching: A New Translation Based on the Recently Discovered Ma-wang-tui Texts*.

When I first began work on the translation of the *Laoꝫi* and Wang's commentary, I often found myself amending the texts of both to accord with readings suggested by Tao Hongqing in his *Du ꝫhuꝫi ꝫhaji* (Reading notes on the philosophers). I soon realized, however, that Tao was doing far more than merely amending these texts; he was actually radically rewriting them to fit with his own understanding of them: he rewrote them so they would mean what he thought they meant. Both Hatano and Lou always cite Tao's readings and interpretations but sometimes reject them as superfluous or wrong, and, as this happened with enough frequency, I began to suspect almost all of Tao's suggested readings. I then went back and started again, throwing out all but a few of Tao's suggestions, determined to meddle with the texts as little as possible.

My translation largely follows the base text established by Lou Yulie for his critical edition of *Laoꝫi* and the Wang Bi commentary. Lou's base text follows the so-called Wang Bi version or Wang Bi recension of the *Laoꝫi*, which he amends throughout by reference to other editions, often repeating the work of Hatano Tarō. As is commonly known in scholarly circles, however, the

Wang Bi commentary to the *Laoʐi* is written in such a way that it obviously refers in many places to a text of the *Laoʐi* that must have differed significantly from the Wang Bi recension. Further complicating this already complicated situation is the fact that the two texts of *Laoʐi* recovered from the early second century B.C.E. tomb at Mawangdui are also significantly different in places from the text that Wang appears to have known. As Hatano and Lou cite most of these discrepancies and suggest amending the text of *Laoʐi* accordingly, when appropriate, I have included their findings in notes to problematic passages. It is by no means certain, however, which exact text of the *Laoʐi* Wang Bi knew. To help with establishing what that text might have been, I have also utilized two other excellent pieces of textual scholarship that deal with this problem: William G. Boltz, "The *Lao-tʐu* Text that Wang Pi and Ho-shang Kung Never Saw," and Rudolf G. Wagner, "The Wang Bi Recension of the *Laoʐi*." Much time and effort were spared by consulting Kitahara Mineki, *Rōshi Ō Hitsu chū sakuin* (Concordance to Wang Bi's commentary to *Laoʐi*).

Another work that has proved especially helpful—both in interpreting many individual passages of Wang's commentary and for developing my overall understanding of Wang Bi's thought—is Alan K. L. Chan, *Two Visions of the Way: A Study of the Wang Pi and the Ho-shang Kung Commentaries on the Lao-Tʐu*. Although I do not always come to the same conclusions as Dr. Chan, I have given careful consideration to the way he reads and explains the Wang Bi commentary, and I am sure my translation is the better for having done so.

Of course, I have also benefited greatly from reading and consulting a large number of other works, many of which are cited in the notes and annotations, and all of which are listed in the bibliography.

The reader should note that two previous translations of Wang Bi's commentary to the *Laoʐi* exist: Paul J. Lin, *A Translation of Lao Tʐu's* Tao Te Ching *and Wang Pi's* Commentary, and Ariane Rump and Wing-tsit Chan (who had translated the text of the *Laoʐi* earlier), *Commentary on the Lao Tʐu by Wang Pi*. I have not found either the Lin or the Rump translation helpful, so neither is cited in the notes and annotations.

My translation of institutional terms and official titles follows Charles O. Hucker, *A Dictionary of Official Titles in Imperial*

China, although I have lowercased most titles according to contemporary usage.

Finally, the reader should also be aware that two earlier translations of Wang's *Laozi zhilue* have appeared: appendix 2, "An Expository Outline of Lao Tzu's Subtle Meaning," in Chung-yue Chang, *The Metaphysics of Wang Pi (226–249)* 223–45, and Rudolf G. Wagner, "Wang Bi: The Structure of the Laozi's Pointers (*Laozi Weizhi Lilüe*)—A Philological Study and Translation." As Chang's and Wagner's translations differ significantly from each other in many places, mine also differs significantly from both of theirs. I have not argued these differences in my notes and annotations, wishing to spare the patience of reader and writer alike, but if the reader wishes to compare the three translations, all are now in the public sphere, and it could easily be done.

Wang Bi's commentary and Outline Introduction together constitute a long and difficult text. Despite all the help available from the Chinese and Japanese traditions of exegesis and textual criticism and from modern Western scholarship, and despite my best efforts to overcome my own shortcomings, I am sure that some old problems still remain unsolved, while fresh errors may have crept in to this new translation. In any event, this project has been an enriching experience, and I am grateful for all those difficult, splendid hours spent with Wang Bi and Laozi.

NOTES

1. A biographical notice on Li Er, which refers to him as Laozi and attributes the *Daodejing* to him, appears in Sima Qian's (ca. 145–85 B.C.E.) *Shiji* (Records of the Grand Historian); see *Shiji*, 63:2139–43. A translation of this notice, along with a discussion of the life of Laozi and his authorship of the Daodejing utilizing traditional sources as well as the views of modern scholars such as Gao Heng and Qian Mu, appears in W. Chan, *The Way of Lao Tzu*, 35–53.

2. Welch, *Taoism: The Parting of the Way*, first published in 1957, is still the best general introduction to the differences and affiliations between philosophical and religious Daoism. For greater historical detail and scope, see Maspero, *Taoism and Chinese Religion*. More recent studies by scholars of Chinese religions tend to subsume philosophical

Daoism into religious Daoism and downplay—if not reject—the fact that there existed an independent, nonreligious Daoist philosophical tradition. See, for example, Robinet, *Taoism: Growth of a Religion*, and Schipper, *The Taoist Body*.

3. A detailed account of the Wang clan, with a focus on Wang Can, Wang Bi's great-uncle, is presented in "The Life of Wang Ts'an," in Miao, *Early Medieval Chinese Poetry*, 36–123. Howard L. Goodman provides much of the same material *Exegetes and Exegeses of the Book of Changes in the Third Century A. D.*, 116–41, which Dr. Goodman says (p. 117 n. 31) is based on Professor Miao's *A Critical Study of the Life and Poetry of Wang Chung-hsüan* (Ph.D. diss., University of California, Berkeley, 1969), the forerunner of his later book. Finding both treatments unsatisfactory in places, I have consulted all the original sources again, helped in the process by Wang Xiaoyi, *Wang Bi pingzhuan* (Critical biography of Wang Bi), 166–92.

4. Wang Gong's biography is contained in the *HouHan shu* (History of the latter Han era), 56:1819–21.

5. For a succinct account of the *qingyi* movement and its subsequent influence on the development of the procedure for evaluating and ranking civil officials under the Wei dynasty, the so-called nine ranks and impartial evaluation (*jiupin zhongzheng*) system, see Hsiao, *A History of Chinese Political Thought*, 631–33.

6. Biographies of Huang Xian and Chen Fan are found in *HouHan shu*, 53:1744–45 and 66:2159–71, respectively.

7. Wang Chang's biography is found in *HouHan shu*, 56:1823–26.

8. See Miao, *Early Medieval Chinese Poetry*, and, for a brief historical and critical treatment, Jean-Pierre Diény, "Wang Ts'an," in Nienhauser, *The Indiana Companion to Traditional Chinese Literature*, 879–80.

9. *Quan HouHan wen*, 91:5b–6a (965A–65B).

10. See Wang Xiaoyi, *Wang Bi pingzhuan*, 175–183.

11. See the biography of Wang Can in *Weishu* (History of the Wei era), in Chen Shou, *Sanguo zhi* (Chronicles of the Three Kingdoms; hereafter referred to simply as *Sanguo zhi*), 21:599 n. 2, where the commentary of Pei Songzhi (372–451) quotes Cao Cao's statement as it appears in Zhi Yu's (late third century) *Wenzhang zhi* (Treatise on letters).

12. See Pei Songzhi's commentary to *Sanguo zhi*, 28:796 n. 1 (last paragraph), where Sun Sheng's (ca. 302–73) *Weishi chunqiu* (Spring and autumn annals of the Wei) is quoted: "Since Emperor Wen had

executed the two sons of Wang Can, he thus made Wang Ye the legitimate heir of Wang Can."

13. See Pei Songzhi's commentary to *Sanguo zhi*, 28:796 n. 1 (penultimate paragraph), where a passage from Zhang Hua's (232–300) *Bowu ji* (Record of erudition) is quoted. Not included in the bequest were books Cai Yong had given to his daughter Cai Yan (b. ca. 178), about which Cao Cao inquired after he had her ransomed and returned (probably in 206) from Central Asia, where she had lived as the wife of a chieftain of the Xiongnu after having been abducted from Chang'an during the turmoil of 192:

> Cao Cao took this opportunity to ask: "I have heard that in your family home there used to be many classical works. Are you still able to recall any from memory?" Wenji [Cai Yan] replied: "The more than four thousand scrolls that my late father gave to me are scattered hither and yon as dust and ashes; none have survived. Those that I can recite from memory number somewhat over four hundred works." Cao Cao then said: "I shall now assign ten clerks to you to write these down." Wenji replied: "I have heard that the separation of men and women is such that propriety forbids the personal exchange of items between them. I beg you to provide me with brush and ink so I can write them out in formal or cursive script to fulfill your command."
>
> Thereupon, she made copies and sent the texts to him, all of which were absolutely free of omission and error.
>
> (*HouHan shu*, 84:2801)

One wonders how Cai Yong's bequest of books to Wang Can survived the same period of trouble.

14. Wang Xiaoyi draws our attention to the significance of the style names of the two Wang brothers; see *Wang Bi pingzhuan*,168.

15. See Pei Songzhi's commentary to *Sanguo zhi*, 28:796 n. 1 (last paragraph), where Zhang Hua's (232–300) *Bowu ji* is quoted.

16. *Quan HouHan wen* (Complete prose of the Latter Han era), 91:4b–5a (964B–965A). Cf. Wang's commentary to section 7; section 41, fourth passage; section 38, paragraph 1; section 64, first passage; section 73; section 77, first passage; and section 81, fourth passage.

17. He Shao's biographical notice is also contained in Lou Yulie, *Wang Bi ji jiaoshi*, 2:639–44. Most of the information provided by the biography is also found in Liu Yiqing's (403–44) *Shishuo xinyu* (A new

account of tales of the world), where it is divided among a number of entries, often in passages worded differently. Liu's work also contains a few other details concerning Wang's life. See the biographical notice and index in Mather, *Shih-shuo hsin-yü*, pp. 593 and 722, respectively. When these passages add something new to He Shao's account, I have made references to them in the notes below.

Zhong Hui (225–264) was the editor of the *Siben Lun* (Treatise on the four basic relations between talent [*cai*] and human nature [*xing*]) and a strict Confucian who was opposed to the subversive (as seen by the Sima forces) Daoist-based pure conversation (*qingtan*) circle. He was an ally of the Sima party at the Wei court, but when the Sima usurped power in 264, Zhong attempted a countercoup against his own troops, which had joined the revolt, and was killed.

18. Pei Hui was the father of Pei Kai (237–291), who also rose to high office. Hui gained a reputation for his expertise in the *Laozi* and the *Classic of Changes*.

19. When Sun Fang (b. ca. 327) was a child, he was asked by Yu Liang (289–340) what his style name was. Sun replied that it was Qi-zhuang, "Equal Zhuang," which prompted Yu to inquire further, "Which Zhuang?" When Sun answered that it was Zhuang Zhou (Zhuangzi), Yu wondered why he did not wish to emulate Confucius instead. Sun replied: "Since the Sage was wise at birth [*shengzhi*], I could not possibly hope to emulate him," an answer that greatly pleased Yu Liang. See Liu Yiqing, *Shishuo xinyu*, A2:86, and cf. Mather, *Shih-shuo hsin-yü: A New Account of Tales of the World*, 54–55. A slightly different version of this episode appears in the brief biographical notice of Sun Fang appended to the biography of his father, Sun Sheng (ca. 302–73). There, Yu Liang is said to have praised Sun Fang's reply by referring to He Shao's biography of Wang Bi and saying: "Wang Fusi's reply was not any better than this!" See *Jin shu* (History of the Jin era), 82:2149.

20. Fu Gu was a member of He Yan's circle of friends dedicated to pure conversation [*qingtan*] who broke with He and joined the Sima party in 249, thus avoiding execution. He authored one of the essays in Zhong Hui's *Siben lun*.

21. *Lunyu* (Analects), 9:22. Cf. the following:

When Ho Yen [He Yan] was serving as president of the Board of Civil Office [240–49] he enjoyed both status and acclaim. Conver-sationalists of the time thronged the seats of his home. Wang Pi [Bi], who was then not yet twenty, also went to visit him. Since

Yen had heard of Pi's reputation, he culled some of the best arguments from past conversations and said to Pi, "These arguments
I consider to be the ultimate. Do you care to raise any objections?"
Pi then proceeded to raise objections, and after he was finished
the whole company considered that Yen had been defeated. Pi
then went on, himself acting as both "host" (*chu* [*zhu*]) and "guest"
(*k'o* [*ke*]) for several "bouts" (*fan*). In every case he was unequaled
by anyone else in the whole company.

(Mather, Shih-shuo hsin-yü, 95)

See Liu Yiqing, *Shishuo xinyu*, A4:151.

22. The translation of this passage here corrects the version given
in Lynn, *The Classic of Changes*, 11: ". . . long time, giving the impression
that no one could equal him in explaining any aspect of it—so Cao
jeered at him." I am grateful to Professor Donald Holzman, University
of Paris, for pointing out the error and for suggested the present version
(personal communication, March 16, 1998).

23. *Touhu* (pitch [arrows] into the pot) was an elegant game played
at formal or ritual feasts.

24. Cf. Sun Sheng's (ca. 302–73) *Weishi chunqiu* (Spring and autumn
annals of the Wei): "In his discussion of the Dao, Wang Bi's ability to
keep the beauty of language under control was inferior to that of He
Yen, but Wang's unique insights into the Natural outstripped anything
of He's." Sun's comment is quoted in Liu Jun's (462–521) commentary to Liu Yiqing, *Shishuo xinyu*, A4:152. For a somewhat different
translation, see Mather, *Shih-shuo hsin-yü*, 96.

25. Part of this work seems to have been incorporated into Han
Kangbo's commentary to the *Xici zhuan* (Commentary on the Appended
Phrases), Part One, of the *Changes of the Zhou* (Classic of Changes).
See *Zhouyi zhengyi* (Correct meaning of the *Changes of the Zhou*), 7:20–
21a; Lynn, *The Classic of Changes*, 60–61.

26. Master Yan, Yanzi (also called Yan Hui or Yan Yuan), was
supposedly the most virtuous of Confucius's disciples. See *Lunyu*
(Analects), 11:18.

27. This is translated and annotated in its entirety in the Outline
Introduction to the *Laozi*, below.

28. See Lynn, *The Classic of Changes*. A discussion of Wang's complete works, both lost and extant, follows this biography.

29. Cf.: "When Ho Yen's [He Yan's] commentary on the *Lao-tzu*
[*Laozi*] was barely completed, he went to visit Wang Pi [Bi]. After

observing how thorough and remarkable Wang's commentary was, he yielded to Wang's superiority, saying, 'With such a person one may discuss the frontier [relationship] between Heaven and Man!' For this reason he converted what he had commented on into two treatises, one on the Way (*tao* [*Dao*]), and one one the Power (*te* [*de*])" (Mather, *Shih-shuo hsin-yü*, 95). Cf. also "He Yen had been writing a commentary on the *Lao-tzu* and had not yet finished when he went to visit Wang Pi. Wang explained the gist of his own commentary on the *Lao-tzu*. Ho's ideas for the most part were inferior to Wang's, so he never got to make a sound, except only to answer, 'Quite so, quite so.' After that he did not go on with his commentary, but composed separate treatises on the Way (*tao* [*Dao*]) and the Power (*te* [*de*]) instead" (Mather, *Shih-shuo hsin-yü*, 97). See Liu Yiqing, *Shishuo xinyu*, A4:152 and 153.

30. See Pei Songzhi's commentary to *Sanguo zhi*, 28:795–96 n. 1.

31. Fan's diatribe is contained in his biography in *Jin shu* (History of the Jin era), 75:1984–85. For background, see Mather, "The Controversy over Conformity and Naturalness," 160–80.

32. See *Laozi*, section 38.

33. For an explanation of Liu's title, see Owen, *Readings in Chinese Literary Thought*, 185.

34. Liu Xie, *Wenxin diaolong*, 325.

35. Ibid.

36. This passage appears in the biography of Wang Yan in the *Jin shu*, 43:1236. Pei Wei's treatise was called *Chung you lun* (Treatise in praise of actuality/being). For a description and discussion of the feud between Wang Yan and Pei Wei, see Mather, *Shih-shuo hsin-yü*, 561 and 597, which give references to it in the text of the *Shishuo xinyu*, and idem, "The Controversy over Conformity and Naturalness," 160–80.

37. See Wang's commentary to section 38, paragraph 4.

38. Wang observes that animals also are subject to the dangers of acting out of something, that is, acting artificially. See his commentary to section 50, second passage, paragraph 2.

39. Although it should become immediately obvious when one begins to read it, I should note here that Wang's commentary is addressed, in the first place, to rulers, and it can be said that he regards the *Laozi* primarily as a treatise of political philosophy. By extension, of course, the truth of the *Laozi* applies to all.

40. I intend to bring out in the future a book-length study of the thought of Wang Bi and its contributions to Chinese thinking. In the meantime, the reader is directed to such works as Zücher, *The Buddhist*

Conquest of China, which discusses Wang's role in the transmission of Buddist concepts and terms in some detail in a dozen or more places and from various angles; W. Chan, "The Evolution of the Neo-Confucian Concept *Li* as Principle"; and A. Chan, *Two Visions of the Way*, especially 44, 52, 54, 65, 66, and 190.

41. See Wang Xiaoyi, *Wang Bi pingzhuan*, 382–83

42. For the transmission of the Wang Bi commentary on the *Laozi*, see Chan, *Two Visions of the Way*, 37–44.

43. See Wang Xiaoyi, *Wang Bi pingzhuan*, 380–82. Professor Wang also surveys the modern scholarship on the question of Wang's authorship of this work.

44. See Wang Xiaoyi, *Wang Bi pingzhuan*, 382, and Lynn, *The Classic of Changes*, 23 n. 9 and 72 n. 36.

45. See Wang Xiaoyi, *Wang Bi pingzhuan*, 384.

46. See ibid.

OUTLINE INTRODUCTION TO

THE *LAOZI* (*Laozi zhilue*)

by Wang Bi

1. The way things come into existence and efficacy [*gong*] comes about is that things arise from the formless [*wuxing*] and efficacy emanates from the nameless [*wuming*]. The formless and the nameless [the Dao] is the progenitor of the myriad things.[1] It is neither warm nor cool and makes neither the note *gong* nor the note *shang* [i.e., is not subject to the sense of touch or that of hearing]. You might listen for it, but it is impossible to get a sense of its sound; you might look for it, but it is impossible to get a sense of its appearance; you might try to understand what it is like, but it is impossible to get it in terms of understanding; or you might taste it, but it is impossible to get it in terms of flavor.[2] Thus try to conceive of it as a thing, and it will turn out to be amorphous and complete;[3] try to capture it as an image, and it will be utterly formless;[4] try to hear it as a tonality, and it will greet you as an inaudible sound; try to experience it as a flavor, and it will have an indistinguishable taste. Thus it is capable of serving as the progenitor and master of things in all their different categories, of covering and permeating everything in Heaven and Earth, so that nothing is allowed to escape the warp of its weave. If it were warm, it could not be cold; if it were the note *gong*, it could not be the note *shang*. If it had a form, it would necessarily possess the means of being distinguished from other things; if it made a sound, it would necessarily belong somewhere among other sounds.[5]

Thus an image that takes an actual form is not the great image;[6] a note that makes an actual sound is not the great note.[7] However, if the four [basic] images[8] did not take actual forms, the great image would have no way to manifest itself, and if the five notes did not make actual sounds, the great note would have no way to express itself. The four basic images take forms, but, because things are not subject entirely to them, the great image manifests itself. The five notes take sounds, but, because our human hearts/minds [musical tastes] are not restricted entirely to them, the great note expresses itself. Thus if one holds fast to the great image, the whole world will come to him,[9] and if one uses the great note, folkways and customs will undergo moral transformation. When the formless is manifested, the whole world comes, and this coming is impossible to explain. When the inaudible sound is expressed, folkways and customs undergo moral transformation, but this transformation is impossible to analyze. Heaven may have produced the five things [metal, wood, water, fire, earth], but it is nothingness [*wuwu*] that brings about their utility.[10] The Sage [Confucius] may have promulgated the five teachings [i.e., concerning the five human relationships], but it is those who do not speak who bring about moral transformation.[11] Therefore "the Dao that can be described in language is not the constant Dao; the name that can be given is not its constant name."[12] The mother of the five things is neither hot nor cold, neither soft nor hard. The mother of the five teachings is neither bright nor dark,[13] neither kind nor cruel.[14] Although the past and the present differ and folkways and customs change with time, this [the Dao] never changes. It is what the *Laozi* means when it says, "from antiquity until now, its name has never been revoked."[15]

If Heaven did not operate in this way, things could not come into existence, and if government did not operate this way, its efficacy could not occur. Thus, as the past and the present are interchangeable and endings and beginnings are identical, by holding fast to the Dao of old one can control what happens in the present, and by taking evidence from the present, one can understand how things were at the beginning of time [*gushi*].[16] This is what is meant by "constancy" [*chang*]. It has neither a bright nor a dark appearance, neither a warm nor a cool image, so "to understand constancy is called 'perspicacity' [*ming*]."[17] When a thing comes into existence or when efficacy occurs, it never happens but that it comes forth from this [the constancy of the Dao]. Thus "we use it [constancy] to convey what the father of everything is [*zhongfu*]."[18]

2. Even if you could hurry by running with the speed of lightning, it would still not be fast enough to get there and back in a single instant. Even if you could travel by riding the wind, it would still not be fast enough to arrive in a single breath. Being good at making quick progress lies in not hurrying, and being good at reaching goals lies in not forcing one's way.[19] Thus even the most replete [Dao], as long as it can still be expressed in words, would never have the capacity to govern Heaven and Earth, and the greatest thing that can possibly have form would never be large enough to house the myriad things.[20] This is why no sighing in admiration of it could ever completely express how beautiful it is, and no singing of its praises could ever tell how great is its size. Any name for it would fail to match what it is. Any comparison for it would fail to express all that it is. A name necessarily involves how one thing is distinct from other things, and a comparison necessarily involves how the tenor of one thing depends on the vehicle of another. Making distinctions, any name would fail to be inclusive; being dependent, any comparison would fall short of all that it is. As it cannot be perfectly inclusive, any name for it would deviate greatly from the truth; as it is cannot express all that it is, any comparison for it would fail to designate what it really is. This may be clarified by further elaboration.

The term "Dao" is derived from the fact that it is that on which the myriad things make their way. The term "mysterious" [*xuan*] is derived from the fact that it is that which emerges from the secret and the dark. The term "profound" [*shen*] is derived from the fact that you might try to plumb to the bottom of it but can never reach that far. The term "great" [*da*] is derived from the fact that you might try to fill it all in or pull it all together but can never ultimately do it.[21] The term *yuan* "far-reaching" is derived from the fact that it stretches on so far that you can never reach the end of it. The term "subtle" [*wei*] is derived from the fact that it is so elusive and inconspicuous that you can never see it. Because this is so, although each of the words "Dao," "mysterious," "deep," "great," "subtle," and "far-reaching" possesses something of its meaning, none of them can express all of what it is. Thus something that can never be entirely filled in or all pulled together certainly cannot be termed "tiny," and something that is so subtle and marvelous that it has no form certainly cannot be termed "great." This is why sections [of the *Laozi*] say such things as "So style it 'Dao' [Way]"[22] and "we refer to them ["origin" and "mother"] as mystery [*xuan*]"[23] but never give it a name. As such, those who speak of it do violence to its constancy; those who give it a name separate themselves from its authenticity; those who try to make deliberate use of it ruin its nature; and those who try to hold on tight to it lose contact with its source.[24] Thus, as the sage does not confuse words for it with its sovereignty, he does nothing in opposition to its constancy; as he does not confuse names for it with its constancy, he does not separate himself from its authenticity; as he does not try to make deliberate use of it to conduct affairs, he does not ruin its nature; as he does not hold on to it as a set of rules, he does not lose contact with its source.

Thus, as far as the text of the *Laozi* is concerned, those who try to explicate it though rational argument do violence to its intent, and those who blame it for misuse of names do violence to the concepts involved.[25] Thus it is that its fundamental goal is to discuss the source of the primordial beginning in order to clarify the nature of the Natural and to elaborate on the ultimate reaches of the secret and the dark in order to put an end to confusion arising from doubt and bewilderment. It [the text of the *Laozi*] responds [to the Dao] and does not act [initiate anything of its own],[26] effaces itself and does not assert,[27] venerates the roots and forgoes the branch tips,[28] and holds fast to the mother in order to preserve the child.[29] It disparages cleverness and craft,[30] for action should occur before the need arises.[31] It would have no blame placed on others but insists that it be found in oneself.[32] These are its essential features.

The Legalists [Fazhe], however, place high value on uniformity and would control the people through the use of punishment.[33] The Nominalists [Mingzhe] place high value on defining actuality [*zhen*] and would correct how they behave through the use of language.[34] The Confucians [Ruzhe] place high value on complete love [*quanai*] and would encourage them to practice it through the use of praise.[35] The Moists [Mozhe] place high value on frugality and would manage the people through the use of self-denial.[36] The Eclectics [Zazhe] place high value on the most attractive elements of these and would act on the people through the combined use of all of them. But if one tries to control people with punishments, cleverness and treachery will surely arise; if one tries to define with names how people should behave,[37] order [*li*] and consideration [*shu*] will surely be lost;[38] if one tries to encourage people [to practice "complete love"] through the use of praise, contention over who should be exalted will surely arise;[39] if one tries to manage the people with self-denial, contradictory behavior will surely ensue;[40] and if one tries to act by using eclectic elements, weedy disorder will surely prosper.[41] All these approaches consist of using the child while discarding the mother, which means that once the people lose their support [the mother], it [the child] is never up to protecting them.[42]

Although as a place can be the same when roads to it differ, so an ultimate congruence [of thought] can be achieved when approaches to it disagree,[43] students [of the *Laozi*] are confused about where it is going and baffled about the approach it takes. When they observe references to uniformity, they call it "Legalist"; when they detect references to defining actuality [*zhen* (authenticity)], they call it "nominalist"; when they discover references to complete love [*chunai*], they call it "Confucian"; when they find references to frugality, they call it "Moist"; and when they see a lack of affiliation, they call it "Eclectic." They adjust the name they apply to it in accordance with what they find and insist on interpreting it in terms of what they like. Therefore, if there are discussions of it marked by stupefying muddle or contention about it because of different analytical approaches, it all happens because of this. Also the text is composed in such a way that it verifies a beginning by fulfilling the conclusion to which it leads, and it fulfills a conclusion by establishing from where it begins.[44] It offers openings but does not go all the way; it leads but does not drag you there.[45] Only after searching for it can you arrive at what it means; only after pursuing inferences can you fully understand the principles involved. It starts its discussions by excellently revealing how things begin and concludes its arguments by lucidly showing how things converge. Therefore, if those who sympathize with its approach are moved to express themselves, none fail to praise how it serves as the starting point that inspires them to speak and, in doing so, elaborate on it. If those who differ with its aims write something original of their own, none fail to be pleased at evidence for a congruence of views and, as such, corroborate what they say in it. Although roads differ, they all bring one back to the same place, and, although there might be hundreds of ways to deliberate, there is an ultimate congruence in thought. Thus it is that it [the *Laozi*] cites the ultimate nature of such congruence to cast light on perfect principle [*zhili*].[46] Therefore let it be those who think in terms of corresponding analogies [*chulei*], and none will fail to take delight in the correspondences [*ying*] its thought makes and, as such, grasp the concepts [*yi*] they seek in it.[47]

3. That by which existence is preserved is actually the opposite of its phenomenal manifestation [*xing*] [i.e., nonexistence, ruin]. That by which one's efficacy [*gong*] is realized is actually the opposite of the reputation [*ming*] it involves [i.e., no reputation].[48] He who continues his existence does not regard existence as a matter of existence but as the result of not forgetting about ruin [*wang*]. He who is secure [*an*] does not regard security as a matter of security but as the result of not forgetting about danger [*wei*]. Thus he who regards his existence as safe comes to ruin, but he who does not forget about ruin continues to exist. He who regards his position as secure puts himself in danger, but he who does not forget about danger remains secure.[49] One may consider his strength excellent when all he does is lift an autumn hair or consider his hearing excellent when all he does is hear thunder, [but this is not true excellence]: this is how the Dao stands in opposition to phenomenal manifestation [*xing*].[50] The secure would substantiate their security, but it [the *Laozi*] says this would negate the way security becomes secure.[51] The existent would substantiate their existence, but it says this would negate the way existence maintains existence. Lords and princes would substantiate honor, but it says this would negate how honor becomes honor.[52] For Heaven and Earth, people would substantiate their greatness, but it says that this would negate the capability of that greatness.[53] For sagely merit, people would substantiate its existence, but it says that one should repudiate the establishment of sagehood.[54] For the virtue of benevolence, people would substantiate its existence, but it says one should do away with the existence of the virtue of benevolence.[55] Therefore let it be those whose vision is limited to physical manifestations and does not reach the Dao, and none will fail to feel anger at the words they find in it [the *Laozi*]. If one wishes to determine what the original substance [*ben*] of things is, although they might be near, he must verify where they start far away. If one wishes to cast light on

where things come from, although they might be perfectly obvious, he must trace their roots where they emerge out of the dark.
Thus it is that one takes from what is outside Heaven and Earth
[the Dao] to cast light on what is within phenomenal appearance
[*xinghai*] and to cast light on what it means for lords and princes
to be "the orphan" or "the widower."[56] It is by thus tracing things
back to the unity of the Dao that one makes clear where they all
begin. Therefore let it be those whose scrutiny is limited to the
nearby and does not reach the source from which all things flow,
and none will fail to regard its [the *Laozi*'s] words as absurd and
think there is nothing in them. This is why people talk on and on
about it, each one trying to explain what it means, and everybody
finding the confusion delightful. Some find its words utterly im-
practical, while others ridicule its arguments. That some seem
to understand it but are really in the dark or others appear to
bring order to it but really create confusion is all because of this.

4. To name [*ming*] is to determine [*ding*] objects [*bi*]. To
designate [*cheng*] is to follow what things are conventionally
called. A name arises from the object, but a designation issues
from the subjective [*wo*]. Therefore, if we set out on it as that
which absolutely nothing fails to follow, we call it the Dao [Way],
and, if we seek it as that from which absolutely no subtlety fails
to emerge, we call it mystery [*xuan*]. Subtleties emerge from
mystery, and all things follow the Dao. Thus that which "gives
them life and nurtures them," neither obstructing nor blocking,
and so allows all people to fulfill their natures is the Dao.[57] That
which "gives them life, yet possesses them not," "acts, yet does
not make them dependent," and "matures them, yet he is not
their steward" is the virtue of mystery.[58] "Mystery" is what we
name the utterly deep, and "Dao" [Way] is what we designate
the utterly great. The name arises from how it appears to us, and
the designation emerges from our setting out on it and seeking
from it. Names do not arise without reason, and designations do
not emerge without cause, so any name will always greatly fail
to capture what it really is, and no designation will ever exhaust
everything it really means. This is why when the text [of the
Laozi] mentions "mystery," it says that it is the "mystery upon
mystery,"[59] and when it designates the Dao, it says of it that
"within the realm of existence there are the four greats."[60]

5. As a book, the *Laozi* can almost be covered completely with a single phrase: Ah! It does nothing more than encourage growth at the branch tips by enhancing the roots.[61] [In other words,] observe where things come from, and follow them to where they inevitably return. In what one says, do not put the progenitor [the Dao] at a distance, and, in what one undertakes, do not neglect the sovereign [the Dao].[62] Although its text consists of five thousand words, there is a single unity that runs through all of them. Although the ideas [*yi*] in it range across a vast perspective, together they all are of the same kind. If one understands how the above single phrase covers it, nothing hidden in it will fail to yield to recognition. But if each matter is taken to involve a separate concept [*yi*], no matter how much argument there is about them, more and more confusion will result. Let us try to discuss this in these terms: How can the occurrence of depravity ever be attributed to what the depraved do? How can the occasion of licentiousness ever be attributed to what the licentious invent? Thus it is that the prevention of depravity depends on the preservation of sincerity[63] and not on the perfection of scrutiny,[64] and the cessation of licentiousness depends on eliminating superficial frivolity [*hua*][65] and not on the proliferation of laws and regulations.[66] The eradication of banditry depends on the elimination of desire and not on making punishment more severe,[67] and the cessation of litigation depends on the avoidance of exaltation[68] and not on the perfection of adjudication.[69] Therefore do not try to govern what the people do but encourage their disinclination to do anything depraved. Do not try to forbid their desires but encourage their disinclination to desire anything.[70] Plan for things while they are still in a premanifested state [*weizhao*] and act on them before they begin.[71] This is all one has to do. Therefore, instead of drying up one's sagehood and intelligence in the attempt to keep cleverness and treachery under control,[72] it would be better to display one's pristine simplicity and thereby still desire among the common folk.[73] Instead of promoting benevolence and righteousness to bring solidity to flimsy social customs, it would be better to embrace the uncarved block and thereby bring the practice of sincerity and honesty to all. Instead of increasing cleverness and sharpness in order to promote the availability of goods and services,

it would be better to minimize one's own personal desires and thereby bring an end to wrangling over the objects of frivolous appeal.[74] Therefore repudiate scrutiny, keep [the ruler's] perspicaciousness and intelligence hidden, eliminate recommendations and promotions, prune away decorative praise, cast aside clever contraptions [that make life easier], and denigrate precious goods.[75] Everything depends on arranging things so covetousness and desire will not arise among the common folk; it does not depend on keeping their practice of depravity under control. Thus it is that the ruler repudiates sagehood and intelligence by the display of pristine simplicity and gets rid of cleverness and sharpness by minimizing his own personal desires. All this is what is meant by encouraging growth at the branch tips by enhancing the roots.

6. However, if the Dao of pristine simplicity does not prevail and an endorsement for liking and desire is not suppressed, although one might exhaust one's sagely brightness in scrutiny of it and dry up one's intelligence and power of inference [*lü*] in how to control it, ever more refined will be the thought behind cleverness and ever more varied the shapes treachery will take. The more severe the attempts to control it, the more assiduous attempts at evasion will be.[76] Then the intelligent and the stupid will try to hoodwink one another, and those involved in the six human relations will treat each other with suspicion. Once the uncarved block fragments and authenticity is lost, all human affairs become permeated by villainy.[77]

If one neglects the roots and attacks the branch tips, although one might have the ultimate degree of sagehood and intelligence, the more he attacks them, the more he will invite such disaster to arrive. And how much more likely this will be if it is a ruler of merely inferior skills and devices![78] If one presses down on the people with pristine simplicity, they will regulate themselves without any conscious action taken against them,[79] but if one attacks them with sagehood and intelligence, the common folk will grow rich in cleverness as they become ever more impoverished. Therefore pristine simplicity may be embraced, but sagehood and intelligence may be discarded. As scrutiny is curtailed, attempts to evade it will also be curtailed, but as the brightness of one's intelligence dries up, ways to evade it will become ever more perceptive. Curtailment here results in minimizing harm to the uncarved block, but intensifying it results in ever more serious cleverness and treachery. Well, those who can employ skills and devices that extend discernment and discover secrets, they can only be the sage and the wise, can they not? Yet the harm that they have done, can one ever account for all of it? Therefore, "benefit a hundredfold" is no exaggeration.[80]

If one cannot distinguish among names [*ming*], it is impossible to discuss principles [*li*] with such a person. If one cannot determine how names apply, it is impossible to discuss actualities [*shi*] with him either. All names arise from forms [phenomenal manifestations, (*xing*)]; never has a form arisen from a name. Therefore, if there is this name, there must be this form, and, if there is this form, there must be its separation [*fen*] [from all other forms].[81] If "benevolence" [*ren*] cannot be called "sagehood" [*sheng*] or "intelligence" [*zhi*] called "benevolence," each must have its own actuality. Discernment of the most minute indicates the ultimate of perspicacity [*ming*]. Discovering what lies completely hidden indicates the ultimate power of inference [*lü*]. One who can extend perspicacity to the ultimate, can this be other than the sage? One who can extend the power of inference to the ultimate, can this be other than the wise? So, when we read the phrase "repudiate sagehood" in the light of this comparison of actualities and determination of names, can there be any doubt what it means?[82]

If the virtues of honesty and the uncarved block are not given prominence but the splendors of reputation and conduct are instead publicized and exalted, one will cultivate that which can exalt him in hope of the praise involved and cultivate that which can lead to it in the expectation of the material advantage involved. Because of hope for praise and expectation of material advantage, he will conduct himself with diligence, but the more splendid the praise, the more he will thrust sincerity away, and the greater his material advantage, the more contentious he will be inclined to be.[83] The heartfelt feelings that fathers, sons, older brothers, and younger brothers should have for one another will lose their authenticity. Obedience [*xiao*] will not be grounded in sincerity, and kindness [*ci*] will no longer be grounded in actuality.[84] All this is brought about by the publicizing of reputation and conduct. Worrying about how reputations soar as social customs become ever more flimsy, a ruler might try to promote the veneration of benevolence and righteousness, but the more he attempts this, the more extreme such falsehood will become. And how much more likely this will be if it is a ruler whose skills and devices are even inferior to this! Therefore to "repudiate benevolence and discard righteousness" in order to bring back filial piety and parental kindness would not be too sweeping a solution![85]

7. As city walls increase in height, siege machines grow taller. As material advantages soar, expectations deepen. If the ruler remained free of desire, although he rewarded them to do it, people would not steal,[86] but as his selfish desires express themselves, the power of cleverness and sharpness to muddle their hearts/minds ever increases. Therefore, if one repudiated cleverness, discarded sharpness, and, in place of them, encouraged minimal desire, the fact that thieves and robbers did not exist would not deserve any praise [i.e., it would be taken for granted].

Sagehood [*sheng*] and intelligence [*zhi*] designate the highest degree of human talent [*cai*]; benevolence [*ren*] and righteousness [*yi*] designate the greatest level of human behavior [*xing*]; and cleverness [*qiao*] and sharpness [*li*] designate the best of human resources [*yong*]. If one encourages these three beauties to flourish without preservation of the roots, harm will still occur in the same way as described above.[87] And how much worse this will be if, just because one's skills and devices are really sharp, one is inclined to treat pristine simplicity with neglect.[88]

Therefore a man of antiquity sighed and said: "Truly! What a difficult thing this is to understand! I knew that not being sagacious was not being sagacious, but I never knew that to be sagacious was not sagacious. I knew that not being benevolent was not being benevolent, but I never knew that being benevolent was not benevolent." However, thus it is that only after repudiating sagehood can the efficacy of sagehood be fully realized; only after discarding benevolence can the virtue of benevolence become really deep. To hate strength does not mean that one desires not to be strong but refers to how the conscious use of strength results in the negation of strength. To repudiate benevolence does not mean that one desires not to be benevolent but refers to how the conscious use of benevolence turns it into something false. Once one tries to govern deliberately, chaos ensues; once one deliberately tries to maintain his security, danger results.

Place oneself in the rear, and one will find himself in front. Finding oneself in front is not possible by trying to place oneself in front. Put aside one's person, and one's person will be preserved. Preservation of one's person cannot be done by trying to preserve one's person.[89] Efficacy [*gong*] cannot be had for the seizing, as praise [*mei*] cannot be had for the applying. Thus it is that one must do nothing except hold fast to the mother that provides efficacy [the Dao].[90] As a section [of the *Laozi*] says, "Once one knows the child," he must "hold on to the mother."[91] If one followed this principle, what venture would ever fail to achieve complete success!

NOTES

1. Cf. Wang's commentary to section 1, second passage.

2. Cf. section 14, first passage.

3. Cf. section 25, first passage.

4. Cf. section 41, penultimate passage.

5. Cf. section 41, thirteenth passage.

6. Cf. section 41, penultimate passage.

7. Cf. section 41, thirteenth passage.

8. Cf. *Xici zhuan* (Commentary on the Appended Phrases), Part One, of the *Changes of the Zhou* (Classic of Changes), which reads: "Therefore, in change there is the great ultimate. This is what generates the two modes [the yin and yang]. The two basic modes generate the four basic images, and the four basic images generate the eight trigrams" (Lynn, *The Classic of Changes*, 65–66). See also *Zhouyi zhengyi* (Correct meaning of the *Changes of the Zhou*), 7:28b– 29a. The four basic images consist of (1) two yang (unbroken) lines, (2) a yin (broken) and a yang line, (3) two yin lines, and (4) a yang and a yin line.

9. Cf. section 35, first passage.

10. Cf. section 11.

11. Cf. section 2, third passage.

12. Section 1, first passage.

13. Cf. section 14, second passage.

14. Cf. section 5, first passage.

15. Section 21, fifth passage.

16. Cf. section 14, last passage.

17. Section 16, fifth passage. See also section 16, sixth passage.

18. Section 21, penultimate passage.

19. Cf. *Xici zhuan* (Commentary on the Appended Phrases), Part One, of the *Changes of the Zhou* (Classic of Changes), which reads: "It is the numinous [*shen*] alone that thus allows one to make quick progress without hurrying and reach goals without forcing one's way" (Lynn, *The Classic of Changes*, 63). See *Zhouyi zhengyi*, 7:25b.

20. Cf. Wang's commentary to section 4, paragraph 4.

21. Cf. *Xici zhuan* (Commentary on the Appended Phrases), Part One, of the *Changes of the Zhou* (Classic of Changes), which reads: "And so it [the *Changes*] shows how one can fill in and pull together the Dao of Heaven and Earth" (Lynn, *The Classic of Changes*, 51; see also *Zhouyi zhengyi*, 7:9a); that is, as if patching fabric and pulling together seams, fill in the parts missing in one's understanding of the Dao.

22. Section 25, fifth passage.

23. Section 1, last passage.

24. Cf. section 29.

25. It is likely that Wang refers here to the *ming-shi* (name-actuality) problem that preoccupied many thinkers of the late Han and early Wei eras, when many were attacked for supposedly failing to ensure that the names they used matched the realities to which the names pointed or, in other words, for using "false" names. The most important figure concerned with the *ming-shi* problem at this time was Xu Gan (170–217), who died a little less than a decade before Wang Bi was born. For a detailed history and analysis of the name-actuality issue and Xu Gan's contributions, see Makeham, *Name and Actuality in Early Chinese Thought*. Wang, of course, is saying that those who try to fault the *Laozi* on such grounds are missing the point: because of its limited nature and limiting function, a name cannot ever designate ultimate reality—the Dao—in any of its aspects.

26. Cf. Wang's commentary to section 10, fifth passage.

27. "Efface" translate *sun* (diminish). Cf. Wang's commentary to section 42, paragraph 3, which reads: "The more one has, the farther removed he is, but being diminished (*sun*) gets him closer to it [the One]. When diminution goes as far as it can go, there its ultimate value [the One, the Dao] is obtained." That is, the text of the *Laozi* diminishes (effaces) itself to the utmost (makes absolutely no assertions of its own) and so gets as close as possible to the Dao. Lou Yulie declares that the text does not make sense as it stands, suggests that *sun* (diminish, efface) is wrongly written for *shun* (follow), and amends the text to read "fol-

lows and does not assert" (Lou, *Wang Bi ji jiaoshi*, 204 n. 40). This reading, however, simply repeats the same idea as the previous clause.

28. Cf. Wang's commentary to section 52, second passage.

29. Cf. section 51, first and second passages.

30. Cf. section 19, first passage.

31. Cf. section 64, especially the third passage.

32. Cf. section 79, third passage.

33. Cf. section 17, fourth passage, and section 27, fifth passage.

34. Cf. section 2, third passage. Makeham, *Name and Actuality in Early Chinese Thought*, is the best study of the early Chinese Nominalists in English.

35. *Quanai*, "complete love," should not be confused with the *jianai*, "universal love," of the *Mozi* (a heterogeneous text of the fourth–third centuries B.C.E.), despite their apparent similarity. Whereas *jianai* is love without discrimination—without reference to kinship or social relationship—the term *quanai*, "complete love," is probably best understood as *fanai*, "broad love," as it appears in the *Lunyu* (Analects), 1:6: "The Master said: A young man, when at home, should be obedient to his parents and, when abroad, should behave as a younger brother to others. He should be attentive and sincere, have broad love [*fanai*] for the common people, and develop close relationships with the benevolent [*ren*]. If he still has energy after doing these things, he should use it to improve his cultural knowledge." The basic meaning of *fan* in *fanai* is "flood," which does suggest a sense of disinterested generality. Nevertheless, although "complete" or "broad" love might indicate affection and caring for people in general, it does not replace or override the specific, differentiated love for one's parents, family, or peers. In any case, Wang's commentary to the *Laozi* states that such efforts are counterproductive and doomed to failure; cf. section 20, third passage, and section 70, first passage. Note also that the text soon refers again to "complete love" and does not use the term *quanai* but *chunai*; cf. the term *qunchuan*, "complete." Later, Han Yu (768–824), in his famous defense of Confucianism, *Yuan dao* (Tracing the origin of the Dao), uses a similar term, *boai*, "broad love": "Broad love is called benevolence [*ren*], the practice of which when suitably applied is called righteousness [*yi*]" (*Quan Tang wen* [Complete prose of the Tang era], 558:2501C).

36. "Self-denial" translates *jiao*. Cf. *Feiming* (Against fatalism), in *Mozi*, part 2, which reads: "They [the notorious evil rulers of antiquity]

did not deny themselves [*jiao*] the desires of eye and ear and so pursued the perversities of heart and thought" (*Mozi*, 9:254A).

37. Cf. section 18, second passage.

38. Cf. section 18, third passage.

39. Cf. section 3, first passage.

40. Cf. Wang's commentary to section 25, twelfth passage, which reads: "It is by taking his models from Earth that Man avoids acting contrary to Earth and so obtains perfect safety."

41. Cf. Wang's commentary to section 59, first passage.

42. Cf. Wang's commentary to section 20, last passage; section 38, paragraph 5; and section 52, second passage.

43. Cf. Wang's commentary to section 47, first passage.

44. That is, because arguments are carried through to correct conclusions, this proves that they started from correct assumptions, and, because they start from correct assumptions, they inevitably led to correct conclusions.

45. Zheng Xuan and Kong Yingda, *Liji zhushu* (Record of rites, with commentaries and subcommentary), 36:11b:

> Thus it is that the teaching of the noble man is metaphorical. It leads but does not drag, is strong but does not force, and starts you off but does not take you all the way. Because it leads but does not drag, you go along harmoniously. Because it is strong but does not force, you go along easily. Because starts you off but does not take you all the way, it makes you think. Anything that makes you think while in a state of harmony and ease can be said to be the best of all metaphors.

46. Cf. Wang's commentary to section 42, second passage, and section 47, first passage.

47. Cf. *Xici zhuan* (Commentary on the Appended Phrases), Part One, of the *Changes of the Zhou* (Classic of Changes), which reads: "With the eight trigrams, we have the small completions. These are drawn upon to create extensions [Their extension results in the sixty-four hexagrams (Han Kangbo's commentary).], and, as they are also expanded through the use of corresponding analogies [*chulei*], all the situations that can happen in the world are covered" (Lynn, *The Classic of Changes*, 61—62; see *Zhouyi zhengyi*, 7:22b–23a).

48. Cf. section 40, first passage.

49. Cf. section 64, first passage.

50. That is, whereas phenomenal manifestation [*xing*] is perceptible to all, its grasp requiring no "excellence," the Dao lies beyond phenomenal manifestation, is imperceptible, and can only be grasped in terms of the opposite of phenomenal manifestation, that is, its absence or negation. This is true "excellence" of perception. Cf. the passage *Xing* (Phenomenal manifestation) in the *Sunzi bingfa* (Master Sun's art of war) (fifth century B.C.E.):

> If, in foreseeing victory, one's knowledge does not exceed what the masses know, such "excellence" is not really excellence, and, when the battle actually results in victory and all under heaven call it "excellent," such "excellence" is not really excellence either. Thus it is that to lift an autumn hair does not attest to much strength; to see the sun or moon does not attest to keen eyesight; or to hear a clap of thunder does not attest to sharp hearing. Those in antiquity who excelled at warfare had neither reputation for wisdom nor acknowledged merit for bravery. This is why their victories in battle invariably occurred without variance. "Without variance" indicates that whatever they tried was sure to result in victory, for it was victory over the already defeated.
>
> (*Sunzi*, 4:416B–417B.)

51. "Substantiate" translates *shi*: to regard, name, and treat something as actual, definite, and "permanent"; that is, to regard *hsing*, phenomenal manifestations [*xing*], as if they were actualities [*shi*] that enjoyed real permanence and to depend on them and frame behavior in terms of them. John Makeham's summary of such distinctions is useful to keep in mind: whereas *xing* is "external shape," equivalent to *mao*, "visible features," and implies *wei*, the "false" or "artificial," and *wen*, "external pattern," *shi* is "inner substantiality," equivalent to *qing*, the "genuine" or "how things are in themselves," or *zhi*, "basic stuff." See Makeham, *Name and Actuality in Early Chinese Thought*, 8–9.

52. Cf. section 13.

53. Cf. Wang's commentary to the *Tuanzhuan* (Commentary on the Judgments) to Hexagram 24, *Fu* (Return), which reads:

> *Return* as such means "to revert to what is the original substance [*ben*]," and for Heaven and Earth we regard the original substance to be the mind/heart. Whenever activity ceases, tranquillity results, but tranquillity is not opposed to activity. Whenever speech ceases,

silence results, but silence is not opposed to speech. As this is so, then even though Heaven and Earth are so vast that they possess the myriad things in great abundance, which, activated by thunder and moved by the winds, keep undergoing countless numbers of transformations, yet the original substance of Heaven and Earth consists of perfectly quiescent nonbeing [*wu*, nothingness]. . . . If Heaven and Earth were to have had being [substance, actuality] instead for this heart/mind, then it never would have been possible for all the different categories of things to become endowed with existence.

(Lynn, *The Classic of Changes*, 286; see
Lou, *Wang Bi ji jiaoshi*, 336–37)

54. Cf. section 19, first passage.

55. Cf. section 19, first passage.

56. Cf. section 39, fourth passage.

57. Section 10, seventh and eighth passages.

58. Section 10, last passage.

59. Section 1, last passage.

60. Section 25, tenth passage.

61. Cf. Wang's commentary to section 57, first passage.

62. Cf. section 70, second passage.

63. Cf. *Wenyan* (Commentary on the Words of the Text) to Hexagram 1, *Qian* (Pure Yang) in the *Classic of Changes*, which reads: "The Master [Confucius] says: 'This refers to one who has a dragon's virtue and has achieved rectitude [*zheng*] and centrality [*zhong*, the Mean]. He is trustworthy in ordinary speech and prudent in ordinary conduct. He wards off depravity and preserves his sincerity' " (Lynn, *The Classic of Changes*, 133; see *Zhouyi zhengyi*, 1:12b).

64. Cf. Wang's commentary to section 49, fifth passage, paragraph 2; and section 58, second passage.

65. Cf. Wang's commentary to section 20, last passage.

66. Cf. section 57, fourth passage.

67. Cf. Wang's commentary to section 65, fifth passage.

68. Cf. section 3, first passage.

69. Cf. Wang's commentary to section 49, fifth passage, paragraph 3.

70. Cf. section 19.

71. Cf. section 64, first passage.

72. Cf. Wang's commentary to section 38, paragraph 11.

73. Cf. section 57, last passage.

74. Cf. section 19.

75. Cf. section 3.

76. Cf. Wang's commentary to section 38, paragraph 11.

77. Cf. section 18; and section 28, penultimate passage.

78. Cf. section 57, first passage.

79. Cf. section 37, third and fourth passages.

80. Cf. section 19, first passage, which reads: "Repudiate sagehood and discard wisdom, and the people would benefit a hundredfold."

81. Cf. Wang's commentary to section 25, fourth through sixth passages.

82. Cf. section 19, first passage.

83. Cf. section 44.

84. Cf. section 18, especially the last passage

85. Cf. section 19, first passage.

86. Cf. *Lunyu* (Analects), 12:18, which reads: "If you [as a ruler] were free of desire, although you rewarded them to do it, people would not steal." Cf. also section 3, first passage.

87. Cf. Wang's commentary to section 19.

88. Cf. section 63, third passage.

89. Cf. section 7.

90. Cf. Wang's commentary to section 28, fifth passage, and the first sentence of this essay, above.

91. Section 52, second passage.

L A O Z I

with the Commentary of Wang Bi

PART I

SECTION   I

The Dao that can be described in language is not the constant Dao; the name that can be given it is not its constant name.

> *The Dao that can be rendered in language and the name* [ming] *that can be given it point to a thing/matter* [shi] *or reproduce a form* [xing],[1] *neither of which is it in its constancy* [chang]. *This is why it can neither be rendered in language nor given a name.*

Nameless, it is the origin of the myriad things;[2] named, it is the mother of the myriad things.

> *Anything that exists originates in nothingness* [wu], *thus, before it has forms and when it is still nameless, it serves as the origin of the myriad things, and, once it has forms and is named, it grows them, rears them, ensures them their proper shapes, and matures them as their mother.[3] In other words, the Dao, by being itself formless and nameless, originates and brings the myriad things to completion. They are originated and completed in this way yet do not know how it happens. This is the mystery* [xuan] *beyond mystery.*

Therefore, always be without desire so as to see their subtlety.[4]

> *Subtlety* [miao] *is the absolute degree of minuteness. As the myriad things reach completion only after originating in minuteness, so they are born only after originating in nothingness. Thus always be without desire and remain empty, so that you can see the subtlety with which things originate.*

And always have desire so as to see their ends.

Jiao [usually "frontier" or "border"] here means the ends to which things revert. If anything that exists is to be of benefit [li], it must function out of nothing. Only when desire is rooted in such a way that it is in accord with the Dao will it prove beneficial [ji]. Thus always have such desire so that you can see those ends to which things finally arrive.

These two emerge together but have different names. Together, we refer to them as mystery: the mystery upon mystery and gateway of all subtleties.

The "two" are origin and mother. "Emerge together" means that they emerge together from mystery. They "have different names" because what these apply to cannot be the same. At the start, it [mystery] is referred to as "origin," and, at the end, it is referred to as "mother." Mystery is the dark, where in silence absolutely nothing exists. It is where origin and mother come from. We cannot treat it as something to be named. Thus the text cannot say, "Together, they have the same name: Mystery," but instead says, "Together, we refer to them as mystery." The reason it refers to them in this way is that there is no other way that they may be treated. Because it has to refer to them in this way, it could not just stop and restrict their meaning to the single word "mystery." If it had restricted their meaning to the single word "mystery," this name certainly would have been far off the mark. Thus the text says, "mystery upon mystery." All subtleties emerge from mystery. Thus the text says that it is "gateway of all subtleties."

NOTES

1. *Zhishi* (point to the thing) is the first of Xu Shen's (fl. ca. 100 A.D.) six graphic principles [of Chinese characters] (*liushu*): the simple ideogram. *Zaoxing* (reproduce the form/make a semblance of something) is probably a variant of *xiangxing* (image the form), Xu's second graphic principle: the simple pictogram. See Xu Shen, *Shuowen jiezi Duan zhu* (Explanations of simple and compound characters, with the commentary of Duan [Yucai]), 15A:3a–3b. Wang Bi here reminds his reader of the limited way language functions, too limited to capture the entirety of the Dao because it always has to refer to things in the specific. *Zaoxing* also occurs in the *Zhuangzi*: "Although your lordship

would practice benevolence and righteousness, it almost amounts to counterfeit versions of them! Their forms certainly may be reproduced [*ɹao xing*], but if you were successful, it would unquestionably provoke attack, and, once such abnormality occurred, foreign states would attack you without fai" (*Zhuangɹi yinde*, 65/24/21; cf. Watson, *Complete Works of Chuang Tɹu*, 264). Wang Bi probably had this passage in mind as well: not only is language limited to naming specific things, it consists of names that at best only approximate the real nature of specific things and, as such, are inevitably false or counterfeit.

   2. The base text reads "Nameless, it is the origin of Heaven and Earth," but Wang's commentary clearly refers to a text similar to that which occurs in the two Mawangdui versions of the *Laoɹi* (designated "A" and "B" in these notes), so I have altered it accordingly, following a suggestion by William G. Boltz, "The *Lao-tɹu* Text that Wang Pi and Ho-shang Kung Never Saw," 34–35. See also *Mawangdui Hanmu boshu* (Silk manuscripts from the Han tomb at Mawangdui), 114; and Wagner, "The Wang Bi Recension of the *Laoɹi*," 50.

   3. Cf. section 51, fourth passage.

   4. Wing-tsit Chan draws our attention to the fact that beginning with Song era commentators such as Wang Anshi (1021–86), Sima Guang (1019–86), Su Che (1039–1112), and Fan Yingyuan (1240–69), it has been the tradition to punctuate this and the following line in the *Laoɹi* differently, resulting in a very different reading: "Thus let there always be nothingness, so we may see their subtleties; let there always be existence, so we may see their ends" Cf. Chan, *The Way of Lao Tɹu*, 97 and 99 n. 5. Many modern annotators and translators of the *Laoɹi*, Chan among them, follows this later tradition.

SECTION   2

Once all under Heaven knew beauty as "beauty"; at that moment "ugliness" was already there. Once all knew goodness as "goodness"; at that moment "not good" was already there. Thus it is that presence and absence generate each other; difficulty and ease determine the sense of the other; long and short give proportion to the other; highs and lows are a matter of relative inclination; instrumental sounds and voice tones depend on one other for harmony; and before and after result from their relative places in a sequence.

The beautiful [mei] *is what induces pleasure in the human heart/ mind* [xin],[1] *and the ugly* [e] *is what brings aversion and disgust to it. To praise* [mei] *or censure* [e] *something is just the same as being delighted or angry with it. To regard something as good or not good is just the same as approving* [shi] *or disapproving* [fei] *of it. Delight and anger have the same root, and approval and disapproval come from the same gate, thus they cannot be used with bias* [pian]. *These six [existence or absence, difficulty or ease, long or short, instrumental sounds or voice tones, highs or lows, and before or after] are all terms that express what is natural* [ziran] *and cannot be used with bias.*

Therefore, the sage [*sheng*] tends to matters without conscious effort

That which by nature is already sufficient unto itself will only end in defeat if one applies conscious effort [wei] *to it.*[2]

And practices the teaching that is not expressed in words. The myriad folk model their behavior on him, yet he does not tell them to do so.[3] He gives them life, yet he possesses them not. He acts, yet they do not depend on him.[4]

Because such intelligence is complete in itself, conscious effort would result in falsehood.[5]

And he achieves success yet takes no pride in it.[6]

Because he acts in accordance with things, success is achieved though them, and this is why he takes no pride in it.

It is just because he is not proprietary that he does not lose it.

If he supposed that success depended on himself, such success could not last long.

NOTES

1. Premodern Chinese thought attributed both intellectual and emotional dimensions to *xin*; although the context often indicates which dimension is emphasized, I have chosen to use the composite term, "heart/mind" throughout instead of rendering *xin* sometimes as "heart" and sometimes as "mind."

2. Cf. Wang's commentary to section 20, first passage.

3. The base text (*diben*) reads *buci*, "does not tell them [to do so]," but it is possible that the text should read *fu*[*bu*]*shi*, "does not start [them

to do so]," as it occurs in the Mawangdui *Laoẓi* B text, or *buwei shi*, "does not serve as a starting point for them," which appears both in the Fu Yi composite edition and in a quotation from the *Laoẓi* in Wang's commentary to section 17, first passage. See also Wagner, "The Wang Bi Recension of the *Laoẓi*," 50. For other variants see Hatano, *Rōshi Dōtokukyō kenkyū*, 48; see also *Mawangdui Hanmu boshu* (Silk manuscripts from the Han tomb at Mawangdui), 114. *Buci*, "does not tell [them to do so]," also occurs in the base text instead of *bushi*, "does not start [them to do so]," in section 34, second passage, in a line similar to the one here, but this line does not occur in the Mawangdui texts. See *Mawangdui Hanmu boshu*, 123.

4. Cf. section 10, last passage; section 51, fifth passage; and section 77, second passage.

5. Hatano Tarō cites a marginal note to this passage made by the Edo era *kangakusha* (scholar of classical Chinese studies) Momoi Hakuroku (1722–1801), in which Momoi draws attention to the similar structure of this and the previous sentence in Wang's commentary and suggests that the *wei* (conscious effort) in the second sentence is redundant, probably a scribal error for *yan* (speech) and that the passage should read "speech would result in falsehood." See *Rōshi Dōtokukyō kenkyū*, 49, which is quoted, without attribution to Momoi, in Lou, *Wang Bi ji jiaoshi* (Critical edition of the works of Wang Bi with explanatory notes), 1:7 n. 6.

6. Cf. section 77, second passage.

SECTION   3

Do not exalt the worthy [*xian*], and so keep the common folk from contention. Do not value goods hard to get, and so stop the common folk from becoming thieves. Do not let them see desirable things, and so spare the hearts/minds of the common folk from disorder.[1]

"The worthy" [xian] *is like saying "the resourceful"* [neng]. *"Exalt" is a name by which we recogniẓe excellence, and "value" is a term for assigning high worth. If only the resourceful were given office, what would be the point of exalting them? If things were used only because they were useful, what would be the point of valuing them? However, because we exalt the*

worthy and make their names illustrious, giving more honor than their offices deserve, people act as if they are always in shooting contests, trying to determine who is the more able, and, because we put more value on goods than their use warrants, those who covet such things compete to rush after them, even digging through or climbing over walls[2] to ransack chests,[3] risking their lives in thievery. Therefore, if desirable things are not seen, hearts/minds will not be subject to such disorder.

Therefore the way the sage governs is to keep their hearts/minds empty and their bellies full.

The heart/mind cherish knowledge and the belly cherishes food, so he keeps that which has the capacity for knowledge empty and that which lacks the capacity for knowing filled.

He keeps their wills weak and their bones strong.

Their bones, lacking the capacity for knowing, provide the means for them to stand trunklike; their wills, prone to stir things up, are the agents of disorder. (If the heart/mind is empty, the will is weak.)[4]

He always keeps the common folk free from the capacity for knowing and from feeling desire.

He preserves their authenticity [zhen].

And prevents the knowledgeable from ever daring to act.

The knowledgeable [zhi] refers to those who know how to act.

Because he acts without conscious effort, nothing remains ungoverned.

NOTES

1. Cf. section 12, second passage; section 27, fifth passage; section 49, fifth passage, paragraph 1; and section 64, seventh passage.

2. Cf. *Lunyu* (Analects), 17:12.

3. Cf. *Zhuangzi yinde*, 23/10/1.

4. Although many editions of Wang's commentary include the sentence in parentheses, it actually is an interpolation from Lu Deming's (556–627) gloss on this passage in his *Laozi yinyi* (Pronunciation and meaning of terms in the *Laozi*), included in the *Jingdian shiwen* (Explication of the texts of the classics), 25:1404. See Hatano, *Rōshi Dōtokukyō kenkyū*, 54, and Lou, *Wang Bi ji jiaoshi*, 10 n. 8.

SECTION 4

The vessel of the Dao is empty, so use it but do not try to refill it.[1] It is such an abyss, oh, that it appears to be the progenitor of the myriad things. It blunts the sharp, cuts away the tangled, merges with the brilliant, and becomes one with the very dust.[2] Its depth is so deep, oh, that it seems somehow to exist. I do not know whose child it could be, for it appears to have been born before the Lord.

1. Adhering strictly to the measures of one noble household cannot keep that household whole, and adhering strictly to the measures of one state cannot keep that state intact. Even if one were to use up all his strength in lifting heavy burdens, it could not be of any use.[3] Therefore, although one might know about government as it applies to the myriad folk, if he governs without regard to the Dao with its two modes [the yin and the yang],[4] he cannot serve to support them.

2. Although Earth consists of physical forms with their earthbound souls,[5] if it did not takes its models from Heaven, it could not keep its quietude intact. Although Heaven consists of embryonic essences with their images,[6] if it did not takes its models from the Dao, it could not preserve its purity.[7] Used as an empty vessel, its [the Dao's] use is inexhaustible, but if one tries to fill it in order to make it into something full [shi], *if any filling is brought to it, it just overflows. Thus "the vessel of the Dao is empty, so use it but do not again try to refill it," for what makes it inexhaustible already fills it completely![8]*

3. No matter how vast a physical form [xing], *nothing could hamper its [the Dao's] power to embody* [ti]. *No matter how great an undertaking* [shi], *nothing could utilize its entire capacity* [liang]. *If the myriad things were to abandon it and seek a different master, where would such a master be found? Indeed, is it not true that "it is such an abyss, oh, that it appears to be the progenitor of the myriad things"? It blunts the sharp but suffers no damage; it cuts away the tangled but is not worn out; it merges with the brilliant but does not soil its power to embody* [ti]; *it becomes one with the very dust but does not compromise* [yu] *its authenticity* [zhen].[9] *Indeed, is it not true that "its depth is so deep, oh, that it seems somehow to exist"?*

4. As Earth must keep its physical forms [xing], *its virtue* [de] *cannot exceed what it upholds, and, as Heaven must remain content with its images* [xiang], *its virtue cannot exceed what it covers. Thus neither Heaven nor Earth can equal it [the Dao]. Indeed, is it not true that "it appears to have been born before the Lord"? "The Lord" [Di] means the Lord of Heaven [Tiandi].*

NOTES

1. "Do not try to refill it" translates *you buying*, but the base text reads *huo buying*, "it might not [need] again be filled." Wang's commentary indicates that he knew the text as it appears in Mawangdui B or Fu Yi's composite edition. See *Mawangdui Hanmu boshu*, 114. See also Wagner, "The Wang Bi Recension of the *Laozi*," 50. Cf. section 45, second passage

2. Cf. section 56, third through sixth passages, and Wang's commentary to section 77, second passage.

3. This alludes to one of the devices that the Chen family used to gain popular support and usurp power from the Jiang family in the ancient state of Qi: "Yanzi [Master Yan] said, 'This is Qi's last age. I may know nothing, but Qi will belong to the Chen family. The duke abandons the common folk, and they find a new home with the Chen family. Qi for a long time has had four measures, *dou, ou, fu,* and *zhong. . . .* Ten *fu* equal one *zhong*. The Chen family doubles the size of the first three, so its *zhong* is very large. They lend in family measures but take returns in the state's measures'" (Third year in the reign of Duke Zhao [538 B.C.E.] in Kong, *Chunqiu Zuozhuan zhengyi* [Correct meaning of *Zuo's Commentary* on the *Spring and Autumn Annals*], 42:9b–10a; cf. Legge, *The Chinese Classics*, 5:589). By manipulating the size of measures, commodities from Chen lands were sold or loaned to the rest of Qi at large discounts, a surefire way to win sympathy and popular support, especially given that the Qi state was imposing heavy taxes and a harsh criminal code: "It was thus natural that the Ch'en [Chen] family gradually overcame the other noble families and finally took control of the entire state" (Hsu, *Ancient China in Transition*, 91). All human measurements are arbitrary, artificial, and subject to manipulation and abuse. No such measurements can apply to the Dao.

4. Cf. *Xici zhuan* (Commentary on the Appended Phrases), Part One, in the the *Yijing* (Classic of changes), sections 5 and 11 of which read in part:

> The reciprocal process of yin and yang is called the Dao. . . .
>
> Therefore, in change [*yi*] there is the great ultimate [*taiji*]. This is what generates the two modes [*liangyi*: the yin and yang]. The two basic modes generate the four basic images [*sixiang*: yang + yang, yin + yang, yin + yin, yang + yin], and the four basic images generate the eight trigrams [*bagua*] [by adding first one yang (unbroken line) to each, then one yin (broken line)]. The eight trigrams determine good fortune and misfortune, and good fortune and misfortune generate the great enterprise [*daye*].
>
> Therefore, of things that serve as models for images, none are greater than Heaven and Earth.
>
> (Lynn, *The Classic of Changes*, 53 and 65–66;
> see *Zhouyi zhengyi* [Correct meaning of the
> *Changes of the Zhou*], 7:11a and 7:28b–29a)

5. Cf. *Liji zhushu* (Record of rites, with commentary and subcommentary), 26:21b, which reads: "Ethereal spirits with their pneumas [*hunqi*] are drawn to Heaven, and physical forms with their earthbound souls (*xingpo*) are drawn to Earth."

6. "Embryonic essences and images" translates *jingxiang*, stars and images ("counterparts" or "simulacra" that stars form either singly or in constellations). See Schafer, *Pacing the Void*, 42–44 and 55–56.

7. It has been argued that "purity" (*jing*) is a textual error for "clarity" (*qing*); see Lou, *Wang Bi ji jiaoshi*, 1:12 n. 7. This seems a needless emendation, however, because purity is a well-attested attribute of Heaven, as in, for example, the following description of *Qian*, the power and action of Heaven, which appears in the *Wenyan* (Commentary on the words of the text) to Hexagram 1, *Qian* (Pure Yang) in the *Yijing* (Classic of changes): "The power in *Qian* to provide origins is such that it can make all under Heaven fit by means of its own beautiful fitness. One does not say how it confers fitness; it is just great! How great *Qian* is! It is strong, dynamic, central, correct, and it is absolutely pure [*jing*] in its unadulteratedness and unsulliedness" (Lynn, *The Classic of Changes*, 130; see *Zhouyi zhengyi* [Correct meaning of the *Changes of the Zhou*], 1:17b–18a).

8. That is, even though infinite, the capacity of the empty vessel of the Dao is already "filled" with emptiness, so no room exists in it for anything else. Cf. Wang's commentary to section 45, second passage.

9. Cf. section 41, ninth passage; and Wang's commentary to section 70, last passage.

SECTION 5

Heaven and Earth are not benevolent and treat the myriad things as straw dogs

> *Heaven and Earth allow things to follow their natural bent and neither engage in conscious effort nor start anything, leaving the myriad things to manage themselves. Thus they "are not benevolent." The benevolent* [ren] *have to establish institutions and influence behavior, for they are prone to use kindness and make conscious effort. But when institutions are established and behavior influenced, people lose their authenticity, and when subject to kindness and conscious effort, they no longer preserve their integrity. If people do not preserve their integrity, they no longer have the capacity to uphold the full weight of their existence. Heaven and Earth do not make the grass grow for the sake of beasts, yet beasts eat grass. They do not produce dogs for the sake of men, yet men eat dogs. Heaven and Earth take no conscious effort with respect to the myriad things, yet because each of the myriad things has what is appropriate for its use, not one thing is denied support. As long as you use kindness derived from a personal perspective, it indicates a lack of capacity to leave things to themselves.*

The sage is not benevolent and treats the common folk as straw dogs.

> *Because the sage makes his virtue conform to that of Heaven and Earth,*[1] *he likens the common folk to straw dogs.*[2]

The space between Heaven and Earth, is it not just like a bellows or a mouth organ! Empty, it can never be used up. Active, it produces all the more.

> *Tuo [open-ended sack] here means a* paituo *[bellows], and* yue *[pipe] means a* yueyue *[mouth organ].*[3] *The interior of a*

bellows or a mouth organ is completely empty and free of both innate tendencies [qing] and deliberate action [wei]. Thus, though empty, it can never be used up, and, when it is in action, it is impossible to exhaust its strength. The space between Heaven and Earth just lets things follow their natural bents without the least stricture, thus it can never be used up, just as with the bellows or the mouth organ.

Many words lead to quick exhaustion; better to maintain emptiness within.

The more you apply conscious effort to something, the more you will fail. If you set up a policy of kindness toward your people and establish words for dealing with matters, without kindness you will have no way to provide relief [ji] and without words you will have no way to establish order. All of which is sure to result in quick exhaustion. As with the mouth organ, maintain emptiness within, and exhaustion will never happen; take yourself out of it and leave things to themselves, and nothing will ever lack order. If the mouth organ itself intentionally tried to make sounds, it would no longer have the capacity to provide the player with what he needs.

NOTES

1. "Conform" translates *he*. Qian Zhongshu glosses *yu tiandihe qi de* (makes his virtue conform to that of Heaven and Earth) as *shifa tiandi* (emulates Heaven and Earth). See Qian, *Guanzhui bian* (The pipe-awl collection), 3:420. Cf. Wang's commentary to section 16, eleventh passage; and section 77, first passage.

2. The prominent historian and geographer Wei Yuan (1794–1856) also did a commentary to the *Laozi*, in which he addresses the significance of "straw dogs" (*chugou*): "People bound grass together to make dogs and used them as sacrificial offerings, but when they had concluded the ritual, they cast them aside and trampled on them" (Wei, *Laozi benyi* [Original meaning of the *Laozi*], A:6).

3. Although most commentators interpret *tuoyue* as a compound word, "bellows," Wang reads it as two words. "Bellows" is clear enough, but it is uncertain what he meant by *yueyue*, obviously some kind of wind instrument. A *yue* is the short reed pipe, and *paituo*,

probably a variant of *painang* (bellows), coupled with *yue* (pipe[s]), gives us [*pai*]*tuo yue*, a "bellows (sack) reed pipes," a name unknown in the sources but that seems to describe the well-known classical Chinese musical instrument the *sheng* (reed mouth organ; Japanese *shō*). The *sheng* resembles another instrument, the *paixiao* (panpipes) but has an additional sacklike resonance box (wood or metal) at the bottom or is enclosed in a *pao* (bottle gourd), which also serves as a resonance box, into which the player blows. Both the bellows and the mouth organ are empty inside, but when this emptiness is activated, the apparatus or instrument starts to function. Modern physics explains that this is all due to the action of air pressure, but the ancients thought it was the functioning of nothingness (*wu*).

SECTION 6

The Valley Spirit never dies, and we call it the "Mysterious Female." The gate of the Mysterious Female is referred to as the "root of Heaven and Earth." On and on,[1] with only apparent existence, it functions inexhaustibly.

> *The Valley Spirit* [Gushen] *is the nothingness in the center of the valley. It has neither form nor appearance and is utterly free of contrariness or disobedience. Lying low and unmoving, it maintains its quiescence and never weakens. Even though all things are completed by it, we do not see its form, for this is the most perfect thing. Lying low and maintaining quiescence, it cannot be grasped in order to give it [the Dao] a name, so the text refers to it as the Mysterious Female* [Xuanpin]. *(The root of Heaven and Earth, on and on, with only apparent existence, functions inexhaustibly.)*[2] *The gate is the place from which the Mysterious Female comes. Because it is rooted in that from which it comes, it is the embodiment of the [great] ultimate* [yu ji tong ti], *and this is why the text refers to it as "the root of Heaven and Earth."*[3] *Do you wish to say that it does exist? Well, we do not see its form. Do you wish to say that it does not exist? Well, the myriad things are produced by it.*[4] *Thus the text says, "On and on, with only apparent existence." Not one single thing fails to be completed, yet it never tires. Thus the text says, "it functions inexhaustibly."*

NOTES

1. "On and on" translates *mianmian*, which seems equivalent to the "on and on" (*shengsheng*) of Wang's commentary to section 14, first passage. Both expressions describe unbroken continuity.

2. The sentence in parentheses has been proven to be an interpolation. See Tao Hongqing (1860–1918), *Du zhuzi zhaji* (Reading notes on the philosophers), 6; Hatano, *Rōshi Dōtokukyō kenkyū*, 72–74; and Lou, *Wang Bi ji jiaoshi*, 18 n. 6.

3. Cf. section 23, fourth and fifth passages.

4. Cf. Wang's commentary to section 14.

SECTION 7

Heaven is everlasting, and Earth endless. That they can last forever and go on without end is because they do not try to exist for themselves.

If one exists for oneself, he will contend with others, but if he does not exist for himself, others will come to him in submission. Thus they can exist forever. As such, the sage places himself in the rear yet finds himself in front. He puts aside his person, yet his person is preserved.[1] Is this not because he is utterly free of self-interest? This is how he can achieve self-fulfillment.

To be utterly free of self-interest [wusi] *means to make no conscious effort for one's own sake. Such a person will always find himself in front and his self preserved. Thus the text says, "he can achieve self-fulfillment."*

NOTES

1. Cf. section 66; and section 67, fourth section.

SECTION 8

The highest good is like water. The goodness of water lies in benefiting the myriad things without contention, while locating itself in places that common people scorn.

> *What common people scorn is the lowly.*

Therefore it is almost exactly like the Dao.

> *Whereas the Dao has no physical existence, water does have existence. Thus the text says "almost exactly like."*

Goodness in position depends on location; goodness in heart/mind depends on profundity; goodness in association depends on benevolence; goodness in words depends on sincerity; goodness in government depends on order; goodness in affairs depends on ability; goodness in action depends on timeliness. And it is only by avoiding contention that no blame occurs.

> *This states how, like water, one should always be in resonance thus with the Dao.*[1]

NOTES

1. The translation here takes a slight liberty with the text, which literally reads: "This states how water is always in resonance thus with the Dao." The wording of the sentence differs among various editions, and some actually read "This states how man always should be." However, the alternate reading of "water" (*shui*) for man (*ren*) has been rejected by most textual scholars (see Lou, *Wang Bi ji jiaoshi*, 21 n. 3, and Hatano, *Rōshi Dōtokukyō kenkyū*, 77). Because the context strongly suggests that a three-part analogy is involved—as water resembles the Dao, so should human action emulate water—I have rendered it here accordingly.

SECTION 9

With it firmly in hand, he goes on to fill it up, but it would be better to quit.

> *"Firmly in hand" means not to let virtue [de] go. Not only does he not let his virtue go, he goes further and fills it up [ying].*[1] *The power [shi] of such a one will surely be toppled. Thus "it would be better to quit," which means that it would be even better if one had no virtue or sense of achievement at all.*

If, having forged it, one goes on to sharpen it, it could not last long.

If one forges the end of a sword to a point but goes further and grinds it sharper, it snaps off, its characteristic property [shi] *destroyed. Thus "it could not last long."*

Gold and jade fill the hall, but none can keep them safe.

It would be better to put an end to them.

If one is arrogant because of wealth and rank, he will give himself a blameworthy fate.

Such a one could not last long.

Once achievement has occurred, one retires, for such is the Dao of Heaven.

The four seasons move on in turn: once one achieves what it should, it gives way to the next.

NOTES

1. Like the Dao itself, virtue should remain "empty" (cf. section 4), that is, free of conscious value, motive, procedure, or goal. Instead of grasping the cup of virtue and attempting to fill it with one's subjective, self-conscious sense of what virtue should be (and the self-satisfaction that one has it), better to abandon it completely.

SECTION 10

Stay where your earthbound soul is protected, and embrace integrity: can you do this with never a deviation?

Zai [usually "uphold"] means something like "stay in" [chu]. "Where your earthbound soul is protected" [yingpo] is where one permanently dwells.¹ "Integrity" [yi] is a person's authenticity [zhen].² In other words, the text says: "Can you stay in the dwelling in which you permanently live, embrace integrity with a pure spirit, and do this with never a deviation? If so, the myriad folk will subject themselves to you spontaneously."

Rely exclusively on your vital force, and become perfectly soft: can you play the infant?

Zhuan [rely exclusively on] is the same as ren [trust entirely to], and zhi [become perfectly] is the same as ji [extend/attain to the utmost]. In other words, the text says: "Can you trust entirely to the vital force endowed by nature [ziran zhi qi], *attain the harmony characteristic of perfect softness* [zhirou zhi he], *and, like the infant, be utterly without conscious desire* [yu]*?"*[3] *If so, people will achieve their proper span of life and fully realize their natures* [wu quan er xing de].

Cleanse your vision into the mystery of things: can you make it spotless?

> Xuan *[mystery] means the ultimate extent and subtlety of things* [ji]. *In other words, the text says: "Can you cleanse away the misleading and the specious and so attain vision capable of grasping the ultimate and the subtle, not allow things to get in the way of its brightness or flaw its numinous power* [shen]*?" If so, it will be one with mystery from beginning to end.*

Cherish the people and govern the state: can you do this without intelligence?

> *Intelligence is concerned with seeking success by using arts and techniques or uncovering what is hidden by plumbing the workings of fate. When vision into the mystery of things is without flaw, it is as if one had repudiated sagehood* [sheng]. *When one governs the state without intelligence, it is as if he had discarded wisdom.*[4] *"Can you do this without intelligence?" If so, the people will not hide, and the state will be governed.*[5]

The gateway of Heaven, whether it is to be open or shut: can you play the female?[6]

> *"The gateway of Heaven" is a term for that through which all under Heaven passes, and "open or shut" refers to moments that decide good order or chaos. Whether open or shut, the effect prevails equally throughout all under Heaven. Thus the text says, "The gateway of Heaven, whether open or shut." The female joins in but does not start the singing, responds but does not act.*[7] *This is what is meant when the text says, "The gateway of Heaven, whether it is to be open or shut: can you play the female?" If so, things will subject themselves to you spontaneously, and your position will be secure as a matter of course.*

Your bright understanding casts its light over the four quarters: can you stay free of conscious effort?

> *This is to say, one's perfect brightness might cast its light over the four quarters without delusion or doubt, yet can such a one refrain from making conscious effort? If so, nurture of the people*

[wuhua] *will indeed take place! This is what is meant when we say the Dao never engages in conscious effort. If any lord or prince were able to hold to this, the myriad folk would be nurtured spontaneously* [zihua].[8]

He gives them life

He does not block the source of their existence.

And nurtures them.

He places no stricture on their natures.

He gives them life, yet he possesses them not. He acts, yet does not make them dependent. He matures them, yet he is not their steward.[9] This we call mysterious virtue.[10]

Do not block the source of their existence, and people will manage life on their own, so what merit is there to that? Place no stricture on their natures, and people will find their own relief [ji], *so on whose actions do they depend? People march along with broad steps all by themselves, and this is not the result of one's stewardship. To have virtue but not exercise mastery, if this is not mysterious, what is it? Whenever we speak of mysterious virtue, it always pertains to one who has virtue, but they* [his people] *are unaware of his being master, for it emerges from the secret and the dark.*[11]

NOTES

1. In interpreting *yingpo* (where your earthbound soul is protected) as a place that provides long-term safety for one's earthly, physical existence, Wang's commentary differs markedly from that of Heshang Gong, which equates *yingpo* with *hunpo* (ethereal spirit and earthbound soul), which almost all later commentators and translators follow, usually taking *zai* (settle in) to mean "keep," "preserve," or "sustain": "Can you [or, "if you can"] preserve your ethereal spirit and earthbound soul [your spirit]" (Heshang Gong, *Heshang Gong zhu Laozi Daodejing* [The Heshang Gong commentary to Laozi's *Classic of the Way and Virtue*], 1:7 (15647A), and cf. Erkes, *Ho-shang Kung's Commentary on Lao-Tse*, 25–26. Erkes translates *hunpo* as "the spiritual and the animal souls."

2. Cf. Wang's commentary to section 32, first passage, which reads: "If one embraces the uncarved block, engages in no conscious effort

[*wuwei*], neither lets his authenticity [*zhen*] be hampered by things nor lets his spirit [*shen*] be harmed by desire, then the people will submit to him spontaneously, and he shall attain the Dao as a matter of course." Note that Wang equates *yi* (integrity), *zhen* (authenticity), and *pu* (simplicity).

3. Cf. Wang's commentary to section 49, last passage.

4. Cf. section 19, which reads: "Repudiate sagehood and discard wisdom, and the people will benefit a hundredfold."

5. The base text reads "*min bubi er guo zhi zhi ye*" (the people will not hide, and the state will govern them), but one version of Wang's commentary preserved in the *Daode zhenjing jizhu* (Collected commentaries on the *True Classic of the Way and Virtue*), 2:13 (16957B) reads *guo zhi ye* (the state will be governed), which seems more likely. However, Tao Hongqing thinks that the text ought to read "*guo zi zhi*" (the state will govern itself), which fits the context even better. See Tao's *Du zhuzi zhaji*, 6, and Lou, *Wang Bi ji jiaoshi*, 25 n. 11. A similar passage occurs in Wang's commentary to section 49, fifth passage, paragraph 4: "If there is nothing he [the ruler] investigates them for, what hiding must the common folk do?"

6. The base text reads: *neng wu ci hu*, "can one not be the female" or "can this do without the female," both of which make sense as rhetorical questions, but many editions of the *Laozi* read *neng wei ci hu*, "can you play the female," which seems more straightforward and thus is preferred. See Lou, *Wang Bi ji jiaoshi*, 25 n. 14.

7. Cf. Wang's commentary to First Yin of Hexagram 6, *Song* (Contention), in the *Yijing* (Classic of changes), which reads "It is always yang [the male] that starts singing and yin [the female] that joins in. Yin is never the one to take the lead" (Lynn, *The Classic of Changes*, 172), and to Second Yin of Hexagram 49, *Ge* (Radical Change), which reads "The character of a yin is such that it is incapable of taking the lead and instead should be an obedient follower" (ibid., 446). See Lou, *Wang Bi ji jiaoshi*, 249 and 466. Cf. also Wang's commentary to section 68, second passage.

8. Cf. section 32, first passage; and section 37, third passage.

9. "Steward" translates *zai*. Cf. section 2, third passage; and Wang's commentary to section 17, first passage.

10. Cf. section 2, third passage; and section 51, penultimate and last passages.

11. Cf. Wang's commentary to section 51, last passage; and section 2 of Wang Bi's Outline Introduction.

SECTION 11

Thirty spokes share one hub. It is exactly where there is nothing of it that the functionality of the wheel resides.

> *That the hub can unite and control the thirty spokes depends on the nothingness there. Because it consists of nothingness, it can accommodate anything. This is how the solitary* [gua] *can unite and control the many.*[1]

Mix clay with water to make a vessel. It is exactly where there is nothing of it that the functionality of the vessel resides. Cut doors and windows to make a room. It is exactly where there is nothing of it that the functionality of the room resides. Therefore this is how what is there provides benefit and how what is not there provides functionality.

> *That wood, clay, and wall can form these three things [wheel, vessel, room] depends in each case on achieving functionality* [yong] *through nothingness* [wu]. *In other words, [as for nothingness,][2] that what is there can be of benefit always depends on its achievement of functionality through what is not there.*

NOTES

1. Instead of *gua* (the solitary), the base text has *shi*, which could only make sense as a function word, "really/truly": "This is how it can really [*shi*] unite and control the many." Used as a substantive, "This is how the solid/substantial [*shi*] can unite and control the many," it would contradict both Wang's overall argument and the text of the *Laozi*. Tao Hongqing suggests that *shi* is a scribal mistake for *gua* (the solitary), the graphs being similar. See Tao's *Du zhuzi zhaji* (Reading notes on the philosophers), 6. Lou Yulie agrees with Tao and points out a similar passage in the *Ming tuan* (Clarifying the Judgments) section of Wang's *Zhouyi lueli* (General Remarks on the *Changes of the Zhou*), in the *Yijing* (Classic of changes): "The many cannot govern the many; that which governs the many is the most solitary [*gua*], the One]" (Lynn, *The Classic of Changes*, 25; see Lou, *Wang Bi ji jiaoshi*, 27 n. 2 and 591). It is significant that in section 11 Wang alludes to the ideal ruler in terms of the unity of the Dao: the ruler should act out of nothing—as if he were not there—thus unifying his people and providing functionality

to the state in the same way that the empty hub unifies and provides functionality to the wheel.

2. It is likely that *wuzhe* (as for nothingness) is an interpolation. See Lou, *Wang Bi jijiaoshi*, 27 n. 4.

SECTION 12

The five colors make one's eyes blind; the five notes make one's ears deaf; the five flavors make one's mouth fail; and sport hunting on horseback makes one's heart/mind go crazy.

> Shuang *[err/lose] means fail. One loses the function of the mouth [to taste]. Thus the text says of it that it "fails." The ear, the eye, the mouth, and the heart/mind [xin] all should comply [shun] each with its own character [xing]. When one does not use them in compliance with their character and individual capacity [ming],*[1] *he thus perversely harms what they are by nature [ziran], and this is why the text characterizes them as "blind," "deaf," "failed," and "crazy."*

Goods hard to get cause one to travel the road to harm.[2]

> *Goods hard to get block the correct path [zhenglu]. Thus the text says that they "cause one to travel the road to harm."*

This is why the sage provides for the belly but not for the eye. Thus he rejects the one and keeps the other.[3]

> *To provide for the belly is to use things to nourish oneself. To provide for the eye is to use things to enslave oneself. Therefore the sage does not provide for the eye.*

NOTES

1. Cf. *Tuanzhuan* (Commentary on the Judgments) of Hexagram 1, *Qian* (Pure Yang), in the *Yijing* (Classic of changes): "The change and transformation [*bianhua*] of the Dao of *Qian* in each instance keep the nature [*xing*] and destiny [*ming*] of things correct" (Lynn, *The Classic of Changes*, 129). Kong Yingda's (574–648) commentary here reads: "'Nature' is the character [*zhi*] that is innate in a thing, such as whether it is hard or soft, slow or quick. 'Destiny' is the individual capacity with which one is endowed, such as whether one is noble or base, short- or

long-lived" (*Zhouyi ʒhengyi* [Correct meaning of the *Changes of the Zhou*], 1:6a).

2. Cf. Section 3, first passage; section 27, fifth passage; section 49, fifth passage, paragraph 1; and section 64, seventh passage.

3. Section 3 makes the same argument.

SECTION 13

Favor and disgrace are enough cause for alarm, and self-importance[1] is a great calamity that can cost one his person. What is meant by "favor and disgrace are enough cause for alarm"? Favor, when it is had by an inferior, is as alarming as when it is lost by him. This is what is meant by "favor and disgrace are enough cause for alarm."

> *If one enjoys favor, he inevitably suffers disgrace. If one enjoys honor, he inevitably suffers calamity. Favor and disgrace are equivalent, and honor and calamity mean the same thing. If, when subject to favor or disgrace, honor or calamity, a inferior finds them enough cause for alarm, such a one does not have it in him to govern all under Heaven successfully.*

What is meant by self-importance being "a great calamity that can cost one his person"?

> *"Great calamity" is associated with "honor" and "favor." To place great emphasis on life is certainly to enter the land of death.[2] This is why the text refers to it [self-importance (*gui*)] as a "great calamity." When one confuses his person [shen, i.e., his individual existence] with honor and favor, it means he exchanges it for them. Thus the text says of this that it is "a great calamity that can cost one his person."*

The reason I suffer such a great calamity is that I am bound by my own person.

> *It stems from one being bound by his own person.*

When I am no longer bound by my own person,

> *That is, when one reverts to what is natural* [ziran].

What calamity could befall me? Therefore, because such a one values his own person as much as anything under Heaven, he may be entrusted with all under Heaven.

> *Because there is nothing that he would exchange his person for,*

> *the text says that he "values" it. Such a one thus may be entrusted with all under Heaven.*

Because such a one cherishes his own person as much as anything under Heaven, he may have all under Heaven rendered to his care.

> *Because there is nothing that he would damage his person for, the text says that he "cherishes" it. It is such a one that may have all under Heaven rendered to his care. It is only someone who refrains from harming his own person because of favor, disgrace, honor, or calamity and who would not exchange it for these things who may have all under Heaven handed over to him.*

NOTES

1. "Self-importance" translates *gui*, which, as a noun, can mean "high rank/status/value" or "esteem/prestige/honor" and refer to anything or anyone of value or importance. Wang's commentary immediately below, however, suggests that it should be understood here as "self-importance" or perhaps "self-esteem," as he explains it in terms of *sheng zhi hou* (great emphasis on one's own life).

2. Cf. section 50, first passage.

SECTION 14

When we look for it but see it not, we call it the invisible. When we listen for it but hear it not, we call it the inaudible. When we try to touch it but find it not, we call it the imperceptible. Because these three aspects of it are impossible to probe, it remains a single amorphous unity.

> *It is shapeless, leaving no image, and soundless, leaving no reverberation. Thus it can permeate* [tong] *absolutely everything and reach absolutely everywhere. We cannot get to know it and even less know how to give it a name derived from how it looks, sounds, or feels. Thus, because it is impossible to probe, it remains a single amorphous unity* [hun er wei yi].[1]

Its risings cast no light, and its settings occasion no dark. On and on it goes,[2] unnamable, always reverting to nothingness. This we refer to as the shape of that which has no shape, the image of that which has no physical existence.

You might wish to say that it does not exist, but everything achieves existence because of it, and then you might wish to say that it does exist, but we do not see its form.[3] *This is why the text refers to it as "the shape of that which has no shape, the image of that which has no existence."*

This we refer to as dim and dark.[4]

It cannot be determined.

Try to meet it, but you will not see its head. Try to follow it, but you will not see its tail, so hold on to the Dao of old to preside over what exists now.

"What exists" [you] means the matters that one attends to [you qishi].

It is possible to know how things were at the beginning of time. This we refer to as holding the thread of the Dao.

That which is free from form and nameless is the progenitor of the myriad things.[5] *Although the present and the past differ, customs changing as age gives way to age, not one single thing ever achieved successful order except from it. This is why it is possible to "hold on to the Dao of old to preside over what exists now." Remote antiquity might be far from us, but the Dao then still exists now. Therefore, although we live in the present, it is possible for one to know how things were at the beginning of time [gushi].*[6]

NOTES

1. Cf. section 1 of Wang's Outline Introduction.

2. "On and on" translates *shengsheng*, which seems equivalent to the "on and on" (*mianmian*), of section 6. Both expressions describe unbroken continuity.

3. Cf. Wang's commentary to section 6, first passage.

4. "Dim and dark" translates *huhuang*. Cf. Wang's commentary to section 21.

5. Cf. Wang's commentary to section 1, second passage, and to section 47, first passage.

6. Cf. Wang's commentary to section 47, first and second passages, and the end of section 1 of his Outline Introduction.

SECTION 15

In antiquity, he who was good at being a leader was perfectly in step with mystery in all its subtlety and profundity; so recondite was he that it was impossible to understand him. Now, because he defies understanding, all I can do is force a description of what he was like: he seemed hesitant, as one might be when fording a river in winter.

> *When one fords a river in winter, he is hesitant, as if unsure whether to ford it or not, and his appearance will be such that his real intention cannot be discerned.*

He seemed tentative, as one who fears his neighbors on all four sides.

> *When neighbors on all four sides join together to attack the master in the center, he so equivocates that they do not know which way he will move. A person of superior virtue gives away not the slightest hint, so his intentions can never be discerned—indeed, just as described here.*[1]

He seemed solemn, oh, as if he were the guest. He seemed yielding, oh, just like ice when about to break up. He seemed solid and sturdy, oh, just like an uncarved block of wood. He seemed empty and receptive, oh, just like a valley. He seemed amorphous, oh, just like murky water.

> *All these examples of how he appeared tell us that his appearance permitted neither accurate description nor a precise name.*

Who can take his turbidity and, by stilling it, gradually become clear? Who can take his quietude and, by stirring it long, gradually come alive?

> *When obscure, it is through principles* [li] *that things achieve distinctness; when turbid, it is by stilling that things achieve clarity; and, when quiet, it is by stirring that things come alive. This is the Dao of nature* [ziran]. *The "Who can" indicates how very difficult this is, and "gradually" suggests meticulousness and caution.*

One who keeps this Dao does not wish to be filled.

> *If filled* [ying], *one would surely overflow.*

For it is only by not getting filled that one can avoid having the cover remade.

> *Bi [cover] means* fugai *[cover].*[2]

NOTES

1. Cf. Wang's commentary to section 20, fourth and seventh passages, and section 38, paragraph 2.

2. Throughout the ages, most commentators have rejected Wang's interpretation and instead, following the much more common textual variant *bi* (worn/worn out) or, occasionally, *bi* (exhausted), denigrate his reading as "not making any sense" or "not fitting the text." See Hatano, *Rōshi Dōtokukyō kenkyū*, 111–12. Accordingly, translations such as the following are more the rule: "He is beyond for things wearing out and renewal" (Wing-tsit Chan, *The Way of Lao Tzu*, 126) and "He can wear out without the need to be renewed" Henricks, *Lao-Tzu Te-Tao Ching*, 216–17). Professor Henricks's reading depends on taking *bie* (clothing; to wipe with clothing) (Mawangdui B) as a variant of *bi* (worn out). The injunction "not to fill," however, is always associated with the empty vessel of the Dao metaphor in Wang's commentary, and Wang's interpretation here is consistent with that metaphor: the keeper of the Dao, as a receptacle of the Dao, does not wish to be filled because any attempt at filling would just overflow, and his receptacle cover—i.e., his head—would be ruined and have to be "remade," not an odd idea if we remember that Wang read the *Laozi* primarily as a treatise of political philosophy for "heads" of state. Cf. sections 4 and 9.

SECTION 16

Their attainment of emptiness absolute and their maintenance of quietude guileless,

> *In other words, "attainment of emptiness" refers to the state of absolute guilelessness* [jidu], *and "maintenance of quietude" refers to the state of perfect genuineness* [zhenzheng].[1]

The myriad things interact.

> *This refers to their behavior and growth.*

I, as such, observe their return.

> *With emptiness* [xu] *and quietude* [jing], *one observes their eternal return. Everything that exists arises from emptiness, and action arises from quietude.[2] Thus, although the myriad things interact together, they all ultimately return to emptiness and quietude, which is the state of absolute guilelessness* [jidu].

All things flourish, but each reverts to its roots.

> *Each returns to where it began.*

To return to the root is called "quietude," which means to revert to one's destiny, and reversion to one's destiny is called "constancy."

> *When one returns to the root, he becomes quiet, which is why this state is called "quietude"* [jing]. *When one is quiet, he reverts to his destiny* [ming]. *This is why this state is referred to as "reversion to destiny." When one reverts to his destiny, he fulfills the constant dimensions of his nature* [xing] *and destiny* [ming], *which is why this state is called "constancy"* [chang].

To understand constancy is called "perspicacity." Not to understand constancy results in errant behavior and, with it, misfortune.

> *Constancy as such has neither predilections* [pian] *nor outer signs* [zhang], *exists neither in light nor dark states,*[3] *and results in neither warm nor cold images. Thus the text says: "To understand constancy is called 'perspicacity'* [ming]."[4] *It is only by this reversion [to destiny] that one can perfectly embrace the myriad folk, leaving out absolutely no one, but, if one lacks this and as such sets forth to do something, he will find that deviancy* [xie] *has entered his destiny* [fen] *and that people depart from their destinies.*[5] *Thus the text says: "Not to understand constancy results in errant behavior and, with it, misfortune."*

To understand constancy is to embrace all things.

> *There is nothing that he will not embrace perfectly.*

To embrace things is to be impartial.

> *Because there is nothing one does not embrace perfectly, he attains the state of oceanic impartiality.*

Such impartiality means true kingship.

> *With such oceanic impartiality, he attains the state wherein he has universal presence.*

With true kingship, he is one with Heaven.

> *Because he has universal presence, he attains the state wherein he becomes one with Heaven.*

To be one with Heaven means to be one with the Dao.

> *He makes his virtue conform to that of Heaven and embodies the Dao so that it permeates him completely* [datong].[6] *As such, he attains the state wherein he reaches the absolute limit of emptiness* [xuwu].

To be one with the Dao is to be everlasting.

> *To reach the absolute limit of emptiness* [xuwu] *is to attain the*

constancy [chang] *of the Dao. As such, he attains the state*
wherein absolutely no limits exist.

As long as he lives, no danger shall befall him.[7]

Nothingness is such that no water or fire can harm it and no
metal or stone can destroy it. If it is put to use by the heart/
mind [xin], *the wild water buffalo and the tiger will have no*
way to strike at him with claw or horn, and weapons of war will
have no way to use point or edge against him. So what danger
could there ever be?[8]

NOTES

1. Both Hatano Tarō and Tao Hongqing give evidence that the
text has been corrupted by interpolations (see Hatano, *Rōshi Dōtokukyō
kenkyū*, 23). Lou Yulie extrapolates from Hatano's comments to suggest
that the text should read: "In other words, this refers to the ultimate
degree [*ji*] to which emptiness [*xu*] is attained and the most authentic
state [*zhen*] in which quietude [*jing*] is maintained" (Lou, *Wang Bi ji
jiaoshi*, 37 n. 1). Tao's suggests "The attainment of emptiness and the
maintenance of quietude characterize the perfect genuineness [*zhenzheng*] of things" (Tao, *Du zhuzi zhaji*, 7).

2. Cf. Wang's commentary to section 26, first passage.

3. Cf. section 14, second passage, and the end of section 1 of
Wang's Outline Introduction.

4. Cf. section 55, sixth passage, and the end of section 1 of Wang's
Outline Introduction.

5. Tao Hongqing, among others, thinks that this passage is corrupt
and does not make sense as it stands, but such confusion arises from
trying to read *fen* (destiny, one's fated lot, etc.) as *fen* (to separate;
separation, distinction), as it occurs in Wang's commentary to section
25 and in section of his Outline Introduction. See Lou, *Wang Bi ji jiaoshi*,
39 n. 9, and Tao, *Du zhuzi zhaji*, 7. In my view, the passage makes perfect sense: without an enlightened identification with "the myriad folk,"
one cannot help perverting his own natural fated allotment, his "destiny,"
along with the natural destinies of everyone else.

6. Cf. Wang's commentary to section 5, second passage, and section 77, first passage.

7. Cf. section 52, second passage.

8. Cf. section 50.

SECTION 17

The "very highest" by those below is just known to exist.

> *"Very highest"* [taishang] *refers to the "great man"* [daren].
> *When a great man is above [in the position of sovereign], he is
> referred to as the "very highest." The very highest there above
> "tends to matters without conscious effort and practices the teach-
> ing that is not expressed in words."*[1] *The behavior of the myriad
> folk is modeled on him, yet he does serve as the starting point
> for them.*[2] *Therefore those below know that he exists but nothing
> more. This refers to how they follow the one above.*[3]

The next is he who is a parent to them, in whom they rejoice.

> *This one is incapable of "tend[ing] to matters without conscious
> effort and practic[ing] the teaching that is not expressed in
> words" but instead establishes goodness* [shan] *and promulgates
> its practice, enabling those below to obtain a parent in whom
> they rejoice.*

The next is he whom they fear.

> *This one is no longer able to lead the people with mercy* [en]
> *and benevolence* [ren] *but relies on the power of force.*

The next is he whom they treat with contempt.

> *This one is not able to keep the people in order with governance
> [zheng]*[4] *but instead relies on intelligence* [zhi] *to govern his
> state, so those below know how to circumvent his laws, which are
> not obeyed. Thus the text says, "they treat [him] with contempt."*

If one fails to have trust, a corresponding lack of trust in him
occurs.[5]

> *If one uses one's body in violation of its nature* [xing], *illness
> will occur. If one tries to enhance the condition of the people but
> violates their authenticity* [zhen], *ill will and conflict will arise.
> If one's trust* [xin] *in them fails, he himself will suffer loss of
> trust, for such is the Dao of nature* [ziran]. *Once one finds him-
> self in a situation where trust fails, it is not something that knowl-
> edge can relieve* [ji].

He takes his time, oh, as he weighs his words carefully. And,
when success is had and the task accomplished, the common folk
all say, "We just live naturally."

> *When things happen "naturally," not the slightest prefiguring
> can be seen, so his intentions cannot be discerned. Because no
> person can thus alter what he says, his words will surely elicit*

agreement. Thus the text says, "He takes his time, oh, as he weighs his words carefully." He "tends to matters without conscious effort," "practices the teaching that is not expressed in words," and does not use rules to govern the people.[6] *Therefore, when success is had and the task accomplished, the common folk do not know how it happens.*[7]

NOTES

1. Section 2, second and third passages. Cf. section 63, first passage.

2. Cf. Section 2, third passage; Wang's commentary to section 27, fifth passage; and section 34, second passage.

3. Hatano Tarō argues that this sentence is out of place and actually belongs at the head of Wang's commentary to the fifth passage, "If one fails to have trust, a corresponding lack of trust in him occurs." See *Rōshi Dōtokukyō kenkyū*, 121. Lou, *Wang Bi ji jiaoshi*, 41 n. 2, without acknowledging Hatano, repeats the same argument.

4. Cf. *Lunyu* (Analects) 2:3: "If the people are led by governance [*zheng*] and kept in order by punishment [*xing*], they will evade these without shame." Cf. section 57, fourth section.

5. Identical to section 23, last passage.

6. "Use rules to govern the people" translates *yi xing li wu*, reading *xing* (forms) as "rules" and *li* (establish) as *li* (oversee/govern), but as *xing* (form) and *xing* (punishment) are used interchangeably in early texts, it might equally be translated as "use punishment to govern his people." Besides sharing a phonetic similarity, the two probably are conceptually related: punishment used to shape/form correct behavior (cf. the English expression "whip them into shape"). If we look back to Wang's commentary to the second passage, however, we see that the ruler who cannot "tend to matters without conscious effort and practice the teaching that is not expressed in words . . . establishes [*li*] goodness [*shan*] and promulgates its practice." That is, he establishes forms or rules of good behavior and encourages their habitual application. In contrast, "punishment" should surely be associated with the next, inferior kind of ruler, who can only govern by force. Reading *liwu* (establish the people) as *liwu* (oversee, govern the people) seems likely given that Wang uses a similar expression, *li zhong* (oversee, govern the mass of common folk), in his commentary to the *Xiang zhuan* (Commentary on the Images) to Hexagram 36, *Mingyi* (Suppression

of the Light), in the *Yijing* (Classic of changes): "One who displays brilliance in overseeing [governing] the mass of common folk will harm them and make them false" (Lynn, *The Classic of Changes*, 357–58; see Lou, *Wang Bi ji jiaoshi*, 396). Similar expressions also occur elsewhere in Wang's commentary to the *Laozi* and in the *Laozi* itself; see section 17, last passage, and section 59, fifth passage (*li guo* [oversee, govern the state)); and section 60, second passage (*li tianxia* [oversee [govern] all under Heaven]).

7. Wang's elaboration on the descending order of efficacy in ruler-ship—with spontaneous identification with the Dao rated as the best and government by deliberate application of intelligence as the worst—is reminiscent of similar remarks made by his contemporary, Ruan Ji (210–63) in the *Tong Lao lun* (General discussion of the *Laozi*): "The three august ones were in accord with the Dao; the five sage emperors submitted to virtue; the three kings exercised benevolence; the five hegemons practiced righteousness; and those who managed their states by force depended on intelligence. This accounts for the difference between good rulership and bad and for its degeneration from the substantial to the flimsy" (*Quan sanguo wen* [Complete prose of the Three Kingdoms era], 45:8a [1310B]). For other variations on this theme and its long tradition associated with the *Laozi* and Daoism, see Hsiao, *A History of Chinese Political Thought*, 1:575–82 and 607–30.

SECTION 18

It is when the great Dao is forsaken that benevolence and righteousness appear,

> *When one gives up on tending to matters without conscious effort and replaces it with the practice of mercy* [hui][1] *and the establishment of goodness* [shan], *it means that the Dao has been invested in things* [dao jin wu ye].[2]

When wisdom and intelligence emerge that great falsehood occurs,

> *When one employs methods and uses intelligence to uncover treachery and falsehood, his intentions become obvious, and the form they take visible, so the people will know how to evade them.*[3] *This is why* "*when wisdom and intelligence emerge . . . great falsehood occurs.*"

When the six relations exist in disharmony that the obedient and the kind appear, and when the state is in disorder that loyal ministers arise.

> *The most praiseworthy of names are generated by the greatest censure, for what we know as praise* [mei] *and censure* [e] *come from the same gate.*[4] *"The six relations" are father and son, older and younger brother, and husband and wife. When the six relations exist in harmony and the state maintains good order all by itself, no one knows where the obedient* [xiao] *[child, younger brother, wife] and the kind* [ci] *[parent, older brother, husband] and loyal ministers are to be found. It is when fish forget the Dao of rivers and lakes that the virtuous act of moistening each other occurs.*[5]

NOTES

1. "Practice of mercy" translates *shi hui*, reading *hui* (wisdom) as *hui* (mercy). See Lou, *Wang Bi ji jiaoshi*, 44 n. 1.

2. "It means that the Dao has been invested in things" is glossed by Lou Yulie as: "It means that once the *chunpu* [pristine simplicity or "the uncontaminated uncarved block"] of the Dao is lost, the Dao is invested in *you xing zhi wu* [tangible entities, such as "mercy" and "goodness"]" (*Wang Bi ji jiaoshi*, 44 n. 2). Cf. section 28, penultimate passage ("When the uncarved block [pu] fragments, it turns into implements [qi]"); and section 38 ("One resorts to virtue [de] only after losing the Dao").

3. Cf. Wang's commentaries to section 15, second passage; section 17, last passage; and section 65, third passage.

4. Cf. Wang's commentary to section 2, first passage.

5. Wang paraphrases the *Dazongshi* (The great master teacher) section of the *Zuangzi*: "When sources dry up, fish, finding themselves stranded together on the ground, moisten each other with spit and wet each other with foam, but it would be better if they could forget each other in the rivers and lakes" (*Zhuangzi yinde*, 16/6/22; cf. Watson, *Complete Works of Chuang Tzu*, 80. Traditional commentators, however, do not read *yu xiangwang yu jianghu zhi dao* as "it is when fish forget [are rendered forgetful of] the Dao of rivers and lakes" but insist that *xiangwang yu jianghu* be read as it occurs in the *Zhuangzi*: "forget each other in the rivers and lakes." With such a reading, Wang's passage

does not make sense as it stands, which has led to various attempts to amend his text, including: "Fish forget each other in the rivers and lakes, but when this Dao of forgetting each other is lost, the virtuous act of moistening each other occurs" (Tao Hongqing); "While the Dao of the fish forgetting each other in the rivers and lakes endures, no one knows where the virtue of wetting each other can be found" (Lou Yulie); "It is when fish do not forget each other in the rivers and lakes that the virtuous act of moistening each other occurs" (Momoi Hakuroku); and "It is when fish forget each other in the rivers and lakes that the virtuous act of moistening each other vanishes" (Tōjō Ichidō [1778–1857]). See Lou, *Wang Biji jiaoshi*, 45 n. 8, and Hatano, *Rōshi Dōtokukyō kenkyū*, 130.

SECTION 19

Repudiate sagehood and discard wisdom, and the people would benefit a hundredfold. Repudiate benevolence and discard righteousness, and the people would again be obedient and kind to each other. Repudiate cleverness and discard sharpness, and thieves and robbers would not exist. As for these three pairs of terms,

> Because they serve as mere decoration,
> Give people the chance to identify with something else:
> Exemplify simplicity, embrace the uncarved block
> Curtail self-interest, and have few desires.

Sagehood [sheng] *and intelligence* [zhi] *designate the best of human talent* [cai]; *benevolence* [ren] *and righteousness* [yi] *designate the best of human behavior* [xing]; *and cleverness* [qiao] *and sharpness* [li] *designate the best of human resources* [yong].[1] *However, the text directly says that these should be repudiated. Because such "decoration"* [wen] *is utterly inadequate, one does not give people the chance to identify with these expressions and so never does anything that exemplifies what they mean. Thus the text says: Because these three pairs of terms serve as mere decoration, they are never adequate. Therefore, when allowing people to identify with something, let them identify with your simplicity and minimal desires.*

NOTES

1. "Cleverness" (artfulness) and "sharpness" strongly imply deceit, as in such English expressions as "artful dodger" and "cardsharp."

SECTION 20

Repudiate learning, and stay free of worry. Really, how distant can approval be from disapproval? Or, how far apart can praise and censure be?[1] One feared by others must also fear others accordingly.[2]

> As it is said in the second part [of the Laozi], "The pursuit of learning means having more each day, but the pursuit of the Dao means having less each day."[3] As such, learning seeks to increase what one can do and advance what one knows, but, if one were free from desire and thus content, what should he ever seek to get by having more? And if one could stay on the mark without knowing how it is done [buzhi er zhong], what should he ever seek to learn by advancing his knowledge?[4] For,

> Finches have mates,
> As do doves.
> People who live in wintry climes
> Are sure to know one fur from another.
> That which by nature is already sufficient unto itself
> Will only come to grief if one tries to add to it.[5]

> Therefore what is the difference between lengthening the duck's legs and cutting down the legs of the crane?[6] And why should the fear of praise that leads to promotion be any different from the fear of punishment? For how far is approval from disapproval or praise [mei] from censure [e]?[7] Therefore, feared by others, I also should be afraid of them. And I never dare rely on such things [approval/disapproval, praise/censure] as reasons for action.[8]

A gulf so vast, oh, it is truly infinite!

> One sighs that the distance that sets him off from the vulgar crowd is so great.

Common people, caught up in the pursuit of happiness, behave as if feasting at a great sacrifice or ascending a springtime terrace.

> *Common people, befuddled by praise and advancement and*
> *excited by honor and reward, let their desires advance and their*
> *hearts/minds contend.*[9]

I alone am quiet and indifferent, oh, in an entirely premanifest
state [*weizhao*],[10] just like an infant who has not yet smiled,

> *In other words, I, in my solitude, have no form that can be named*
> *and provide no hint that can be detected, just like an infant who*
> *is yet unable to smile.*[11]

Utterly aimless, oh, just as if I had no place to go home.

> *I seem to have no place to live.*

Common people all have more than enough, but I alone seem to
have lost all.

> *Without exception, common people have longings and ambitions,*
> *which fill their breasts to overflowing. Thus the text says "all have*
> *more than enough." In solitude, I alone engage in no conscious*
> *effort and have no desires, as if I had lost all capacity for them.*

Mine is really the heart/mind of a stupid man!

> *The heart/mind* [xin] *of a completely stupid man are innocent*
> *of distinctions, and his thoughts are free of any consideration*
> *of good and bad. As such, my tendencies* [qing] *cannot be dis-*
> *cerned.*[12] *Utterly compliant, I am just like him.*

Absolutely amorphous, oh!

> *Innocent of distinctions, I cannot be named.*

Common people are clearly obvious.

> *They make their brilliance shine.*

But I alone am cryptically obscure.

Common people are meticulously discriminating,

> *They discriminate between each and every thing.*

But I alone muddle everything together.

Floating indifferently, oh, as if out on the sea,

> *My tendencies* [qing] *cannot be discerned.*

Blown about by the wind, oh, I seem to have no place to stop.

> *I have no ties to anything.*

Common people all would have purpose.

> *Yi* [use] *means* yong [purpose]. *Everyone wishes to have the*
> *chance to fulfill some purpose.*

But I alone am doltish and rustic.[13]

> *I have nothing that I want to do. I am so muddled and oafish*
> *that I appear to know nothing at all. Thus the text says, "doltish*
> *and rustic."*

I alone wish to be different from others[14] and so value drawing sustenance from the mother.

"Drawing sustenance from the mother" refers to the root of life [the Dao]. Everyone forsakes the roots from which the common folk draw sustenance and instead values the blossoms [hua] decorating the branch tips [superficial frivolity]. Thus the text says, "I alone wish to be different from others."

NOTES

1. The base text has *shan* (goodness) instead of *mei* (praise), but both the text as paraphrased in Wang's commentary and as it appears in the two versions of the *Laozi* recovered from Mawangdui read not *shan* but *mei*, "praise." See Lou, *Wang Bi ji jiaoshi*, 50 n. 9; *Mawangdui Hanmu boshu*, 119; and Wagner, "The Wang Bi Recension of the *Laozi*," 50.

2. The base text reads *ren zhi suowei buke buwei*, "what people fear one cannot but fear," but Wang's commentary, *ren zhi suowei wu yi wei yan*, "feared by others, I also should be afraid of them," supports the Mawangdui B text reading of this passage: *ren zhi suowei yi buke yi buwei ren*, "one feared by others must also fear others accordingly." See *Mawangdui Hanmu boshu*, 119.

3. Section 48, first and second passages.

4. Cf. section 64, penultimate passage.

5. Cf. Wang's commentary to section 2, first passage.

6. Cf. Wang's commentary to the *Tuanzhuan* (Commentary on the Judgments) to Hexagram 41, *Sun* (Diminution), in the *Yijing* (Classic of changes): "The natural substance of things in each case determines the measure of the thing involved. 'The short as such cannot be taken for insufficiency,' and 'the long as such cannot be taken for excess'" (Lynn, *The Classic of Changes*, 388; see Lou, *Wang Bi ji jiaoshi*, 421). Both commentaries allude to a passage in the *Zhuangzi*: "The long as such cannot be taken for excess, and the short as such cannot be taken for insufficiency. This is why, although the duck's legs are short, to lengthen them would cause it grief, and, although the crane's legs are long, to cut them down would cause it distress. Therefore what is by nature long is not something that should be cut down, and what is by nature short is not something that should be lengthened" (*Zhuangzi yinde*, 21/8/8; cf. Watson, *Complete Works of Chuang Tzu*, 99–100).

7. Cf. Wang's commentary to section 2, first passage.

8. "Rely on such things as reasons for action" translates *shi zhi yi wei yong*, which might also be rendered "[try to] achieve functionality through such things." Cf. *lai wu yiwei yong*, "[that what is there can be of benefit always] depends on its achievement of functionality through what is not there," from Wang's commentary to section 11, second passage.

9. Cf. Wang's commentary to section 70, first passage.

10. Cf. section 64, first passage.

11. Cf. Wang's commentary to section 15, second passage.

12. Cf. Wang's commentary to section 15, second passage.

13. "Doltish and rustic" translates *wan qie bi*, but the base text reads *wan si bi*, "doltish as a rustic." Wang's commentary indicates that it should be "doltish and rustic," a reading supported by Fu Yi's (554–639) edition of the *Laozi*, based on several old manuscripts, *Daode jing gubenpian* (An edition compiled from old manuscripts of the *Classic of the Way and Virtue*), 1:6a, in which the text has *qie* instead of *si*. Fu Yi's text is also included in *Mawangdui Hanmu boshu*, 119.

14. The base text reads "I alone am different from others," but Wang's commentary indicates that it should be "I alone wish to be different from others," a reading that also appears in Fu Yi's composite edition. The two versions of the *Laozi* recovered from Mawangdui read "I alone wish to be different from others"; see Lou, *Wang Bi ji jiaoshi*, 52 n. 27, and *Mawangdui Hanmu boshu*, 119.

SECTION   2 1

A capacity for the virtue of emptiness, this alone allows conformance with the Dao.

> *Kong [usually "great"] here means* kong *[empty]. Only by embracing emptiness* [kong] *as virtue* [de] *can one ensure that one's actions conform with the Dao.*

The Dao as such is but dim, is but dark.

> *"Dim" and "dark" refer to the appearance*[1] *of that which is formless and not attached to anything.*

Dark, oh, dim, oh, but within it some image is there. Dim, oh, dark, oh, but within it something is there.

> *It [the Dao] originates things thanks to its formlessness and brings things to completion thanks to its freedom from attachments. The myriad things are originated and completed in this way yet do not know how it happens.*[2] *Thus the text says: "Dark,*

oh, dim, oh, but within it some image is there. Dim, oh, dark,
oh, but within it something is there."[3]

Abstruse, oh, indistinct, oh, but within it the essence of things is
there.

"Abstruse" and "indistinct" refer to an appearance of unfathom-
able profundity [shenyuan].[4] *It [the Dao] is so unfathomably*
profound that we cannot treat it as something seen, yet the myriad
things all proceed from it. Because we cannot see it and so fix
what its authentic existence [zhen] *is, the text says: "Abstruse,*
oh, indistinct, oh, but within it the essence of things [jing] *is there."*

Its essence is most authentic, for within it authentication occurs.

Xin *[trust] means* xinyan *[authentication]. When things revert*
to the unfathomably profound, the ultimate state of authentic
essence [zhenjing zhi ji] *is attained and the natures* [xing] *of*
all the myriad things are fixed. Thus the text says: "Its essence
is most authentic, for within it authentication occurs."

From antiquity until now,[5] its name has never been revoked.

The ultimate of perfect authenticity [zhizhen] *cannot be named.*
Because it is "nameless" [wuming], *this is its name. From now*
back to antiquity, nothing has ever become complete except
through it. Thus the text says: "From antiquity until now, its
name has never been revoked [qu]."

We use it to convey[6] what the father of everything is.[7]

Zhongfu *[father of everything] means the origin of things. We*
use "nameless" to convey what the origin of the myriad things is.

How do I know that the father of everything is so? It is by this.

"This" means what has just been said above. In other words, if
you ask how I know that the myriad things originate in nothing-
ness, I know it by this.

NOTES

1. The base text reads *tan* (exclamation) instead of *mao* (appearance), which would result in " 'dim' and 'vague' are exclamations signifying that which. . . ." However, *mao* (appearance) instead of *tan* occurs
in a quotation of this passage in Li Shan's (ca. 630–89) commentary to
Wang Jin's (d. 505) *Toutuo si beiwen* (Dhūta Temple stele inscription),
in *Wenxuan,* 59:3b, which seems more likely. See Hatano, *Rōshi*
Dōtokukyō kenkyū, 154.

2. Cf. Wang's commentary to section 1, second passage.

3. Cf. Wang's commentary to section 6

4. The base text reads " 'abstruse' and 'indistinct' are exclamations [*tan*] signifying unfathomable profundity"; however, *mao* (appearance) instead of *tan* occurs in a quotation of this passage in Li Shan's commentary to Shen Yue's (441–513) first of five *Zhongshan shi ying Xiyang wang jiao* (Poems on Mount Zhong written in response to instructions received from the Prince of Xiyang), in *Wenxuan*, 22:15a, which seems more likely. See Hatano, *Rōshi Dōtokukyō kenkyū*, 156.

5. The base text of the *Laozi* and Wang's commentary both read "from antiquity until now," as does the quotation of this line in section 1 of Wang's Outline Introduction. As both Mawangdui texts read "from now back to antiquity" (*Mawangdui Hanmu boshu*, 119), this is one more indication that Wang knew a different version of the *Laozi*.

6. "Convey" translates *yue*, which usually means "observe" or "inspect." Instead of *yue*, the two Mawangdui texts have *shun* (comply): "We use it to comply [*shun*] with what the father of everything is" (*Mawangdui Hanmu boshu*, 119). *Yue* comes close to the meaning of *shun* in some contexts, where it can be read as "contain" or "gather." Jiao Hong (1541–1620) suggests in his commentary to this passage that *yue* should be read as it occurs in Lu Ji's (261–303) *Tan shi fu* (Lamentation on death): "A river gathers (*yue*) water and so becomes a river, / And water flows on with each passing day. / An age gathers [*yue*] men and so becomes an age, / And men move gradually toward the twilight of life." See *Wenxuan*, 16:11a; and Jiao Hong, *Laozi yi* (Wings to *Laozi*), A2:9. "Convey" attempts to bridge the meanings of "comply" and "gather": the term "nameless" (the Dao) complies with and gathers together what is meant by "the father of everything." See also the end of section 1 in Wang's Outline Introduction.

7. As both Mawangdui texts have *fu*, "father," the *fu* in *zhongfu* should be understood as "father" and not "origin." See *Mawangdui Hanmu boshu*, 119.

SECTION 22

Stepping aside[1] keeps one's wholeness intact.

> *Avoid flaunting yourself, and your brilliance will remain unimpaired.*[2]

Bending makes one straight.

> *Avoid insisting that you are right, and your rightness will commend itself.*

Being empty makes one full.

> *Avoid boasting about yourself, and your merit will be acknowledged.*

Being worn out keeps one new.

> *Avoid self-importance,*[3] *and your virtue will long endure.*

Having little gives one access. Having much leads one astray.

> *This is the Dao of nature* [ziran], *just like a tree. The more* [duo] *a tree has, the farther it is from its roots; the less* [shao] *it has, the closer it is to its roots. The more one has, the farther he is from his authenticity* [zhen]. *This is why the text uses the expression, "leads one astray." The less one has, the better the access to his roots* [de qiben].[4] *This is why the text refers to "access"* [de].[5]

In this way, the sage embraces the One and becomes a model for all under Heaven.

> *One* [yi] *is the ultimate degree of "little." Shi [model] means the same thing as* ze *[model].*

He does not flaunt himself, thus he shines.[6] He does not insist that he is right, thus his rightness is manifest. He does not boast about himself, thus his merit is acknowledged. He avoids self-importance, thus he long endures. It is because he does not contend that none among all under Heaven can contend with him.[7] As the ancient saying has it, "Stepping aside keeps one's wholeness intact." How could this ever be an empty saying! Truly, such a one will revert to it [nonexistence][8] with his wholeness intact.

NOTES

1. "Stepping aside" translates *qu* (literally, "curved"), a sense suggested by Momoi Hakuroku's reading of this passage: "According to Wang's commentary, what is kept whole is one's brilliance, so *qu* must be the *qu* of *pianqu* [out of the way], and if one is out of the way, he is sure to be obscure [*an*]. If a person himself steps aside [i.e., out of the way], his whole being will fully shine forth" (quoted in Hatano, *Rōshi Dōtokukyō kenkyū*, 161). This is slightly different from the usual gloss of *qu* as "yielding," which seems to derive originally from Guo Xiang's

(d. 312) commentary to the *Zhuangzi*: "[Laozi said] . . . others all seek good fortune, but he [the sage] alone keeps his wholeness intact [*quan*] by yielding [*qu*]." Guo's commentary reads: "By yielding [*weishun*] to perfect truth, he always keeps his wholeness intact. Thus he has no good fortune to seek, as he already has all the good fortune he needs" (*Zhuangzi zhu* [Commentary to Zhuangzi], 10:86b). Most later commentators, however, gloss *qu* in this section of the *Laozi* as "yield to others," which is how Wing-tsit Chan, among others, has it in *The Way of Lao Tzu*, 139.

2. This and the next three passages of commentary are identical with the second, third, fourth, and fifth passages of Wang's commentary to section 24. Yi Shunding (1858–1920) notes how much closer these four lines fit the second to fifth passages of section 24 and concludes that they must have been copied from there to section 22 by some later hand. See Yi Shunding, *Du Lao zhaji* (Reading notes on *Laozi*), A:18a–18b; see also Hatano, *Rōshi Dōtokukyō kenkyū*, 161 and 170.

3. "Worn out" translates *bi*, which Wang seems to understand in its figurative sense, as a term of self-deprecation: "worn out/exhausted one," "humble I." That is, if one behaves with humility, he will never be worn out (humbled) and will remain forever "new," which, keeping with the metaphor, would mean "respected," "regarded as capable/important."

4. Cf. section 48.

5. "Access to one's roots" implies "success" (*de*) and the possession and exercise of "virtue" (*de*), while "being led astray" implies "failure" (*shi*) and the loss of "virtue." Cf. Wang's commentary to section 23, passages 4 and 5.

6. Cf. section 24, second passage.

7. Cf. section 66 and section 73, fifth passage.

8. Cf. section 14, second passage, where, instead of "reverting to it," the text reads "reverting to *wuwu* [nothingness]." That is, such a one will live out his life with his wholeness intact.

SECTION 23

The "inaudible" is a way of referring to the Natural.

> *"When we listen for it but hear it not, we call it the inaudible."* [1]
> *A later section says: "When the Dao is spoken of, how bland: it has no flavor at all! We look for it, but not enough is there to see*

anything. We listen for It, but not enough is there to hear any-
thing."[2] *As that is so, such expressions as "no flavor at all" and*
"not enough there to hear anything" are actually the most appro-
priate ways of referring to the Natural.

Thus a whirlwind does not last an entire morning, and a rainstorm does not last an entire day.[3] What is it that causes them? It
is Heaven and Earth. If even Heaven and Earth cannot make
them last long, how much less can man?

In other words, praise arising all at once[4] *does not last long.*

Thus, to undertake things in accordance with the Dao, the man
of Dao becomes one with the Dao.

Cong shi [undertake things] means managing affairs in accor-
dance with the Dao. The Dao completes [cheng] *and benefits*
[ji] *the myriad things without form or conscious effort. Thus*
one who undertakes things in accordance with the Dao "tends to
matters without conscious effort and practices the teaching that
is not expressed in words."[5] *On and on, he has only apparent*
existence, yet through him the people achieve authenticity.[6] *He*
is an embodiment of the Dao.[7] *Thus the text says, "becomes*
one with the Dao" [tong yu dao].

The man of virtue becomes one with virtue.

Virtue/success [de] *results from having little* [shao]. *"Having*
little gives one access [de], *"*[8] *and this is why the text here refers*
to virtue/success [de, *access*]. *If one practices virtue/success,*
such a one embodies virtue/success. Thus the text says that he
"becomes one with virtue."[9]

The man of failure becomes one with failure.

Failure [shi] *results from being entangled in having much* [duo].
If one is entangled in having much, he fails, and this is why the
text refers to "failure." If one practices failure, such a one embodies
failure. Thus the text says that he "becomes one with failure."

He who becomes one with virtue, the Dao also endows with virtue; he who becomes one with failure, the Dao also endows with
failure.[10]

In other words, the Dao reacts to one's practices and so responds
in kind.

If one fails to have trust, a corresponding lack of trust in him
occurs.[11]

When one's faith in those below fails, "a corresponding lack of
trust in him occurs."

NOTES

1. Section 14, first passage.

2. Section 35, third passage.

3. Cf. Wang's commentary to section 30, last passage.

4. "Praise arising all at once" translates *meixing*. Cf. Wang's commentary to section 30, last passage: "A whirlwind does not last an entire morning, and a rainstorm does not last an entire day. Thus a sudden rise [*baoxing*] surely goes against the Dao and will come to an early end." Commentators have found *meixing* problematic, however. Lou Yulie thinks the text is corrupt and, referring to the section 30 commentary, says that it should not read *baoji meixing buchang* (praise arising all at once does not last long) but *baoxing buchang* (sudden arisings do not last long);see *Wang Bi ji jiaoshi*, 59 n. 4. Another possibility, suggested by Momoi Hakuroku, is to read *xing* (arising) as *yu* (reputation), which would yield "a fine reputation [*meiyu*] that occurs all at once does not last long"; see Hatano, *Rōshi Dōtokukyō kenkyū*, 165.

5. Section 2, second and third passages. Cf. Wang's commentary to section 17, first passage. However, the text here reads *yiwuwei wei jun*, "reigns as sovereign without conscious effort." Because the same phrasing, *yi wuwei wei ju*, occurs in Wang's commentary to section 63, it is likely that *jun* (sovereign) here should be read as *ju* (tend to matters), a suggestion made by Jiang Xichang in his notes to section 2 of the *Laozi*; see *Laozi jiaogu* (Collations and glosses to *Laozi*), 14. Cf. Hatano, *Rōshi Dōtokukyō kenkyū*, 166–67, and Lou, *Wang Bi ji jiaoshi*, 59 n. 5.

6. Cf. Wang's commentary to section 6, first passage, and section 14, second passage.

7. "Is an embodiment of the Dao" translates *yu dao tong ti*, literally, "shares the same body with the Dao," which should be understood metaphorically. It is unlikely that *ti* here should be thought of as the abstract, metaphysical "substance" of the later Neo-Confucians. This is Alan K. L. Chan's conclusion in *Two Visions of the Way*, 66–67, where he draws attention to the syntax as it occurs identically in each of the next two passages of Wang's commentary—*yu de tong ti* (is an embodiment of success) and *yu shi tong ti* (is an embodiment of failure)—where the metaphorical dimension is more obvious. Cf. also Wang's commentary to section 6.

8. Section 22, fifth passage.

9. Wang identifies *de* (virtue) with *de* (success) and associates *de* (success) with the expression *de qiben*, "have access to one's roots,"

i.e., be successful in getting at them. One's "roots" are one's essentials, his "authenticity" (*zhen*), that which is a pure embodiment of the Dao. Creative, spontaneous, and natural, one's roots compare to the "root of Heaven and Earth." Cf. section 6.

10. This translates the sixth passage of section 23 as it is found in the Mawangdui *Laozi* B text; see *Mawangdui Hanmu boshu*, 120. The base text reads: "He who becomes one with the Dao, the Dao also gladly endows with virtue/success; he who becomes one with virtue/success, virtue/success also gladly endows with virtue/success; he who becomes one with failure, failure also gladly endows with failure." Wang's commentary contains no reference to the odd expression "gladly" (*le*), so it is unlikely that this is the text he knew. Even before the Mawangdui discovery, commentators have suspected that Wang's commentary did not fit the base text there; however, the Heshang Gong commentary is obviously written to it. See *Heshang Gong*, 2:6 (15653B); Hatano, *Rōshi Dōtokukyō kenkyū*, 168–69; and Lou, *Wang Bi ji jiaoshi*, 60 n. 8.

11. Identical to section 17, fifth passage.

SECTION 24

One up on tiptoes does not stand firm.

> *If one prizes advancement, he neglects security. Thus the text says, "One up on tiptoes does not stand firm."*

One who takes big strides does not move;[1] one who flaunts himself does not shine.

> *Avoid flaunting yourself, and your brilliance will remain unimpaired.*[2]

One who insists that he is right is not commended.

> *Avoid insisting that you are right, and your rightness will commend itself.*

One who boasts about himself has no acknowledged merit.

> *Avoid boasting about yourself, and your merit will be acknowledged.*

One filled with self-importance does not last long.

> *Avoid self-importance, and your virtue will long endure.*

In respect to the Dao, we can say about such behavior, too much food is an excrescence making the rounds.

> *Discussing such things in respect to the Dao, a good simile for Que Zhi's [sixth century B.C.E.][3] behavior is that it is like too*

*much food at a sumptuous feast. Although the basic dishes might
be very fine, anything more is wasteful extravagance. Although
Que Zhi's basic accomplishments deserved merit, because he
bragged about them, this excessive behavior was regarded as an
excrescence.*

The people always hate this, so one who has the Dao has nothing
to do with it.

NOTES

1. This line does not occur in the Mawangdui texts; as Wang does
not refer to it, it is likely that it was not part of the text that he knew.
However, the Heshang Gong commentary refers explicitly to it. See
Heshang Gong, 2:6 (15653B), and cf. Erkes, *Ho-shang Kung's Commentary
on Lao-Tse*, 51.

2. This and the next three passages of commentary are identical
with the first four passages of Wang's commentary to section 22. See
the note to Wang's commentary on the first passage there.

3. "When he [Que Zhi] conversed with Duke Xiang of Shan, he
was quick to boast of his accomplishments. The heir apparent of Shan
said to the grandees of court, 'Wenji [Que Zhi] is finished! Positioned
beneath seven others, he seeks to eclipse those above him. He is amass-
ing resentment, which has become the root of disorder. He increases
the resentment and would use the disorder as steps upward, but how
could he manage to stay in office doing that!' " (see sixteenth year in
the reign of Duke Cheng [574 B.C.E.] in Kong, *Chunqiu Zuozhuan zhengyi*
[Correct meaning of *Zuo's Commentary* on the *Spring and Autumn
Annals*], 28:18b–19a.) Cf. Legge, *The Chinese Classics*, 5:399.

SECTION   25

There is something, amorphous and complete, that was born
before Heaven and Earth.

*Amorphous, we are unable to know it, yet the myriad things by
it are made complete. Thus the text says it is "amorphous and
complete."[1] We do not know whose child it could be, therefore it
"was born before Heaven and Earth."*

Obscure, oh, and, immaterial, oh, it stands alone, unchanged.

Jiliao [ordinarily, "silent and empty/vague"] means "without physical form or substance" [wu xingti]. Nothing exists to match it. Therefore the text says: "it stands alone." In the end it always transforms itself back to what it was at the start, never losing its constancy. Thus the text says that it is "unchanged."

It operates everywhere but stays free from danger, thus we may consider it the mother of all under Heaven.[2]

Operating everywhere, nothing out of its reach yet never in any danger, it begets and keeps whole the great physical form [daxing].[3] Thus it may be considered the mother of all under Heaven.

We do not know its name

Names [ming] are used to determine forms [xing], but, amorphous and complete, it has no form, so we cannot make any such determination. Thus the text says that "we do not know its name."

So style it "Dao" [Way].

Names [ming] are used to determine forms, and style names [zi] are used to designate [cheng] attributes [ke]. To speak of "Dao" [Way] is derived from the fact that absolutely nothing fails to follow it and because, of all the terms that might be used to address the "amorphous and complete," this one has the broadest meaning.

Forced to give it a name, we call it "great."

The reason we style it "Dao" is that, of all the terms that might be used to address it, this one has the broadest meaning. Seeking the reason why this style name is assigned to it, we find that it is connected with the notion of greatness. But once such a connection [xi] exists, separation [fen] is sure to occur, and, once separation occurs, all sense of what it ultimately means is lost. Thus the text says, "forced to give it a name, we call it 'Great.'"

"Great" refers to the way it goes forth.

"Goes forth" means "operates," so the meaning here is not restricted just to the single sense of great as in "great body." As it operates everywhere, there is no place it does not reach. Thus the text says: "goes forth."

"Goes forth" describes how it is far-reaching, and "far-reaching" describes its reflexivity.

"Far-reaching" means "to reach the ultimate." As it operates everywhere, there is both nothing that lies beyond its infinite

reach and no particular direction of operation that it favors over
any other. Thus the text says: "far-reaching." Because it does
not subordinate itself to that to which it goes, as substance, it
"stands alone." This is why the text refers to its "reflexivity."

Thus the Dao is great, Heaven is great, Earth is great, and the
king is also great.

"Between Heaven and Earth, of all things endowed with life,
Man is the most valued,"[4] *and the king is the master of men.*
Although he might not be in charge of something great, he is
still great and a cohort of the other three.

Within the realm of existence there are the four greats,

The "four greats" are the Dao, Heaven, Earth, and the king.
All things have designations or names, but, as such, these are
not what they ultimately are. As for speaking of "Dao," this
has a derivation. First there is this derivation and only then do
we refer to it as "Dao." Although this is the greatest of all
equivalents for it, however, it falls short of the greatness of that
for which no equivalents exist. That for which no equivalents
exist cannot be named. Thus the text says "realm of existence."
The Dao, Heaven, Earth, and the king are all included among
that for which no equivalents exist. Thus the text says: "Within
the realm of existence there are the four greats."

And the king has title to one of these.

He occupies the position of a "great" as the master of men.

Man takes his models from Earth; Earth takes its models from
Heaven; Heaven takes its models from the Dao; and the Dao
takes its models from the Natural.

"To take models from" means "to follow the example of." It is
by taking his models from Earth that Man avoids acting contrary
to Earth and so obtains perfect safety. It is by taking its models
from Heaven that Earth avoids acting contrary to Heaven and
so achieves its capacity to uphold everything. It is by taking its
models from the Dao that Heaven avoids acting contrary to the
Dao and so achieves its capacity to cover everything. It is by
taking Its models from the Natural that the Dao avoids acting
contrary to the Natural and so realizes its own nature. To take
models from the Natural means that when it exists in a square,
it takes squareness as its model, and when it exists in a circle, it
takes circularity as its model: it does nothing that is contrary to
the Natural. "The Natural" is a term for that for which no equiv-

*alents exist, an expression for that which has infinite reach and
scope.[5] As using knowledge falls short of being without the capacity for knowing, so physical forms and earthbound souls fall
short of embryonic essences and images; embryonic essences and
images fall short of being free from forms, and to have the modes
[yin and yang] falls short of being without them.[6] Thus each
takes its models from the other in turn. The Dao complies with
the Natural, which results in Heaven having something to rely
on [the Dao]; Heaven takes its models from the Dao, which
results in Earth having something to emulate [Heaven]; Earth
takes its models from Heaven, which results in Man finding
images there [in the Earth]. The way the king becomes master
is by treating what he rules as a single entity.*

NOTES

1. Cf. section 1 of Wang's Outline Introduction.

2. Cf. section 52, second passage.

3. "The great physical form" refers to the sum of all physical existence: the grand, total embodiment of the Dao. See *Jundao* (The Dao
of the sovereign), in *Xunzi* (The sayings of Master Xun) (ca. 310–ca.
200 B.C.E.), 8:317B; cf. *On the Grand Embodiment of the Perfect Way*, in
Knoblock, *Xunzi*, 2:184–85: "Thus, the Son of Heaven does not look
yet sees, does not listen yet hears, does not think yet knows, does not
move yet accomplishes: rather, like a clod of earth he sits alone on his
mat, and the world follows him as though it were of a single body with
him, just as the four limbs follow the dictates of the mind. This may
indeed be described as the Grand Embodiment." That is, the perfect
ruler operates like the Dao itself.

4. Wang quotes *Shengzhi* (Government of the sage), section 9 of
the *Xiaojing* (Classic of filial piety); see Xing Bing et al., *Xiaojing zhushu*
(Commentaries and subcommentaries on the *Classic of Filial Piety*),
5:1a.

5. Evidence suggests that the text here might be corrupt: In his
commentary to Sun Chuo's (314–71) *Tiantaishan fu* (Rhapsody on
roaming the Celestial Terrace Mountains), Li Shan (ca. 630–89) quotes
Wang Bi's commentary to this passage, "Heaven takes its models from
the Dao; and the Dao takes its models from the Natural," but instead
of *wucheng zhi yan* (a term for that for which no equivalents exist) his

quotation has *wuyi ʒhi yan* (a term for that for which there is no meaning). See *Wenxuan*, 11:3b. In addition, the Qing era scholar Hong
Yixuan (1765–1837) in his *Dushu ʒonglu* (Collected notes on works read)
observes that the Tang monk Falin in his polemical treatise against
Daoism, the *Bian ʒheng lun* (Treatise on determining what is correct;
dated 626), cites this passage in the *Laoʒi* and appears to quote from a
version of Wang Bi's commentary that is quite different: "As such, the
Dao of Heaven and the Dao of Earth are not at all contrary to each
other, and this is why the text refers to the 'taking of models.' 'The
Natural' is an expression for that for which no equivalents exist and
which has infinite reach and scope. 'The Dao' is a term of the utmost
wisdom and ingenuity." I suspect that Falin is paraphrasing rather than
quoting Wang's text and cannot agree with Hong Yixuan when he uses
this discrepancy as evidence that Wang's commentary to the *Laoʒi*, here
at least, was "patched together" by later writers. See Lou, *Wang Bi ji
jiaoshi*, 68 n. 28.

    6. Cf. section 4.

SECTION 26

The heavy is the foundation of the light, and quietude is the
sovereign of activity.

> *For all things, the light cannot uphold the heavy, and the small
> cannot press down the large. The one who does not act causes
> action, and the one who does not move causes movement. This
> is the reason that the heavy is surely the foundation of the light
> and quietude is surely the sovereign of activity.*[1]

This is why the sage travels throughout the day yet does not
separate himself from his retinue.

> *Because he treats the heavy [himself as sovereign] as the foun-
> dation [of the state], he does not separate himself from it [the
> protection of his retinue].*

So despite the presence of glorious scenery, he remains relaxed
and detached.

> *His heart/mind is not captivated by it.*[2]

How could one be the master of ten thousand war chariots and
yet treat his own person lighter than all under Heaven![3] If he
treats it lighter, he will lose his foundation. If he engages in activity, he will lose his sovereignty.[4]

If he treats it lighter, he will not hold down [pacify/stabilize]
what is heavier [all under Heaven]. "Lose his foundation"
means he will lose his life. "Lose his sovereignty" means he
will lose the position of sovereign.

NOTES

1. Cf. Wang's commentaries to section 16, third passage, and section 45, last passage. His commentary to Top Yin of Hexagram 32, *Heng*
(Perseverance), in the *Yijing* (Classic of changes) reads: "Quietude is
the sovereign of activity, and repose is the master of action. Thus repose
is the state in which the one at the top [the ruler] should reside, and it is
through quietude that the Dao of everlasting duration works" (Lynn,
The Classic of Changes, 339; see Lou, *Wang Bi ji jiaoshi*, 380). Qian Zhongshu cites another relevant passage from the *Yijing* to help elucidate this
passage; it is from the *Tuanzhuan* (Commentary on the Judgments) to
Hexagram 24, *Fu* (Return): "In *Fu* [Return] we can see the very heart
and mind of Heaven and Earth!" To which Wang Bi comments:

> *Return* as such means "to revert to what is the original substance
> [*ben*]," and for Heaven and Earth we regard the original substance
> to be the mind/heart. Whenever activity ceases, tranquillity results,
> but tranquillity is not opposed to activity. Whenever speech ceases,
> silence results, but silence is not opposed to speech. As this is so,
> then even though Heaven and Earth are so vast that they possess
> the myriad things in great abundance, which, activated by thunder
> and moved by the winds, keep undergoing countless numbers of
> transformations, yet the original substance of Heaven and Earth
> consists of perfectly quiescent nonbeing [*wu*, nothingness]. Thus
> it is only when earthly activity ceases that the heart/mind of
> Heaven and Earth can be seen. If Heaven and Earth were to have
> had being [substance, actuality] instead for this heart/mind, then
> it never would have been possible for all the different categories
> of things to become endowed with existence.
>
> (Lynn, *The Classic of Changes*, 286;
> see Lou, *Wang Bi ji jiaoshi*, 336–37)

2. Wang's commentary suggests that the base text is the text he knew.
In place of "glorious scenery" (*rongguan*), however, the Mawangdui

texts have "walled hostelry" (*huanguan*), and it is likely that Text A, which has "only" (*wei*) in place of "despite" (*sui*), is the more authentic reading: "Only when there is a walled hostelry to which he can retire can he become detached" (*Mawangdui Hanmu boshu*, 121). Wang's commentary is obviously not to this version. See Henricks, *Lao-Tʐu Te-Tao Ching*, 238.

3. Cf. section 13, fourth and fifth passages.

4. The sage should reside in quietude and not get caught up in activity. Cf. Wang's *Zhouyi lueli* (General Remarks on the *Changes of the Zhou*), *Ming tuan* (Clarifying the Judgments): "The many cannot govern the many; that which governs the many is the most solitary [*gua*, he One]. Activity cannot govern activity; that which controls all activity that occurs in the world, thanks to constancy, is the One. Therefore for all the many to manage to exist, their controlling principle must reach back to the One, and for all activities to manage to function, their source cannot but be the One" (Lynn, *The Classic of Changes*, 25; see Lou, *Wang Bi ji jiaoshi*, 591).

SECTION 27

One good at traveling leaves no tracks or prints.

> *He follows the path of the Natural, neither formulating nor implementing, thus things attain perfection without his leaving track or print on them.*[1]

One good at words says nothing flawed or blameworthy.

> *He follows the nature of things, neither distinguishing nor discriminating, thus no flaw or blame can be laid at his door.*

One good at reckoning does not use bamboo tallies.

> *He follows the count of things without relying on external forms.*

One good at locking up has no lock yet what is locked cannot be opened. One good at tying up has no cord yet what is tied cannot be untied.

> *He follows the natural bent of people, neither formulating nor implementing, thus, though he uses neither lock nor cord, no opening or untying can occur. These five [traveling/acting, using words, reckoning, locking up, and tying up] all refer to how one should avoid formulating and implementing. Instead, he should follow the nature of the people and not try to carve [zhi] them into shapes according to forms external to them.*[2]

This is how the sage is always good at saving people, so no one is discarded,

> *The sage does not establish punishments and names in order to impose restraints on the people.[3] Nor does he create promotions and honors[4] in order to cull and discard the unworthy. He enhances the natural state of the myriad folk but does not serve as the starting point for them.[5] Thus the text says, "no one is discarded." Because he does not exalt the worthy and the resourceful, the common folk do not contend. Because he does not value goods hard to get, the common folk do not become thieves. Because he does not allow them to see desirable things, the hearts/minds of the common folk are not subject to disorder.[6] It is because he keeps the hearts/minds of the common folk from desire and from going astray that "no one is discarded."*

Always good at saving things, and so nothing is discarded. This is what is known as maintaining the light. Thus the good man is the teacher of men who are not good.[7]

> *He fosters goodness as a means to teach those who are not good. Thus the text refers to such a one as "teacher."*

Men who are not good are material for the good man.

> *Zi [material] means qu [included].[8] The good man relies on goodness to keep in order those who are not good; he does not[9] rely on goodness to discard those who are not good. This is why men who are not good are included by the good man.*

But if they do not value their teacher, and he does not cherish his material, no matter how wise, one will become greatly lost.

> *No matter how much intelligence one has, if he depends on that intelligence but does not conform to [the natural bent of] things, he is sure to get lost on the way ["way" (dao) is a pun on "Dao"]. Thus the text says, "one will be greatly lost."*

This is called the "profoundly subtle."[10]

NOTES

1. *Xing*, "travel," can also mean "act." Alan Chan provides a translation (significantly different from mine in places) of Wang's commentary to section 27 and compares it to the Heshang Gong commentary in *Two Visions of the Way*, 165–67.

2. Cf. Wang's commentary to section 28, last passage.

3. The base text reads "forms" (*xing*) instead of "punishments" (*xing*), However, "punishments" is the more likely; cf. section 2 of Wang's Outline Introduction, which reads: "If one tries to control people with punishments, cleverness and treachery will surely arise; if one tries to define with names how people should behave, order and consideration will surely be lost." However, see also section 17, last passage.

4. "Promotions and honors" translates *jinshang*, but the base text has *jinxiang*, "direction of advance," which does not make sense in this context. See Lou, *Wang Bi ji jiaoshi*, 73 n. 9. Lou thinks that *jinshang* should be construed as verb plus object, "promote the worthy." I think it more likely that it is a noun-plus-noun construction, parallel to the "punishments and names" of the previous sentence.

5. Cf. section 2, third passage; Wang's commentary to section 17, first passage; and section 64, last passage.

6. Cf. section 3, first passage; section 12, second passage; section 49, fifth passage, paragraph 1; and section 64, seventh passage.

7. Section 27, fourth, fifth, and sixth passages, as well as Wang's commentary to them, bear comparison with section 49, first through fifth passages, and section 62, second and fourth passages, along with Wang's commentary to all seven.

8. Wang's gloss of *zi*, "assets" or "material," as *qu*, "included," surely derives from the fact that *qu*, "include," is the opposite of *qi*, "discard": if the good man does not "discard" bad men, he must "include" them. *Zi* in its verbal sense means "rely on," "make use of," so, strictly speaking, Wang must have read this passage as "Men who are not good are made use of/worked on by the good man."

9. The base text lacks the negative *bu*, "does not"; however, the overwhelming consensus among textual scholars of Wang's commentary is that the passage must have a negative here to make sense. See Hatano, *Rōshi Dōtokukyō kenkyū*, 193, and Lou, *Wang Bi ji jiaoshi*, 73 n. 13. Without the negative, the passage could only be read as "he relies on goodness to eliminate the lack of goodness," that is, get rid of the sin and not the sinner. In my opinion, this reading is possible but not likely, given the context.

10. "Profoundly subtle" translates *yaomiao*. Although Wang does not comment on this passage, others usually regard it as a summary comment on the section as a whole that refers to the sage described earlier.

SECTION   28

He who knows the male yet sustains the female will be a river valley for all under Heaven.[1] He who is a river valley for all under Heaven never separates himself from constant virtue and always reverts to the infant.

> *The male belongs to that category of being that is in front; the female belongs to that category of being that is in the rear. One who knows that he is foremost among all under Heaven must put himself in the rear. "As such, the sage places himself in the rear yet finds himself in front."[2] The river valley does not solicit anything, yet things come to it as a matter of course. The infant does not use any knowledge of its own, yet it communes with the knowledge of nature.*

He who knows the white yet sustains the black will be a model for all under Heaven.[3]

> Shi *[model] means a* mo *[mold].*

He who is a model for all under Heaven never deviates from constant virtue

> Te *[deviate] means* cha *[differ].*

And always reverts to the infinite.

> *This means the inexhaustible.*

He who knows glory yet sustains disgrace will be a valley for all under Heaven.[4] He who is a valley for all under Heaven is filled completely by constant virtue, for he always reverts to the uncarved block.

> *These three state that it is only with constant reversion to such ends [to the infant, the infinite, and the uncarved block* (pu)*] that virtue completely fills him in whom it resides. A later section says, "Reversion is the action of the Dao."[5] Efficacy is not something that one can seize, for it always resides with the mother.[6]*

When the uncarved block fragments, it turns into implements. As the sage would make use of them, he stands as chief of officials over them.

> *The uncarved block* [pu] *is authenticity* [zhen]. *When authenticity fragments, many different kinds of behavior emerge, and many different types of people appear, just like a variety of implements. Because they are so fragmented, the sage stands as chief of officials over them. He employs good men as teachers*

for those who are not good, and those who are not good become material to be worked on.[7] *By his reformation of customs and transformation of habits, he brings about a reversion to the One.* Thus the great carver never cuts.

Because "the great carver" [dazhi] *takes the heart/mind* [xin] *of all under Heaven as his heart/mind, he never cuts.*[8]

NOTES

1. This might be paraphrased as "A ruler who knows how to be-have as a male yet can sustain female behavior and treatment will. . . ." Cf. section 32, last passage, section 61, first passage, and section 66.

2. Section 7, second passage. Cf. section 66.

3. This might be paraphrased as "A ruler who knows he is inno-cent yet can bear being treated as if he were guilty will. . . ." Cf. Wang's commentary to section 41, seventh passage.

4. This might be paraphrased as "A ruler who knows glory yet can bear disgrace will. . . ." Cf. section 78, second passage.

5. Section 40, first passage.

6. Cf. section 20, last passage; and Wang's commentary to section 38, paragraph 5.

7. Cf. Wang's commentary to section 27, seventh passage.

8. "Cuts" translates *ge*. I suggest that Wang understood "cut" in the way the merely good cook did his cutting, which required him to change his knife once a year, as described in the *Zhuangzi*, in the parable of Cook Ding (Pao Ding), who, completely in step with the Dao, never has to change his knife: "I go along with the natural makeup [natural patterns (*tianli*)], strike in the big hollows, guide the knife through the big openings, and follow things as they are. So I never touch the smallest ligament or tendon, much less a main joint. A good cook changes his knife once a year—because he cuts [*ge*]. A mediocre cook changes his knife once a month—because he hacks" (*Zhuangzi yinde*, 7/3/7, as translated in Watson, *Complete Works of Chuang Tzu*, 51). Other occa-sions of *ge*, "cut," in Wang's commentary (section 41, passages 5 and 11; and section 58, passage 7), also suggest that "cut" always has the sense of "cut wrong," "cut unnaturally," or simply "harm" or "damage"; cf. the English "cut against the grain." For "takes the heart/mind [*xin*] of all under Heaven as his heart/mind," see section 48, first passage. Cf. the "great carpenter" in section 74, second passage.

SECTION   29

As for those who would like to take all under Heaven and act on it, the way I see it, such action would never end, because all under Heaven is the numinous vessel,

> *"Numinous" [shen] is that which is formless [wuxing] and infinite [wufang]. A vessel [qi] is something formed by being combined together [hecheng]. But because it [all under Heaven] is composed without form, we refer to it to as "the numinous vessel."*

Which cannot be acted on. One who acts on it will destroy it; one who tries to grasp it will lose it.

> *The myriad folk follow nature [ziran] in forming their natures [xing]. This is why one can act in accordance with them but not act on them, can identify with them but not interfere with them. People have their constant nature, so if one tries to create something artificial out of them, he is sure to destroy them. People have their own comings and goings, so if one tries to grasp them, he is sure to lose them.*

Thus some people tend to lead and some follow; some breathe in through the nose and some blow out through the mouth;[1] some are strong and some weak; and some are energetic and some lazy. As this is so, the sage rids them of extremism, extravagance, and complaisance.

> *All these examples of "some," because people alternate between cooperation and obstinacy, advocate that one should not take action against or interfere with them. The sage thoroughly understands what human nature [xing] is by nature and allows the innate tendencies [qing] of all the myriad folk full expression. Therefore he follows and does not act, complies and does not interfere. He eliminates what leads people astray and gets rid of what confuses them. Therefore, hearts/minds freed from disorder, human nature is allowed to fulfill itself.*

NOTES

1. Whereas those who "breathe in through the nose" are surely the sedate, the cool, and the calm, those who "blow out through the mouth" are the impetuous, the passionate, and the excitable.

SECTION 30

One who would assist the ruler of men in accordance with the Dao does not use military force to gain power over all under Heaven.

> *Even one who, in accordance with the Dao, assists the ruler of men may not use military force to gain power over all under Heaven, so how much more this is true for the ruler of men who devotes himself to the Dao!*

As for such matters, he is wont to let them revert.[1]

> *Whereas one who consciously works at governing earnestly wants to have effect and make things happen, one who has the Dao earnestly wants things to revert to where no conscious effort [wuwei] is involved. Thus the text says: "As for such matters, he is wont to let them revert."*

Where armies deploy, there thistles and thorns grow. The aftermath of great military operations is surely a year of famine.

> *In other words, an army is a cruel and wicked thing. Not beneficial, it is surely harmful, for it devastates the people and ravages the land. Thus the text says: "there thistles and thorns grow."*

One good at this desists when result is had and dares not use the opportunity to seize military supremacy.

> *Guo [result] means ji [relief]. This says that the good military leader sets out to relieve people from danger and then desists. He does not use military force to gain power over all under Heaven.*

Have result but do not take credit for it; have result but do not boast about it; have result but do not take pride in it;

> *I do not regard the Dao of military leadership worthy of esteem and use it only when there is no other choice, so what is there to take credit for or boast about?*

Have result but only when there is no choice; have result but do not try to gain military supremacy.

> *In other words, although one sets forth to succeed and relieve people from danger, this should only be done in cases where there is no other choice and only to quell violent insurrection. One should not go on to take advantage of such results to gain military supremacy.*

Once a thing reaches its prime, it grows old. We say it goes against the Dao, and what is against the Dao comes to an early end.[2]

"Its prime" refers to the sudden rise of military power and is a metaphor for the use of military force to gain supremacy over all under Heaven. "A whirlwind does not last an entire morning, and a rainstorm does not last an entire day."[3] Thus a sudden rise surely goes against the Dao and will come to an early end.

NOTES

1. Wang's commentary suggests that *qishi haohuan* be translated "as for such matters, he is wont to let them revert." Most commentators, however, seem to read it as "such matters tend to rebound" (cf. "those that live by the sword die by the sword"), an interpretation popular among translators of the *Laozi*.

2. Cf. section 55, last passage.

3. Section 23, second passage.

SECTION   31[1]

Weapons[2] are instruments of ill omen. The people always hate them, so one who has the Dao has nothing to do with them. When the noble man is at home, he honors the left and, when employing troops, honors the right. Weapons are instruments of ill omen; they are not the instruments of the noble man, who uses them only when there is no choice. It is best to be utterly dispassionate [*tiandan*] about them, and, even if they bring victory, one should not praise them. Nevertheless, to praise them means that one delights in slaughtering people, and one who delights in slaughtering people, of course, can never achieve the goal of ruling all under Heaven. For auspicious matters, one honors the left, and, for inauspicious matters, one honors the right. A deputy general takes his place on the left, but a general-in-chief takes his place on the right, where mourning rites are observed. When masses of people are slaughtered, one should weep for them with utmost sadness, so, when victorious in war, one should observe it with mourning rites.

NOTES

1. Sections 31 and 66 have no commentary by Wang Bi. Although throughout the ages many have speculated about these two omissions, the most likely reason for them is that Wang probably considered the two sections self-explanatory and so in need of no commentary. The speculation that the two sections are spurious has now been refuted by the discovery of the two Mawangdui texts, which contain them both. In any case, the phrase "it is best to be utterly dispassionate [*tiandan*] about them" is echoed in Wang's commentary to section 63, first passage, which suggests his familiarity with section 31. Another possibility, of course, is that Wang did write a commentary to these two sections but the texts were lost at some early date. The text of section 31 used here is the base text as given in Lou, *Wang Bi ji jiaoshi*, 80.

2. The base text reads *jiabing*, "beautiful weapons," but both Mawangdui texts simply read "weapons"; see *Mawangdui Hanmu boshu*, 122. I suspect that if *jiabing* had occurred in the text he knew, Wang would have commented on it, perhaps along the lines of the Heshang Gong commentary: " 'Auspicious' refers to good things, but weapons alarm the spirit and muddy an aura of harmony. They are the instruments of bad men, and one should not decorate them" (*Heshang Gong zhu Laozi Daodejing*, 2:13 (15657A); cf. Erkes, *Ho-shang Kung's Commentary on Lao-Tse*, 62).

SECTION 32

The Dao in its constancy is "nameless." Although the uncarved block is small, none under Heaven can make it his servitor [*chen*], but, if any lord or prince could hold on to it, the myriad folk would submit spontaneously.

> *The Dao is formless, not attached to anything,*[1] *and in its constancy cannot be named, so we use "nameless" to refer to it in its constancy. Thus the text says, "The Dao in its constancy is 'nameless.' "*[2] *The uncarved block* [pu] *as such has nothingness* [wu] *for heart/mind* [xin], *and this too is nameless. Therefore, if one would attain the Dao, nothing is better than holding on to the uncarved block. One who is wise may accordingly become a capable minister* [chen]*;*[3] *one who is brave may accordingly be used in a military capacity; one who is clever may accord-*

ingly be assigned bureaucratic duties; and one who is strong
may accordingly be charged with heavy responsibilities. But the
uncarved block as such, all muddled together,[4] *has no such pre-*
dilection [pian] *and almost totally lacks existence. Thus the*
text says, "none . . . can make it his servitor." If one embraces
the uncarved block, engages in no conscious effort [wuwei],
neither lets his authenticity [zhen] *be hampered by things nor*
lets his spirit [shen] *be harmed by desire, then the people will*
submit to him spontaneously, and he shall attain the Dao as a
matter of course.

As when Heaven and Earth unite to send down sweet dew, though
not one of the people are ordered to do so,[5] they live in harmony
of their own accord.

In other words, as when Heaven and Earth unite, sweet dew,
though not sought, falls of its own accord, if I hold on to my
authentic nature, though the people are not ordered to do so,
they will live in harmony of their own accord.

When the cutting of it starts, names come into existence. Once
names exist, one should know to stop. It is by knowing to stop
that danger can be avoided.

"When the cutting of it starts" refers to when the uncarved block
begins to fragment and [the sage] becomes chief of officials.[6]
When he first cuts out senior officials, he cannot help but set up
names and ranks [mingfen] *in order to establish superiors and*
inferiors [zunbei]. *Thus "when the cutting of it [the uncarved*
block] starts, names come into existence." If he lets things go
beyond this, there will be contention over [issues as small as]
the point of a small knife.[7] *Thus the text says: "Once names*
exist, one should know to stop." Eventually, if the names of
official appointments are used to address people, the mother
[natural source/Dao] of government will be lost. Thus "It is
by knowing that it should stop that danger can be avoided."

As an analogy, the relationship between the Dao and all under
Heaven is similar to the way streams and tributaries respond to
the river and the sea.[8]

The relationship between streams and tributaries and the river
and the sea is such that it is not because the river and the sea
summon them but because streams and tributaries gravitate to
them without being summoned or sought. One who practices the
Dao among all under Heaven issues no orders, yet the people

live in harmony of their own accord; he does not seek [the myriad folk], yet he obtains them as a matter of course. Thus the text says: "It is similar to the way streams and tributaries respond to the river and the sea."

NOTES

1. Cf. Wang's commentary to section 21, second passage.

2. Cf. section 1.

3. The *nengchen*, "capable minister," here playfully echoes the *tianxiamo neng chen ye*, "none under Heaven can make it his servitor," of the text.

4. "All muddled together" translates *kuiran*. *Kui* describes confused or unclear—"muddled"—states of the heart/mind, a perfect description of the undifferentiated, nonpurposeful, nonconscious attitudes and activities of the Daoist sage. This reading has been surprisingly overlooked, however, and scholars tend to insist that *kui* (muddled) should be read either as *tui* (meek, compliant) or *yi* (lacking everything, lost all). See Hatano, *Rōshi Dōtokukyō kenkyū*, 219; and Lou, *Wang Bi ji jiaoshi*, 83 n. 5.

5. A passive construction is indicated by Wang's commentary below: "One who practices the Dao among all under Heaven issues no orders yet the people live in harmony of their own accord."

6. See Wang's commentary to section 28, sixth passage.

7. "Once the people know that there is a basis for contention, they will cast propriety aside and base arguments on the written law. Though it might be [matters as small as] the point of a small knife, they will all wrangle over them" (sixth year in the reign of Duke Zhao [535 B.C.E.] in Kong, *Chunqiu Zuozhuan zhengyi* [Correct meaning of *Zuo's Commentary* on the *Spring and Autumn Annals*], 42:9b–10a; cf. Legge, *The Chinese Classics*, 5:609).

8. Cf. section 28, first passage; section 61, first passage; and section 66.

SECTION 33

One who knows others is wise, but one who knows himself is perspicacious.

Knowing others consists in nothing more than using intelligence [zhi], *which falls short of knowing oneself, for this transcends intelligence.*[1]

One who conquers others has strength, but one who conquers himself is powerful.

Conquering others consists in nothing more than using strength, which falls short of conquering oneself, for here there is no one else for whom one saps his strength. Using one's intelligence on others falls short of using one's intelligence on oneself. Using one's strength on others falls short of using one's strength on oneself. If one's perspicacity [ming] *is used to illuminate oneself, no one else will escape from it. If one's strength is used on oneself, no one else will change places with him.*[2]

One who knows contentment is rich.

One who knows contentment is himself not wanting for anything. Thus he is rich.

One who acts with power has his goal fulfilled.

If one acts with diligence and ability, his goal will surely be realized. Thus the text says: "One who acts with power has his goal fulfilled."

One who does not lose his place lasts long.

If one examines himself with perspicacity, acts in accordance with his strength, and does not lose his place, he is sure to enjoy a long reign [jiuchang].[3]

One who dies but is not destroyed has longevity.

Although one dies, thanks to the Dao by which he lives, he is not destroyed [buwang], *and that is how he manages to enjoy longevity to the full. The Dao still exists after one's person* [shen] *ceases to exist, so how more likely is it that the Dao will not cease while one's person does exist!*[4]

NOTES

1. Cf. section 16, sixth passage.

2. "Change places with him" translates *gai yan*, that is, "usurp his throne/replace him as ruler," a reading that breaks with textual scholars such as Hattori Nankaku (1683–1759), Otsuki Joden (1845–1931), Hatano Tarō, and Lou Yulie, who read *gai* as *gong* (attack), making this "launch an attack on him," and those such as Momoi Hakuroku

(1722–1801) who read *gai* as *bai* (defeat), which yields "inflict defeat on him." See Hatano, *Rōshi Dōtokukyō kenkyū*, 226, and Lou, *Wang Bi ji jiaoshi*, 85 n. 2.

3. Cf. Robber Zhi's reply to Confucius, who was trying to persuade him to give up banditry and become a proper ruler: "Now you tell me about this great walled state, this multitude of people, trying to sway me with offers of gain, to lead me by the nose like any common fool. But how long [*jiuchang*] do you think I could keep possession of it?" (*Zhuangzi yinde*, 81/29/26; cf. Watson, *Complete Works of Chuang Tzu*, 326–27).

4. We should note that Wang's commentary cannot have been to the text as it appears in the two Mawangdui versions, both of which read: *si er buwangzhe shou ye*, "Dead yet not forgotten, this is longevity." See *Mawangdui Hanmu boshu*, 123. As for Wang's own reading of this passage, the syntax and wording of his commentary are ambiguous in places, and one has to rely to a great extent on the context of Wang's reading of the *Laozi* as a whole to interpret his argument, which I paraphrase here: Although one has to die, if he lives in accordance with the Dao, he can avoid an early, untimely death. As a ruler devoted to the Dao, he can avoid the danger of rebellion within and conquest from without, reign long and thus enjoy longevity. The Dao will not fail him. Since the Dao will go on operating after he is gone, there is no doubt that it will do so while he is still alive. Alan Chan also does a careful translation and thoughtful analysis of this passage of Wang's commentary (see *Two Visions of the Way*, 163), but I have to disagree with his results. Wang's reading of this passage, of course, also differs sharply from the many interpretations throughout the ages that find evidence in it for a belief in spiritual or physical immortality. It also differs from those who interpret it in terms of identification with the eternal Dao, by which one transcends the dualism of life and death, as, for example, Su Che (1039–1112): "The change that life and death bring about is indeed great! Yet his nature [*xing*] is so profound and tranquil that it does not perish [*buwang*]. This is the perfect man [*zhiren*] of antiquity, one who can free himself from both life and death" (*Daode zhenjing zhu* [Commentary on the *True Classic of the Way and Virtue*], 2:21 [16101A]).

SECTION   34

The way the great Dao floods, oh, it can go left or right.

> *In other words, the Dao floods in such a way that there is no place that it does not go. It functions [yong] with the ability of operating everywhere, left, right, up, or down, thus there is no place it does not reach.*[1]

The myriad folk rely on it for life, but it does not tell them to do so.[2] It achieves success but enjoys no reputation for doing so. It clothes and feeds the myriad folk but does not become their master. It is always without desire and so can be named among the small.

> *The myriad things all derive life from the Dao, but, having life, they do not know where it came from. Therefore, when all under Heaven are without desire, each of the myriad folk will obtain his proper place, and it will be as if the Dao had done nothing for them. Thus it is named among the small.*

The myriad things return to it, but it does not become their master, so it can be named among the great.

> *All the myriad things return to it for life, but it assiduously ensures that they do not know where they come from, which is no small matter. Thus one can again name it among the great.*

Therefore it is because he himself never tries to be great that he fulfills his greatness.[3]

> *"Plan for the difficult while it is still easy; work at the great while it is still small."*[4]

NOTES

1. Cf. *Zhuangzi*, which reads: "Master Tung-kuo [Dongguo] asked Chang Tzu [Zhuangzi], 'This thing called the Way [Dao], where does it exist?' Chang Tzu said, 'There's no place it doesn't exist.' " (*Zhuangzi yinde*, 59/22/43; cf. Watson, *Complete Works of Chuang Tzu*, 240).

2. The base text (*diben*) reads *buci*, "does not tell [them to do so]," as it does in a similar line in section 2, third passage. It is possible, however, that *buci*, "does not tell [them to do so]," should read *bushi*, "does not start [them to do so]." See note 3 in section 2.

3. Cf. section 63, third passage: "Therefore it is because the sage never tries to be great that he fulfills his greatness."

4. Section 63, third passage.

SECTION 35

Grasp the great image, and all under Heaven will turn to you.

The "great image" is the mother of the images of Heaven.[1] *It is neither hot nor cold, neither warm nor cool,*[2] *thus it can perfectly embrace the myriad things, and none suffers any harm. If a ruler grasps it, all under Heaven would turn to him.*

Turning to you means not harm but safety and peace in great measure.

Such a one is formless and without consciousness, has neither predilections [pian] *nor outer signs* [zhang],[3] *thus the myriad folk can turn to him and stay free of harm.*

Music and fine food make the passing visitor stay. When the Dao is spoken of, how bland: it has no flavor at all! We look for it, but not enough is there to see anything. We listen for it, but not enough is there to hear anything.[4] We try to use it, but not enough is there to use up.

This speaks to the profundity and greatness of the Dao. When one hears the words of the Dao, he does not find them at all like music and fine food, which, when one responds to them, cause a reaction of heartfelt pleasure. With music and fine food, one can detain a passing visitor, but the words that come out of the Dao are so bland they are utterly without flavor. We look for it, but not enough is there to see anything, so not enough is there either to please the eye. We listen for it, but not enough is there to hear anything, so not enough is there either to delight the ear. It is as if it has nothing at all inside it, and this is why in using it one finds that it is inexhaustible.[5]

NOTES

1. Section 11 of the *Xici zhuan* (Commentary on the Appended Phrases), Part One, in the *Yijing* (Classic of changes), reads in part: "Heaven hung images [*xiang*] in the sky and revealed good fortune and bad, and the sages regarded these as meaningful signs" (Lynn, *The Classic of Changes*, 66; see *Zhouyi zhengyi* [Correct meaning of the *Changes of the Zhou*], 7:29b). The "images of Heaven" are the sun, moon, planets, and constellations. The "great image" is another way to refer to the Dao.

2. Section 41, fourteenth passage: "The great image is formless," about which Wang comments: "As soon as there is a form, distinctions exist, and, with distinctions, if something is not warm, it must be cool; if not hot, it must be cold, Thus an image that has a form is not the great image." Cf. also Wang's commentary to section 16, sixth passage; section 55, sixth passage; and section 1 of his his Outline Introduction, which reads: "The formless and the nameless [the Dao] is the progenitor of the myriad things. It is neither warm nor cool. . . . Try to capture it as an image, and it will be utterly formless. . . . If it were warm, it could not be cold. . . . Thus an image that takes an actual form is not the great image."

3. Cf. Wang's commentary to section 16, sixth passage.

4. Cf. section 14.

5. Cf. Wang's commentary to section 4 and section 1 of his Outline Introduction, which reads: "You might listen for it, but it is impossible to get a sense of its sound; you might look for it, but it is impossible to get a sense of its appearance; you might try to understand what it is like, but it is impossible to get it in terms of understanding; or you might taste it, but it is impossible to get it in terms of flavor."

SECTION 36

If you would like to gather him in, you must resolve yourself to let him aggrandize himself. If you would like to weaken him, you must resolve yourself to let him grow strong. If you would like to nullify him, you must resolve yourself to let him flourish. If you would like to take him, you must resolve yourself to let him have his way. Such an approach is called subtle and perspicacious.

> *If you would remove the dangerously bold[1] and get rid of the rebellious, you should do so by these four methods. Take advantage of the nature of the man involved, allow him to destroy himself, and do not rely on punishment as the major means to get rid of such harmful elements.[2] Thus the text characterizes such an approach as "subtle and perspicacious." Let such a fellow find satisfaction in his aggrandizement, for, if you allow him satisfaction, he will seek even more aggrandizement, and then he will be gathered in by the mass of common folk.[3] Rather than prevent him from aggrandizing himself to the point where*

it is satisfying and divert him from trying to aggrandize himself
as such, it would be better to let him keep increasing it so that he
brings danger back on himself.[4]

Softness and pliancy conquer hardness and forcefulness. Fish
must not be allowed to escape to the depths. The sharp instruments of the state may not be disclosed to the people.

"Sharp instruments" [liqi] are devices [qi] used to profit the
state [li guo]. Act only in accordance with the nature [xing] of
the people and do not rely on punishment to keep them in order.
It is by ensuring that these devices cannot be seen, thus allow-
ing everyone to obtain his proper place, that they are the "sharp
instruments" of the state. Disclosing them to the people means
relying on punishment. If one tries to use punishment to profit
the state, it will mean loss. If fish escape to the depths, they
certainly are lost. If it is as devices used to profit the state that
one establishes punishments and as such discloses them to the
people, this also surely will mean loss.[5]

NOTES

1. Cf. section 42, last passage.

2. "Harmful elements" translates *qiangwu*, reading *qiang* (harmful)
for the base text *jiang* (about to), which makes no sense. This follows
the suggestion of Hattori Nankaku, cited in Hatano, *Rōshi Dōtokukyō*
kenkyū, 240; see also Lou, *Wang Bi ji jiaoshi*, 90 n. 1.

3. "Gather in" translates *she*, the base text reading. The Mawangdui
A text has *shi* (grab, gather in, harvest); Mawangdui B has *jian* (bind,
grab, gather in, harvest); and Fu Yi's composite text based on old manuscripts has *xi* (gather in, harvest). See *Mawangdui Hanmu boshu*, 124.
The translation of *she* as "contract" or "shrink," favored by many recent
English translations because these words are opposites of "expand" or
"stretch," renderings for *zhang* (aggrandize), seems forced and unlikely
in the light of early textual variants. It certainly is not how Wang read
the text of the *Laozi*. I settled on "gather in" instead of simply "grab"
because I think it fits with the overall theme of this passage that troublemakers should be allowed to swell, ripen, or mature to the point where,
like ripe fruit or grain, they can be "gathered in" or harvested by the
irate common folk; in other words, they should be given enough rope
to hang themselves.

4. Although the text seems to make good sense as it stands, it has been judged corrupt, and various attempts have been made to amend it, none of which, in my opinion, either are necessary or present better readings. See Hatano, *Rōshi Dōtokukyō kenkyū*, 241; and Lou, *Wang Bi ji jiaoshi*, 90 n. 4.

5. Using punishments to keep the people in order will make them hide (avoid authority), just as an inept fisherman scares away the fish by letting them see his fishing tackle (the fisherman's "devices"). For a discussion of this passage and Wang's commentary to it, as well as a different translation of both, see Chan, *Two Visions of the Way*, 68–71. Dr. Chan also notes the reading of this passage from the *Laozi* in *Han Fei zi* (Sayings of Master Han Fei) (late third century B.C.E.), which differs sharply from that of Wang Bi. His translation of two pertinent passages in *Han Fei zi* reads:

> Strong central power is the "deep" [depths] of the ruler of men. Ministers are the "fish" of this power. When the fish is lost to the deep, it cannot be regained. When the ruler of men loses his power to the ministers, he will never get it back. . . . Reward and punishment are the sharp weapon of the state. On the side of the king, they keep the ministers in check. On the side of the ministers, they overpower the king. If the king is the first to show the reward, then the ministers would diminish it by claiming it to be their own virtuous action. If the ruler is the first to show punishment, the ministers would add to it by claiming it to be their own forceful action. The king shows reward and the ministers make use of its power; the king shows punishment and the ministers ride on its force. Thus it is said, "Sharp instruments of the state must not be shown to anyone."
>
> (Chan, *Two Visions of the Way*, 68–71; see *Han Fei zi*,
> 10:1152C [section 31] and 7:1140B [section 21])

SECTION   37

The Dao in its constancy engages in no conscious action,
  It complies with the Natural.[1]
Yet nothing remains undone.[2]
  In either getting its start or achieving its completion, every one

> *of the myriad things, without exception, stems from what is done in this way.*[3]

If any lord or prince could hold on to it, the myriad folk would undergo moral transformation spontaneously.[4] Once nurtured, should desire arise, I would press down on it with the nameless uncarved block.

> *In "once nurtured, should desire arise," "arise" means the for-mation of desire. "I would press down on it with the nameless uncarved block" means that I would not play the master.*

With the nameless uncarved block, they too would stay free of desire.

> *There would be no desire or contention.*[5]

Achieving tranquillity by keeping them free of desire, all under Heaven would govern themselves.[6]

NOTES

1. Cf. Wang's commentary to section 25, last passage.

2. Cf. section 3, last passage; section 48, third passage; and para-graph 2 of Wang's commentary to section 38.

3. The base text reads *ℤhi* (being governed) instead of *shi* (getting its start), but similar statements in Wang's commentary link starting with completion, so it is likely that the text should also read *shi* (start) instead of *ℤhi* (govern) here. Cf. Wang's commentaries to section 1, second and third passages, and section 21, third passage. However, al-though the text seems to make good sense as it stands (except for the *shi / ℤhi* problem), it has been judged corrupt in other places, and various attempts have been made to amend it, none of which, in my opinion, either are necessary or present better readings. See Hatano, *Rōshi Dōtokukyō kenkyū*, 243–44; and Lou, *Wang Bi ji jiaoshi*, 92 n. 1.

4. Cf. section 32, first passage; and section 57, last passage.

5. Cf. Wang's commentary to section 20, third passage, which reads: "Common people, befuddled by praise and advancement and excited by honor and reward, let their desires advance and their hearts / minds contend."

6. Cf. section 57, last passage.

PART 2

SECTION 38

A person of superior virtue is not virtuous, and this is why he has virtue. A person of inferior virtue never loses virtue, and this is why he lacks virtue. A person of superior virtue takes no conscious action and so acts out of nothing. A person of inferior virtue takes conscious action and so acts out of something.[1] When a person of superior benevolence takes action, he acts out of nothing. When a person of superior righteousness takes action, he acts out of something. When a person of superior propriety takes action and no one responds, he pushes up his sleeves and leads them to it.[2] Therefore one resorts to virtue only after losing the Dao, resorts to benevolence only after losing virtue, resorts to righteousness only after losing benevolence, and resorts to propriety only after losing righteousness. Propriety consists of the superficial aspects of loyalty and trust and is thus the beginning of disorder. Foresight consists of the flower of the Dao and is thus the origin of duplicity. This is why the really great man involves himself with its substance and not with its superficial aspects. He involves himself with its fruit and not with its flower. Therefore he rejects the one and takes the other.

    1. Virtue [de] *consists of attainment* [de]. *Because this means constant attainment without loss and benefit without harm, we use "virtue" as the name for it. Where does one attain virtue? One attains it from the Dao. By what does one fulfill the Dao? One fulfills it by functioning out of nothing. If one's functioning is out of nothing, no one will not be upheld* [zai].[3] *Therefore, as far as the people are concerned, if one applies nothing to them, not a single one will be disorderly, but, if one applies something to them, they will lack the means to escape with their lives. This is why, although Heaven and Earth are vast, they have nothingness* [wu] *for heart/mind* [xin],[4] *and, although the sage sovereign is great, his rule is based on emptiness* [xu]. *Therefore I say that if one looks at it in terms of* Fu *[Return], the heart/mind of Heaven and Earth is seen.[5] If we think of it in terms of the solstice, the perfection* [zhi] *of the former kings is witnessed.[6] Therefore, if one is able to extinguish his self-interest and nullify his personal existence, no one within the four seas will fail to look to him, and no one from near or far will fail to gravitate to him.[7]*

2. If one regards oneself as something special and possesses a heart/mind of his own, this one body of his will fail to keep itself whole, its flesh and bones rendered incompatible. This is why the person of superior virtue only functions if it is with the Dao. He does not regard his virtue as virtue, never holds on to it nor makes use of it. Thus he is able to have virtue, and nothing fails to be done. He attains it without seeking it and fulfills it without conscious effort [wei].[8] *Thus, although he has virtue, he does not have a reputation for "virtue."*

3. The person of inferior virtue attains it by seeking it and fulfills it with conscious effort, then he establishes goodness as the way to keep people in order. Thus a reputation for "virtue" is acquired by him. If one tries to attain it by seeking it, he will surely suffer the loss of it. If he tries to fulfill it by making conscious effort, he will surely fail at it. Once the name "goodness" appeared, there was a "not good" corresponding to it.[9] Thus it is that "a person of inferior virtue takes conscious action and so acts out of something." One who acts out of nothing stays free of biased action [pianwei]. *Those who are incapable of acting without conscious effort/deliberate action* [wuwei] *are always persons of inferior virtue, that is, those concerned with benevolence, righteousness, or propriety and etiquette.*

4. The text always clarifies the distinction between superior and inferior virtue by citing examples of inferior virtue to serve as contrasts to superior virtue, so, when it arrives at the person of inferior virtue who still has the lowest possible capacity for acting out of nothing, he turns out to be the person of superior benevolence. That is, he is a person whose capacity is such that he can act out of nothing. Because, when he [the person of superior benevolence] acts, he acts out of nothing, those who act out of something regard it [disinterested benevolence] as calamitous.[10]

5. *The root [of action] is found in no conscious effort [wuwei] and the mother [of action] is found in the nameless [the Dao]. If one rejects the roots and discards the mother and instead turns to the child,*[11] *although one's merit might become great because of it, there surely will be instances when benefit [ji] fails, and, although one might acquire a praiseworthy reputation, falsehood too will surely arise.*[12]

6. *If one is incapable of accomplishment without deliberate action or of ruling without deliberate application, this, of course, means that conscious effort is involved. Therefore there appear those who promote the sweeping application of benevolence and love. Such love may be free of biased self-interest, however. Thus, "when a person of superior benevolence takes action, he acts out of nothing."*

7. *As such love cannot be applied universally, there appear those who, with a little more truing here and a little less straightening there, try to apply righteousness [yi] and moral principles [li]. They rage against the crooked and bless the straight, assisting that one and attacking this one, for they act with something in heart/mind when dealing with matters. Thus, "when a person of superior righteousness takes action, he acts out of something."*

8. *As straightening cannot make people sincere, there appear those who turn cultural institutions and ceremonial etiquette into superficial ornamentation. Because those who esteem cultivation and etiquette interact by wrangling and faultfinding, anger arises where opinions conflict. Thus it is "when a person of superior propriety takes action and no one responds, he pushes up his sleeves and leads them to it."*

9. *The greatest thing possible, how can this be other than the Dao? How could any lesser expression adequately serve to honor it?*[13] *Thus, although its virtue is replete, its enterprise great, and its rich abundance embraces the myriad things,*[14] *each thing still has access to its virtue, but none in itself can encompass all of it. Thus Heaven cannot serve to uphold it, Earth serve to cover it, or man serve to support it.*[15] *Although the myriad things*[16] *are noble, their functioning is based on nothing,*

and they cannot reject having nothingness as their embodiment. If one were to reject having nothingness as his embodiment, he would lose his power to be great. This is what is meant by "one resorts to virtue only after losing the Dao."

10. If one's functioning is based on nothing, he has access to the mother. This is how it is possible, without his laboring at it, for absolutely all people to live an orderly existence. However, if one falls from this, he will lose the mother that gives birth to functioning. If one is incapable of unconscious effort, he will value sweeping application [of benevolence]. If one is incapable of such sweeping application, he will value truing and straightening. If one is incapable of truing and straightening, he will value ornamental etiquette. This is what is meant by one "resorts to benevolence only after losing virtue, resorts to righteousness only after losing benevolence, and resorts to propriety only after losing righteousness." Propriety as such gets its start when loyalty and trust lack sincerity. The frank and unconventional, refusing to go along with such pretense, heap scorn on how superficial this is, while those obsessed with minute detail wrangle over its application. When benevolence and righteousness emerge from within, acting out of them is still false, so how much less likely that efforts at external ornament will long endure! Thus "propriety consists of the superficial aspects of loyalty and trust and is thus the beginning of disorder."

11. Foresight means knowing something before others do, and it refers to those who belong to the "inferior virtue" category of persons. These people dry up their intelligence in the pursuit of foresight and apply their knowledge to devise schemes to deal with the masses. They might get at the innate tendencies of things [qing] but are responsible for the thick spread of treachery. They might enrich their reputations but in doing so ever increase the loss of sincerity and honesty. The more they labor, the more situations become obscure; the more effort they make, the more entangled with filthy weeds the government becomes. The more they dry up their sovereign's sagehood and intelligence, the more harm befalls the common folk. If one discards the self and leaves things alone, peace will be had without conscious effort.[17] If one holds fast to simplicity and the uncarved block,[18] he need not follow any system of criminal law. However, one becomes besotted with what wins him [reputation] and rejects what this

*[the uncarved block] holds for him. Thus "foresight consists of
the flower of the Dao and is thus the origin of duplicity."*

*12. If one has access to the mother that provides success,
"the myriad folk model their behavior on him, yet he does not
tell them to do so,"*[19] *and the myriad affairs are managed by
him, yet he labors not. It is because one functions not by using
forms and rules and not by using names that it becomes possible
for benevolence and righteousness, propriety and etiquette to
manifest and display themselves. If one upholds the people with
the great Dao and presses down on them with the nameless,*[20]
*they will have nothing to exalt and their hearts/minds will have
nothing to scheme for. As each person tends to his own proper
affairs and acts out of his own sense of sincerity, the virtue of
benevolence deepens, the practice of righteousness rectifies itself, and propriety and etiquette become pure accordingly.*

*13. When it [the Dao] is rejected as the means to uphold
[the people] and discarded as the means to sustain their lives,
use is then made of the concrete forms it takes and application
made of what the intelligence perceives of it. If [it takes the
form of] benevolence, one shows it esteem. If [it takes the form
of] righteousness, one wrangles about it. If [it takes the form
of] propriety, one makes it the object of dispute. Therefore the
deepening of the virtue of benevolence is impossible for one who
uses [the form of] benevolence; the rectification of the practice
of righteousness is not achieved by one who uses [the form of]
righteousness; and the purification of propriety and etiquette is
not attained by one who uses [the form of] propriety.*

*14. It is when one upholds them [the people] with the Dao
and unites and controls them with the mother that benevolence
may be manifest but there is no esteem of it, and righteousness and propriety may be displayed but there is no wrangling
over them. It is by making use of the nameless that names
become honest and by making use of the formless that forms
become perfect. If one preserves the child by holding fast to the
mother and makes the branch tips flourish by enhancing the
roots,*[21] *forms and names will all exist, but anomalies will not
occur. Such great beauty* [damei][22] *will make a companion
worthy of Heaven, and superficiality will not arise. Therefore
the mother must not be kept at a distance, and the roots must not
be lost. Benevolence and righteousness are born of the mother;*

they must not be mistaken for the mother. Implements are produced by the artisan; they must not be mistaken for the artisan. When one discards the mother and makes use of the child, rejects the roots and takes the branch tips, if this is manifest in names, there will be distinctions, and, if this is manifest in forms, there will be limits. One may enlarge their size to the utmost, but there is sure to be something they do not encompass.[23] *One may make them as praiseworthy as possible, but there are sure to be those who cause calamity and distress. If success depends on making such conscious effort, how is that worth engaging in?*

NOTES

1. I have followed the base text—*shangde wuwei er wu yi wei xiade wei zhi er you yi wei*—because, from Wang's commentary, this appears to be the text as he knew it. The same "person of superior virtue" sentence occurs partially in the Mawangdui A text and completely in Mawangdui B, but the following "person of inferior virtue" sentence is missing in both. Fu Yi's composite text based on old manuscripts has the same second sentence, but the first sentence reads *shangde wuwei er wu buwei*, "A person of superior virtue takes no conscious action and nothing remains undone," which requires that the second sentence mean something like "A person of inferior virtue takes conscious action and so has nothing for his efforts." See *Mawangdui Hanmu boshu*, 101. The *Han Fei zi* also quotes the text of the *Laozi* as "a person of superior virtue takes no conscious action and nothing remains undone" (6:1136C [section 20]). This passage has attracted much attention from commentators throughout the ages, and preference seems to be for the text as it appears in the Fu Yi composite edition. See Hatano, *Rōshi Dōtokukyō kenkyū*, 248; and Lou, *Wang Bi ji jiaoshi*, 98 n. 12. Wagner suggests that Wang Bi read it this way also (see "The Wang Bi Recension of the Laozi," 51), but I see nothing in Wang's commentary to support this view and a clear indication that he did not.

2. Cf. section 69, second passage.

3. Cf. Wang's commentary to section 34, second passage, which reads in part: "Each of the myriad folk will obtain his proper place, and it will be as if the Dao had done nothing for them." I.e., when the

sage ruler acts out of nothing—in perfect unconscious accord with the Dao—each person will fulfill his natural destiny.

4. Cf. Wang's commentary to section 32, first passage.

5. Cf. *Tuanzhuan* (Commentary on the Judgment) of Hexagram 24, *Fu* (Return), in the *Yijing* (Classic of changes), which reads in part: "In *Fu* (Return) we can see the very heart and mind of Heaven and Earth!" Wang's commentary says:

> *Return* as such means "to revert to what is the original substance [*ben*]," and for Heaven and Earth we regard the original substance to be the mind/heart [*xin*]. Whenever activity ceases, tranquillity results, but tranquillity is not opposed to activity. Whenever speech ceases, silence results, but silence is not opposed to speech. As this is so, then even though Heaven and Earth are so vast that they possess the myriad things in great abundance, which, activated by thunder and moved by the winds, keep undergoing countless numbers of transformations, yet the original substance of Heaven and Earth consists of perfectly quiescent nonbeing [*wu*, nothingness]. Thus it is only when earthly activity ceases that the heart/mind of Heaven and Earth can be seen. If Heaven and Earth were to have had being [substance, actuality] instead for this heart/mind, then it never would have been possible for all the different categories of things to become endowed with existence.
>
> (Lynn, *The Classic of Changes*, 286;
> see Lou, *Wang Bi ji jiaoshi*, 336–37)

6. Cf. *Xiangzhuan* (Commentary on the Images) of Hexagram 24, *Fu* (Return), in the *Yijing* (Classic of changes), which reads: "Thunder in the Earth: this constitutes the image of *Fu* [Return]. In the same way, the former kings closed the border passes on the occasion of the winter solstice, and neither did merchants and travelers move nor sovereigns go out to inspect domains." Wang's commentary says:

> The winter solstice is the time when the yin principle commences its Return [begins to become quiescent], and the summer solstice is the time when the yang principle commences its Return [begins to become quiescent]. Thus to undergo Return as such means to reach perfect stillness and great tranquillity. The former kings behaved in such a way that they acted as do Heaven and Earth.

For activity to be subject to Return means that it becomes quiescent; for movement to be subject to Return means that it comes to a halt; and for matters to be subject to Return means a disengagement from matters [*wu shi*].

(Lynn, *The Classic of Changes*, 286–87;
see Lou, *Wang Bi ji jiaoshi*, 337)

Suggestions hae been made that "perfection [*zhi*] of the former kings" should be read "intention [*zhi*] of the former kings," but, in my opinion, this seems unnecessary and does not result in a better reading. See Hatano, *Rōshi Dōtokukyō kenkyū*, 252; and Lou, *Wang Bi ji jiaoshi*, 97 n. 7.

7. Cf. Wang's commentary to section 7, first passage.

8. Cf. section 47, last passage.

9. Cf. section 2, first passage.

10. The text here is ambiguous and perhaps corrupt, but the drift of Wang's argument is clear. In it, he apparently refers to both Confucians, whose cardinal virtue is benevolence, in such a way that he seems to damn them with faint praise—as if the greatest of Confucians, the person of superior benevolence, could only be the least of Daoists— and the Legalists, who regard all ostensibly disinterested behavior with skepticism and hostility. For attempts to amend the text, in my opinion unnecessary and misleading, see Hatano, *Rōshi Dōtokukyō kenkyū*, 254– 56; and Lou, *Wang Bi ji jiaoshi*, 99 n. 17 and 18.

11. Cf. Wang's commentary to section 52, second passage.

12. Cf. section 18.

13. Cf. Wang's commentary to section 25, fifth and sixth passages.

14. Cf. section 5 of the *Xici zhuan* (Commentary on the Appended Phrases), Part One, of the *Yijing* (Classic of changes), which reads in part: "As replete virtue and great enterprise, the Dao is indeed perfect! It is because the Dao exists in such rich abundance that we refer to it as 'the great enterprise'" (Lynn, *The Classic of Changes*, 54; see *Zhouyi zhengyi* [Correct meaning of the *Changes of the Zhou*]), 7:13a).

15. Cf. paragraph 4 of Wang's commentary to section 4, which reads in part: "As Earth must keep its physical forms [*xing*], its virtue [*de*] cannot exceed what it upholds, and, as Heaven must remain content with its images [*xiang*], its virtue cannot exceed what it covers. Thus neither Heaven nor Earth can equal it [the Dao]"; and paragraph 1, which reads in part: "Therefore, although one might know about government as it applies to the myriad folk, if he governs without regard

to the Dao with its two modes [the yin and the yang], he cannot serve to support them."

16. The text from "but none in itself" to "the myriad things" is not present in the base text but occurs in two editions of Wang's commentary preserved in the *Daozang* (Daoist canon): *Daode zhenjing jizhu* (Collected commentaries on the *True Classic of the Way and Virtue*), 6:9 (17017A); and Wang Bi, *Laozi Daodejing zhu* (Commentary on Laozi's *Daodejing*), 3:2–3 (16064B–16065A).

17. Cf. Wang's commentary to section 5, first passage.

18. Cf. section 19.

19. Section 2, third passage.

20. Cf. section 37, fourth passage.

21. Cf. Wang's commentary to section 57, first passage.

22. Cf. *Zhuangzi*: "Heaven and earth have their great beauties but do not speak of them; the four seasons have their clear-marked regularity but do not discuss it; the ten thousand things have their principles of growth but do not expound on them. The sage seeks out the beauties of Heaven and Earth and masters the principles of the ten thousand things. Thus it is that the perfect man does not act, the great sage does not move: they have perceived [the Way of] Heaven and Earth, we may say" (*Zhuangzi yinde*, 58/22/16; cf. Watson, *Complete Works of Chuang Tzu*, 236).

23. Cf. Wang's commentary to section 25, fourth through sixth passages.

SECTION   39

As for those who obtained the One long, long ago,

> *"Long, long ago" means at the beginning. One is the beginning of numbers as well as the ultimate number of things. Each thing, as such, is produced by the One [Unity], and this is why it is the master of them all. All things achieve completeness by obtaining this One, and, once complete, they exist as complete entities by separating themselves from the One. Once they exist as complete entities, they lose the mother, and this is why all things deteriorate, disintegrate, terminate, dry up, expire, or collapse.*

Heaven is pure by having obtained the One; Earth is stable by having obtained the One; the gods have their spiritual power by having obtained the One; valleys can be filled by having obtained the One; the myriad things live by having obtained the One; lords and princes provide constancy[1] to all under Heaven by having obtained the One. This is how they attain to these states.[2]

> *Each of these, thanks to access to the One, respectively attains purity, stability, capacity to be filled, life, and constancy* [zhen].[3]

If Heaven had not this means to be pure, it would, we fear, deteriorate.

> *It attains purity by making use of the One; it is not pure by making use of purity. Because it holds to the One, its purity is not lost, but if it tried to make use of purity, "it would, we fear, deteriorate." Thus it is that one must not separate from the mother that provides efficacy* [gong]. *For this reason, if all these did not make use of this source of efficacy, they would, we fear, lose their roots [basis of what they are].*[4]

If Earth had not this means to be stable, it would, we fear, disintegrate. If the gods had not this means to have spiritual power, they would, we fear, terminate. If valleys had not this means to achieve fullness, they would, we fear, dry up. If the myriad things had not this means to live, they would, we fear, expire. If lords and princes did not have this means to achieve loftiness and nobility, they would, we fear, collapse. Thus it is that nobility uses humility as its roots and loftiness uses lowliness as its foundation. This is why lords and princes refer to themselves as "the orphan," "the widower," or "the unworthy." Is this not using humility as the roots? Is this not so? Therefore the ultimate number of praises amounts to no praise, so one wants neither "he glows with luster like the jade" nor "he is as hard as hard can be like the stone."

> *Purity cannot provide purity; fullness cannot provide the capacity to be filled. As long as they all keep their mother, they preserve their forms accordingly. Therefore purity is unworthy of being thought noble, and fullness is insufficient to be considered much. Nobility resides with the mother, but the mother is without noble form. Thus it is that "nobility uses humility as its roots and loftiness uses lowliness as its foundation." "Therefore the ultimate number of praises" is really "no praise."[5] Jadestone glows with luster and is hard as can be, but what it embodies is found entirely in its form. Thus one should not want [to be praised as if he were jadestone].*

NOTES

1. "Constancy" translates *zhen*, which is the base text reading. This *zhen* also appears in Wang's commentary to this passage, and, although both Mawangdui texts have *zheng* (governance), Fu Yi's composite text also reads *zhen*. See *Mawangdui Hanmu boshu*, 101. Cf. the *Ming tuan* (Clarifying the Judgments) section in Wang's *Zhouyi lueli* (General Remarks on the *Changes of the Zhou*): "The many cannot govern the many; that which governs the many is the most solitary [the One]. Activity cannot govern activity; that which controls all activity that occurs in the world, thanks to constancy [*zhen*], is the One. Therefore for all the many to manage to exist, their controlling principle must reach back to the One, and for all activities to manage to function, their source cannot but be the One" (Lynn, *The Classic of Changes*, 25; see Lou, *Wang Bi ji jiaoshi*, 591).

2. This translates the base text. Robert Henricks, in his own translation of the *Laozi* based on the Mawangdui manuscripts, renders this line as "Taking this to its logical conclusion we would say," which translates *qi zhi zhiwei* (Mawangdui A) or *qi zhi ye wei* (Mawangdui B) (*Lao-Tzu Te-Tao Ching*, 100–101; see *Mawangdui Hanmu boshu*, 101–2). Wang's commentary to this passage indicates that neither of these readings was available to him.

3. Wang's commentary indicates that the text he knew did not conform to that of the two Mawangdui versions, both of which read "if Heaven remained pure in perpetuity [*wuyi*]." See *Mawangdui Hanmu boshu*, 101; and William Boltz, "The *Lao-tzu* Text that Wang Pi and Ho-shang Kung Never Saw," 495–501.

4. Cf. Wang's commentary to section 38, paragraph 5.

5. The base text reads *yu* (carriage) both in the *Laozi* and in Wang's commentary. The context of the commentary, however, concerned as it is with praise, suggests that Wang read *yu* (carriage) as *yu* (praise). "Carriage" also occurs in the Mawangdui B text, however (Mawangdui A is ambiguous), which leads Robert Henricks to translate the passage as: "Therefore, they regard their large number of carriages as having no carriage. / And because of this, they desire not to dazzle and glitter like jade, / But to remain firm and strong like stone" (*Lao-Tzu Te-Tao Ching*, 100–101; see *Mawangdui Hanmu boshu*, 102). For detailed discussions of the textual problems associated with this passage, in which it is often noted that, beginning at least with the Fu Yi composite edition,

most texts of the *Laoʒi* read "praise" instead of "carriage" and that *yu* should be read as "praise" regardless of which graph occurs in the *Laoʒi* and the Wang Bi commentary, see Hatano, *Rōshi Dōtokukyō kenkyū*, 276–78, and Lou, *Wang Bi ji jiaoshi*, 107 n. 7. Supporting evidence also comes from the *Zhuangʒi*, where a similar expression occurs: *ʒhiyu wuyu*, "perfect [the ultimate amount of] praise is no praise." See *Zhuangʒi yinde*, 46/18/11. Taking the opposite position, Qian Zhongshu, while noting that such annotators as Lu Deming (556–627) and Lü Huiqing (1031–110) read *yu* as "praise," surveys with approval commentaries that read *yu* as "carriage" and concludes, citing the commentary of Su Che (1039–112), that the text should be interpreted as "enumerate all the parts of a carriage and there is still no carriage," Laozi's way of exploding the logical "fallacy of division" (*fensan yuanlun*), that is, that the sum of parts equals a "real" whole. Qian's remarks make fascinating reading, and, while he might be right as far as the meaning of the original text of the *Laoʒi* is concerned, the commentary indicates that Wang did not read it this way. See Qian, *Guanʒhui bian*, 3:440–44.

SECTION 40

Reversion is the action of the Dao.[1]

> *Nobility uses humility as its foundation, and loftiness uses lowliness as its roots.[2] What exists becomes useful by making use of what does not exist.[3] This is what is meant here by "reversion." If action occurs so that it always proceeds to a state of nothingness, all things will go smoothly.[4] Thus the text says: "Reversion is the action of the Dao."*

Softness is the function of the Dao.[5]

> *Because its softness and pliancy embraces all things equally, its capacity is infinite.*

The myriad things under Heaven achieve life in existence. Existence arises from nothingness.

> *All things under Heaven achieve life because of existence, but the origin of existence has nothingness for its roots. If one would have things achieve their full existence, he must allow them to revert to nothingness.*

NOTES

1. Cf. section 65, penultimate passage; and section 78, second passage.

2. Cf. section 39, last passage.

3. Cf. section 11, second passage.

4. This translates *dong jie zhi qi suowu ze wu tong yi*. The *zhi* in the base text, however, is not "proceed" but "know/understand," which requires a different rendering: "As for action, if one always understands its state of nothingness, all things are his to embrace." *Zhi* (proceed) actually occurs in the version of Wang's commentary preserved in the *Daode zhenjing jizhu* (Collected commentaries on the *True Classic of the Way and Virtue*) (late 11th century), 6:18 (17021B). Both Hatano Tarō and Lou Yulie think that *zhi* (proceed) is the better reading, and Lou suggests the paraphrase: "If the action of the myriad things is such that they are all rendered able to return to their fundamental roots, that is, reside in nothingness, one can then embrace the myriad things" (Lou, *Wang Bi ji jiaoshi*, 110 n. 3). See Hatano, *Rōshi Dōtokukyō kenkyū*, 280.

5. Cf. section 10, second passage; section 36, second passage; and section 78, second passage.

SECTION 41

When the superior man hears the Dao, he diligently practices it.
  He has the will to do so.
When the average man hears the Dao, sometimes he retains it, sometimes he forgets it. When the inferior man hears the Dao, he laughs loudly at it. If he did not laugh, what he heard would not be worthy of being the Dao. Therefore, as the established adage has it:
  Jian [established] is similar to li *[established].*
The bright Dao seems dark.[1]
  "He is bright but does not shine."[2]
Advancing on the Dao[3] seems retreat.
  "The sage places himself in the rear yet finds himself in front. He puts aside his person, yet his person is preserved."[4]
The smooth Dao seems rough.
  Lei [entangled, knotted] here means kuai *[rough].[5] The great smooth Dao follows the nature [xing] of things and does not*

grasp the carpenter's level in order to make them smooth. Because its own even smoothness cannot be seen, people take it for the complete opposite, as if it were rough and bumpy.

Superior Virtue is like a valley.[6]

Because it does not regard virtue as virtue,[7] it is devoid of content.

Great whiteness seems soiled.

It is only by "know[ing] the white yet sustain[ing] the black" that great whiteness can be achieved.[8]

Vast virtue seems wanting.

Vast virtue is not filled with anything, for it is so capacious and formless that it cannot be filled.[9]

Established virtue seems stealthy.

Tou [stealthy] suggests "congenial" [pi].[10] Established virtue follows the natural bent of the people and does not set itself up and work on them. Thus it appears stealthily congenial.

Simple authenticity seems compromised.

Simple authenticity [zhizhen] does not take credit for its authenticity [zhen]. Thus it appears compromised [yu]

The great square has no corners.

It is square but does not cut, this is how it has no corners.[11]

The great vessel is slow to form.

The great vessel forms all under Heaven without holding on to anything completely separate from it [as a model to follow],[12] thus, it necessarily is slow to form.

The great note is inaudible.

"When we listen for it but hear it not, we call it the inaudible."[13] The great note is the note that we cannot get to hear. If it had a sound, it would be distinct, and, once distinct, if it were not the note gong, it would be the note shang. If it were distinct, it would not be able to govern all the other notes. Therefore, if it has a sound, it is not the great note.[14]

The great image is formless.[15]

As soon as there is a form, distinctions exist, and, with distinctions, if something is not warm, it must be cool; if not hot, it must be cold. Thus an image that has a form is not the great image.

The Dao may be hidden and nameless, but it alone is good at bestowing and completing.

All these manifestations of excellence are achieved by the Dao. When it exists as an image, it is the great image, but the great image is formless. When it exists as note, it is the great note, but the great note is an inaudible sound. Things are completed by it, but they do not see its form. Thus it is hidden and nameless. When it bestows, this is not limited merely to supplying what something specifically happens to need. Once it makes its bestowal, this is sufficient to make the virtue of that something last until its end. Thus the text says: "It . . . is good at bestowing." The way it completes things is not like the way the carpenter makes something. With it, not a single thing fails to fulfill its form perfectly. Thus the text says: "It . . . is good at . . . completing."

NOTES

1. Cf. section 21, second and third passages.

2. Section 58, last passage. Cf. section 14, second passage; section 20, ninth passage; and Wang's commentary for both.

3. Dao, after all, means "way" or "path."

4. Section 7, second passage. Cf. section 28, first passage; and section 66.

5. *Kuai* transliterates an unusual graph that consists of the "earth" significant (*tu*) on the left and a phonetic *nei* (inner, inside) on the right. Other possible pronunciations include *kui, rui,* and *nie.* It is probably an alternate way of writing *kuai* (broken, in pieces; piece), thus the meaning "rough" seems appropriate here. See Hatano, *Rōshi Dōtokukyō kenkyū,* 282–83, and Lou, *Wang Bi ji jiaoshi,* 114 n. 4.

6. Cf. section 15, third passage.

7. Cf. Wang's commentary to section 38, paragraph 2.

8. Section 28, second passage.

9. Cf. Wang's commentary to section 4. Vast virtue, like the Dao itself, is utterly empty. With no content to it, it seems wanting.

10. Although Lou Yulie says that this line makes no sense and appears corrupt, it seems perfectly intelligible in the context of the passage: the possessor of well-established virtue seems stealthily to acquiesce with the natural bent of the people, as if he were pairing (*pi*) his virtue (making it conform) to their inclinations. After reviewing attempts to amend Wang's statement, Hatano Tarō concludes that the wording is correct as it stands, that *tou* should be understood as *touqie* (steal, stealthy) and *pi* as *pichou* (match, matching), but that the meaning is still unclear and can only be paraphrased as: "One who

establishes his own virtue refrains from conscious action and does not apply it. Thus he does not go out and campaign against others to establish virtue." Hatano then quotes from Wang's commentary to section 27, first passage: "He follows the path of the Natural, neither formulating nor implementing." It seems a short step from these observations to my interpretation of the line, but Hatano did not take it. See Hatano, *Rōshi Dōtokukyō kenkyū*, 284–85; and Lou, *Wang Bi ji jiaoshi*, 114 n. 7. Most recent translators of this line in the *Laozi* seem to follow commentators who gloss *jian* (well established) as *jian* (strong) and *tou* (stealthy) as *duo* (indolent, dissipated, weak).

11. Cf. Wang's commentary to section 58, seventh passage. Like the Dao that does not make things conform to standard models, the sage is "square" (upright), but he does not try to cut others into square shapes (upright and honest human beings).

12. Commentators usually prefer to read *quanbie* (completely separate [from it]) as *fenbie* (distinctions). Although the reading that results—"The great vessel forms all under Heaven without holding to distinctions"—seems plausible, both in terms of the immediate context and the larger context of Wang's commentary as a whole, it does not appear to connect with what follows: "it necessarily is slow (or late) to form." The translation I propose here, which leaves the base text intact, seems to make perfect sense: The great, numinous vessel of the Dao forms all under Heaven without reference to or guidance from anything outside itself and so "has to find its own way," a slower process than if it could simply work from some model. Wang's statement has perplexed many a textual scholar, however, and various ingenious solutions have been proposed, but all these depend on significantly rewriting Wang's statement and sometimes the base text of the *Laozi* itself, so none seems likely. See Hatano, *Rōshi Dōtokukyō kenkyū*, 286–87, and Lou, *Wang Bi ji jiaoshi*, 114 n. 10.

13. Section 14, first passage.

14. Cf. the *Ming tuan* (Clarifying the Judgments) section in Wang's *Zhouyi lueli* (General remarks on the *Changes of the Zhou*): "The many cannot govern the many; that which governs the many is the most solitary [*gua*, the One]" (Lynn, *The Classic of Changes*, 25; see Lou, *Wang Bi ji jiaoshi*, 27 n. 2 and 591). See also section 1 of Wang's Outline Introduction.

15. Cf. Wang's commentary to section 35, first passage. Wang's commentary here also bears comparison with his remarks in section 1 of the Outline Introduction.

SECTION   42

The Dao begets the One; the One begets two; two beget three;
and three beget the myriad things. The myriad things, bearing
yin and embracing yang, form a unified harmony through the
fusing of these vital forces. What people most hate are "the
orphan," "the widower," and "the unworthy," yet lords and
princes use these terms to refer to themselves.[1] Thus it is that
some are augmented by being diminished, and others are diminished by being augmented.

>   *1. Although the myriad things exist in a myriad forms, they all
>   revert to the One. What is it due to that they all ultimately become
>   One? It is due to nothingness* [wu]. *Because it is from nothingness
>   that One comes, One can be called "nothingness." Because we
>   already call it "One," how can there not be a word for it? Because
>   we have this word and because we have the One, how can there
>   not be two? Because we have the One and have these two [the
>   word "one" and the word "two"], this consequently gives birth
>   to three [the word "one," the word "two," and the One]. The
>   numbers involved in the transition from nothingness to exist-
>   ence are all accounted for here. If one passes this point and keeps
>   on going, any such path will not be the course of the Dao.*
>
>   *2. Therefore the myriad things are begotten, and I know
>   the master that controls this. Although they have a myriad forms,
>   the fusion of vital forces makes One out of them all. Each of
>   the common folk has his own heart/mind, and customs differ
>   from state to state, yet any lord or prince who attains to the One
>   becomes master over them all. Because he becomes master thanks
>   to the One, how could the One ever be discarded?*
>
>   *3. The more one has, the farther removed he is, but being
>   diminished gets him closer to it [the One]. When diminution
>   goes as far as it can go, there its ultimate value [the One] is
>   obtained.[2] Because calling it "the One" already brings us to
>   three, how much less likely is it that someone rooted in something
>   other than the One could ever get close to the Dao?[3] So saying
>   that one is "augmented by being diminished and . . . dimin-
>   ished by being augmented" is certainly not mere empty talk!*

What others teach, I also teach.

>   *My teaching of others does not consist of forcing them to follow
>   what I teach but of helping them make use of the Natural* [ziran],

which I cite as perfect principle [zhili], *compliance with which means good fortune and opposition to which means misfortune.*[4] *Thus, concerning what people teach each other, if one opposes it, he surely will bring misfortune on himself. So I also teach others in such a way that I do not oppose them.*

The dangerously bold do not get to die a natural death, so I am going to use them as the fathers of my teaching.

If one is dangerously bold,[5] *he surely will not get to die a natural death.*[6] *People teach each other to be dangerously bold, and this surely is just as good as my teaching them that one should not be dangerously bold, for is not the occasion of the dangerously bold not getting to die a natural death a form of teaching? This is just as good as my saying, "Comply with my teaching, and you will have good fortune." Therefore I have caught those fellows who are lawbreakers, for they are just right to use as the fathers of my teaching.*[7]

NOTES

1. Cf. section 39, fourth passage.

2. Cf. Wang's commentary to section 22, fifth passage.

3. Cf. *Zhuangzi*: "Heaven and Earth were born at the same time as I was, and the ten thousand things are one with me. We have already become one, so how can I not be saying something? The One and what I said about it make two, and two and the original One make three. If we go on this way, then even the cleverest mathematician can't tell where we'll end, much less the ordinary man. If by moving from nonbeing [*wu*, nothingness] to being [*you*, existence] we get to three, how far will we get if we move from being to being? Better not to move, but to let things be!" (*Zhuangzi yinde*, 5/2/52; cf. Watson, *Complete Works of Chuang Tzu*, 43). Alan Chan provides a detailed discussion of this passage in Wang's commentary; see *Two Visions of the Way*, 47–48 and 55–56.

4. Cf. Wang's commentary to section 73, sixth passage.

5. Cf. Wang's commentary to section 36, first passage.

6. Cf. Wang's commentary to section 73, first passage.

7. This is a difficult passage, but I have translated the base text as it stands. Both Tao Hongqing and Hatano Tarō are dissatisfied with the text and suggest various ways to amend it, all of which seem unnecessary and misleading. Lou Yulie, on the other hand, thinks the base text

makes sense and should be read in the light of the previous passage of Wang's commentary. See Hatano, *Rōshi Dōtokukyō kenkyū*, 294; and Lou, *Wang Bi ji jiaoshi*, 119 n. 12.

SECTION   43

The softest things under Heaven gallop through the hardest things.[1]

> *There is no place that air* [qi] *cannot enter, no place that water cannot run through.*

That which has no physical existence can squeeze through where there is no space, so from this I know how advantageous it is to act without conscious purpose.

> *Emptiness is so soft and pliable that there is no place that it cannot penetrate, for that which has no physical existence* [wuyou] *is inexhaustible and the perfectly soft is unbreakable. It is by pursuing this line of thought that we come to understand how advantageous it is to act without conscious purpose* [wuwei].[2]

The teaching that is not expressed in words,[3] the advantage that is had by acting without conscious purpose, rare is it that anyone under Heaven ever reaches them.

NOTES

1. Cf. section 36, second section.

2. In addition to the base text, this passage exists in three variants: (1) "The perfectly soft is unbreakable, and nothingness is inexhaustible. It is by pursuing this line of thought that we come to understand the Dao of acting without conscious purpose and how advantageous it is for dealing with the people. What ever could surpass this!" (*Daode zhenjing jijie* (Collected exegesis on the *True Classic of the Way and Virtue*), 3:13 [16910B]). (2) "Nothingness is inexhaustible, and the perfectly soft is unbreakable. It is by pursuing this line of thought that we come to understand the Dao of acting without conscious purpose and how advantageous it is for dealing with the people" (*Daode zhenjing jizhu* (Collected commentaries on the *True Classic of the Way and Virtue*), ed. Peng Si, 11:15 [17222B]); and *Daode zhenjing zangshi zuanwei pian*

(An edition of collected subtleties from the treasure house of the *True Classic of the Way and Virtue*), 6:12 [17978A]). (3) "So soft and pliable, for emptiness there is no place that it cannot penetrate. The perfectly soft is unbreakable, and nothingness is inexhaustible. It is by pursuing this line of thought that we come to understand how the Dao of acting without conscious effort is advantageous" (*Daode ẓhenjing qushanji* (Selection of superlative remarks on the *True Classic of the Way and Virtue*), 6:21 [17978A]). All variants are critiqued in Hatano, *Rōshi Dōtokukyō kenkyū*, 296, and quoted in Lou, *Wang Bi ji jiaoshi*, 121 n. 3.

3. Cf. section 2, third passage.

SECTION   44

Reputation or one's person, which is dear?

> *When one values reputation and craves high position, his person surely becomes a matter of indifference to him.*

One's person or what he possesses, which is more?

> *When one's covetousness for possessions becomes insatiable, his person surely diminishes.*[1]

Gain or loss, which is harm?

> *If one gains reputation and material advantage [wealth]*[2] *but loses his own person, which one is harm?*

Thus it is that extreme meanness is sure to result in great expense, and much hoarding is sure to result in heavy loss.

> *When in the grip of extreme meanness, one does not identify with the people, and, when addicted to much hoarding, one does not share with them. The more one tries to get, the more numerous will be his attackers, which means that he will be harmed by the people. Thus he will suffer great expense and heavy loss.*

One who knows contentment will not suffer damage to his reputation, and one who knows how to stop will not place himself in danger. As such, he will last long.

NOTES

1. Cf. Wang's commentary to section 22, fifth passage.

2. "Gains reputation and material advantage" translates *de mingli*; however, the base text reads "gains much material advantage" (*de duoli*).

Hatano Tarō, citing the annotations of Wei Yuan (1794–1856) in his *Laoʐi benyi* (The original meaning of the *Laoʐi*), B:52, and Ma Qichang (1855–1930) in his *Laoʐi gu* (Exegesis of the ancient meaning of the *Laoʐi*), agrees with them and suggests that *duo* (much) is a scribal error for *ming* (reputation). See Hatano, *Rōshi Dōtokukyō kenkyū*, 296. Since *mingli* (reputation and material advantage/wealth) is a common compound in classical texts, it is the more likely reading.

SECTION   45

Great completion seems incomplete, but its functioning is never exhausted.

> *Because it completes things as they come along, it never forms one complete image* [xiang], *thus it "seems incomplete* [que]*"*[1]

Great fullness seems empty, but its functioning is limitless.

> *Great fullness is filled with emptiness.*[2] *Because It provides for things as they come along, none get treated with special consideration, thus it "seems empty."*

Great straightness seems crooked.

> *Because it straightens things as they come along, there is no single basis for straightening,*[3] *thus it "seems crooked."*

Great skill seems clumsy.

> *Great skill completes the physical objects of existence* [qi] *in accordance with the Natural and does not work to any other standard, thus it "seems clumsy."*

Great eloquence seems inarticulate.[4]

> *Great eloquence speaks to things as they come along and does not engage in any artfulness of its own, thus it "seems inarticulate."*

Although the heat of activity conquers cold, quietude conquers heat,[5] so pure quietude is the right way to govern all under Heaven.

> *Only when the heat of activity ceases does it conquer cold, and it is by acting without conscious effort* [wuwei] *that quietude* [jing] *conquers heat. It is by pursuing this line of thought that we come to understand that "pure quietude is the right way to govern all under Heaven." If one practices quietude, this will fully realize the authenticity* [zhen] *of the people, but, if one engages in activity, this will violate the nature* [xing] *of the*

people. Thus it is only through pure quietude that one can achieve
all the forms of greatness mentioned above.

NOTES

1. The occurrence together of "image" (*xiang*) and "incomplete"
(*que*) suggests that Wang interprets the "great completion" of the Dao
metaphorically in terms of the image (*xiang*) of the incomplete (*que*)
moon. Except in its brief full phase, the moon continually waxes or
wanes and in either case is "incomplete." The other celestial bodies all
form complete, unchanging images, so only the moon is an appropriate metaphor for the "great completion" of the Dao, which, as it completes things, never reaches a point where everything is complete. The
Dao as such never has a full phase like the moon and always seems
"incomplete."

2. Cf. Wang's commentary to section 4.

3. Cf. Wang's commentary to section 58, penultimate passage.

4. Cf. section 81, third passage.

5. Cf. section 16, third passage; and section 26, first passage.

SECTION   46

When the Dao prevails among all under Heaven, one relegates
coursers to producing manure.

> *"When the Dao prevails among all under Heaven," it means*
> *contentment[1] and knowing to stop.[2] Avoiding all ventures*
> *abroad, each of them [such rulers] does nothing beyond culti-*
> *vating what is at home. Thus they delegate coursers to deal with*
> *the manuring of fields.*

When the Dao does not prevail among all under Heaven, war
horses are born in the fields outside towns.

> *When covetous desire becomes insatiable, they [such rulers] do*
> *not cultivate what is at home, and each engages in ventures*
> *abroad. Thus "war horses are born in the fields outside towns."[3]*

Nothing causes greater disaster than not being content, and
nothing brings about greater blame than craving something.
When contentment fills one perfectly, this is indeed constant contentment!

NOTES

1. Cf. Wang's commentary to section 20, first passage.
2. Cf. Wang's commentary to section 32, third passage.
3. Cf. Huan Kuan (first century B.C.E.), *Yantie lun* (Debates on salt and iron), which reads, in a passage that begins with describing the idyllic age of the sage king Yu:

> Farmers used horses to till the fields, and the common folk did not ride or use them to pull carriages. At that time, they relegated coursers to producing manure, but later, when armies were repeatedly dispatched, war horses became insufficient, so even mares in foal were enlisted in the ranks, which resulted in colts being born out on the battlefields. Because the six domestic animals were neither raised in the homes nor the five grains cultivated in the fields, the common folk did not have enough of even the coarsest food to eat, so there is no question that they ever got tired of eating oranges and pomelos!
>
> (Huan Kuan, *Weitong* (Impasse), *Yantie lun*, section 15, 412)

SECTION 47

Know all under Heaven without even leaving your gate; see the Dao of Heaven without even peering out your window.

Matters have a progenitor, and things have a master.[1] Although roads differ, they all bring one back to the same place, and, although there might be hundreds of ways to deliberate, there is an ultimate congruence in thought.[2] The Dao has its great constancy [dachang], and principle[3] has its great perfection [dazhi], so "hold on to the Dao of old to preside over what exists now."[4] Although we live in the present, it is possible for one to know how things were at the beginning of time.[5] Thus one can know [the Dao] without leaving his gate or peering out his window.[6]

The farther one goes out, the less he will know.

Such a one does not reside in the One but tries to find things out from the many. As for the Dao, he looks for it but sees it not; he listens for it but hears it not; he tries to touch it but finds it not.[7]

> *If he knew it, there would be no need to leave his gate, but if he does not know it, the farther he goes out, the more he will be confused.*

Thus it is that the sage knows without making a move and names without seeing.

> *Because the sage grasps the principle of things perfectly, although he does not make a move, he is able to know what happens just by his power of inference [lü]. Because he recognizes the progenitor of things, although he does not see what happens, which principles of right and wrong are involved are his to name.*

He brings about the completion of things without taking action.

> *He understands the nature [xing] of things and does nothing other than stay in accord with it. Thus, although he does not take deliberate action, he brings about their completion.*[8]

NOTES

1. Cf. Wang's commentary to section 14, last passage, and to section 42, first passage, where the "progenitor" and the "master" are identified as the Dao, the One, and nothingness. Also see Wang's commentary to section 49, fifth passage.

2. Cf. section 5 of the *Xici zhuan* (Commentary on the Appended Phrases), Part Two, in the *Yijing* (Classic of changes), which reads in part: "What does the world have to think and deliberate about? As all in the world ultimately comes to the same end, though the roads to it are different, so there is an ultimate congruence in thought, though there might be hundreds of ways to deliberate about it. So what does the world have to think and deliberate about?" (Lynn, *The Classic of Changes*, 81; see *Zhouyi zhengyi* [Correct meaning of the *Changes of the Zhou*], 8:9b).

3. Cf. Wang's commentary to section 42, second passage. For a discussion of Dao as principle in the thought of Wang Bi, see Alan Chan, *Two Visions of the Way*, 52–57.

4. Section 14, penultimate passage. See also Wang's commentary there.

5. See section 14, last passage, along with Wang's commentary.

6. Wang's commentary here bears comparison with his remarks at the end of section 2 of his Outline Introduction. See also Wang's commentary to section 70, first passage.

7. Cf. section 14, first passage.

8. Cf. Wang's commentary to section 29, second passage.

SECTION 48

The pursuit of learning means having more each day,

> *Such a one earnestly wishes to advance what he can do and increase what he has learned.*

But the pursuit of the Dao means having less each day.

> *Such a one earnestly wishes to revert to emptiness* [xuwu].[1]

Having less upon having less, eventually one reaches the point where one engages in no conscious action, yet nothing remains undone.[2]

> *Because conscious action* [youwei] *results in occasions of failure, no conscious action* [wuwei] *will result in nothing remaining undone.*[3]

One who takes all under Heaven as his charge always tends to matters without deliberate action.

> *Such a one always acts in accordance with things.*

But when it comes to one who does take conscious action,

> *Such a one tries to implement things of his own making.*

Such a one is not worthy to take all under Heaven as his charge.[4]

> *Such a one has lost the roots of rulership.*

NOTES

1. Concerning this and the previous passage, see Wang's commentary to section 20, first passage.

2. Cf. section 37, first and second passages.

3. Cf. Wang's commentary to section 38, paragraph 2.

4. For this and the previous two passages, see Wang's commentary to section 57, first passage.

SECTION 49

The sage has no constant heart/mind [*changxin*] but takes the heart/mind of the common folk as his heart/mind.[1]

Such a one always acts in accordance with things.

The good I regard as good; those who are not good I also regard as good.

If one always handles people in accordance with their usefulness, the good involved will not be lost.

This is to transform goodness into virtue.

No one is discarded.

The trustworthy I trust; those who are not trustworthy I also trust. This is to transform trust into virtue. The sage resides among all under Heaven with perfect equanimity and impartiality and for the sake of all under Heaven merges his heart/mind with theirs. [The common folk all fix their ears and eyes on him,][2]

Each one uses that which is sharp [cong, *i.e., the ears*] *and that which is clear* [ming, *i.e., the eyes*].[3]

And the sage treats them all as his children.

1. All are made harmonious and rendered free of desire, so they are just like infants.[4] "Heaven and Earth established the positions of things, and the sages fully realized the potential [neng] *inherent in them. Whether consulting with men or consulting with spirits, they allowed the ordinary folk to share in these resources* [yuneng]."[5] *One of such resources shares them, but one who hoards goods takes them. If such resourcefulness is important [to the ruler], it will be thought important [by the people]; if goods are valued by him, they will be thought valuable by them.[6]*

2. Matters have their progenitor, and things have their master.[7] If one acts accordingly, cap tassels may cover his eyes, yet he need not fear deception; yellow embroidered ear flaps may block his ears, yet he need not worry about trickery. So why should such a one ever again belabor all the intelligence that he can muster to investigate what tendencies [qing] *are at play among the common folk? If one tries to use the power of bright scrutiny to investigate the people, they will compete with each other to find ways to escape that scrutiny.[8] If one makes demands on the people in a spirit of mistrust, they will compete with each other to find ways to respond in kind.[9] The hearts/minds of all under Heaven are not necessarily the same, so if people dare not differ in the ways they respond, none will be willing to act in accord with their innate tendencies* [qing]. *How terrible! For nothing causes greater harm than such use of bright scrutiny![10]*

3. If one relies on intelligence, people will join in litigation with him. If one relies on force, people will contend with him. If his intelligence comes not from others but one still takes a stand on the field of litigation, it will mean exhaustion! If his strength comes not from others but one still takes a stand on the field of contention, it will mean danger! There has never been a ruler who was able to ensure that no one used his intelligence and strength against him, and, if one follows this course, he has just his one person to pit against others, while they have thousands and tens of thousands to pit against him. If one then increased the net of the law and made punishments more exacting, blocked up the smallest avenues of escape, and assaulted the most hidden refuge, the myriad folk would have to act in violation of Nature, and the common people would be left with nowhere to place a hand or foot, like birds frightened into confusion above or fish scared into chaos below.

4. This is why "the sage resides among all under Heaven with perfect equanimity and impartiality." His heart/mind free of any control, he "for the sake of all under Heaven merges his heart/mind with theirs," so his thought is without tendency to favor or slight.[11] *If there is nothing he investigates them for, what hiding must the common folk do?*[12] *If there is nothing that he demands of them, what response must the common folk make? Free of the need to hide or respond, none will fail to act in accord with his innate tendencies* [qing]. *None will be forced to discard what he is able to do and made to do something he cannot do or forced to discard a strength and made to employ a weakness. If one follows this course, those who speak will talk about things they know, and those who act will do things for which they are capable. The common folk will fix their ears and eyes on me, and I do nothing but treat them all as my children.*

NOTES

1. Cf. Wang's commentary to section 28, last passage. "Constant heart/mind" means fixed, preconceived ideas about how things should be done. Note also that the first five passages of section 49, along with Wang's commentary, bear comparison to section 27, fourth, fifth, and

sixth passages, along with the commentary, and to section 62, second and fourth passages.

2. The base text lacks the text inside the brackets, which occurs in its entirety in the Mawangdui A text, partially in Mawangdui B, and again entirely in Fu Yi's composite text. See *Mawangdui Hanmu boshu*, 104. Wang's commentary to both this and the last passage of section 49 clearly indicates that the text of the *Laozi* he knew included these words.

3. Cf. Wang's commentary to the *Tuanzhuan* (Commentary on the Judgments) to Hexagram 50, *Ding* (The Cauldron) in the *Yijing* (Classic of changes): "When sages and worthies receive nourishment, then the sage himself [i.e., the sovereign] accomplishes things without purposeful action [*wuwei*]. This is why 'it is through *Sun* [Compliance] that the ear and eye become sharp and clear' [i.e., sage and worthy ministers become his eyes and ears]" (Lynn, *The Classic of Changes*, 452; see Lou, *Wang Bi ji jiaoshi*, 469).

4. Cf. Wang's commentary to section 10, second passage.

5. The quotation is from section 12 of the *Xici zhuan* (Commentary on the Appended Phrases), Part Two, of the *Yijing* (Classic of changes), to which Han Kangbo's (d. ca. 385) commentary reads:

> The sages availed themselves of the rightness of Heaven and Earth and so had each of the myriad things realize its potentiality [*cheng qineng*]. "Consulting with men" is equivalent to discussing things with the mass of people in order to determine the chances for failure and success. "Consulting with spirits" is equivalent to resorting to divination in order to examine the possibilities for good fortune and misfortune. Without enslaving their [the sages'] capacity for thought and deliberation [power of inference], failure and success thus came to light by themselves, and, without belaboring their capacity for study and examination, good fortune and misfortune made themselves known. They categorized the innate tendencies of the myriad things and thoroughly explored the reasons that underlie the most obscure and most profound of things. This is why, as the ordinary folk were allowed to share in these resources [*yu neng*], they "delighted in being their [the sages'] advocates and never tired of doing so."
>
> (Lynn, *The Classic of Changes*, 94; see *Zhouyi zhengyi*
> [Correct meaning of the *Changes of the Zhou*], 8:24a,
> or Lou, *Wang Bi ji jiaoshi*, 574)

The quotation at the end of this passage from Han's commentary is from the *Laozi*, section 66 (note that this volume does not use that translation). Although Wang's commentary suggests that he read *yu neng* as something like "share in these resources"—and I think Han Kangbo read *yu neng* this way, too—Kong Yingda (574–648) started a tradition of reading *yu neng* as *ju neng*, "elevate/promote the resourceful/able," which results in: "Whether for consulting with men or consulting with spirits, the ordinary/common folk promoted the resourceful/able [i.e. worthies]." See *Zhouyi zhengyi* (Correct meaning of the *Changes of the Zhou*), 8:24a.

6. Cf. Wang's commentary to section 3, first passage; section 12, second passage; section 27, fifth passage; and section 64, seventh passage.

7. Cf. Wang's commentary to section 47, first passage.

8. Cf. Wang's commentary to section 17, fourth passage; section 52, seventh and eighth passages; and section 58, last passage.

9. Cf. Wang's commentary to section 17, fifth passage.

10. Cf. Wang's commentary to section 65, third passage.

11. Cf. *Lunyu* (Analects), 4:10: "The noble man among all under Heaven finds nothing to favor, nothing to slight."

12. Cf. Wang's commentary to section 10, fourth passage.

SECTION 50

We emerge into life, enter into death.

This refers to how we emerge into the land of life and enter into the land of death.

Three out of ten are adherents of life; three out of ten are adherents of death; and there are three out of ten whose way of life also leads them to death. Why is this so? It is due to placing too much emphasis on life.[1] For I have heard that one good at preserving life, when traveling by land, does not encounter the wild buffalo and, when entering the army, suffers no wound from weapons. The wild water buffalo has no way to strike at him with horn, the tiger has no way to strike at him with claw, and weapons of war have no way to use point or edge against him. Why is this so? It is due to the fact that he stays free of the land of death.[2]

1. "Three out of ten" is like saying "three parts of ten parts."
Those who take the road to life and do everything to live as long

as possible amount to three out of ten people. Those who take the road to death and do everything to die as soon as possible also amount to three out of ten people. When people place too much emphasis on life, it turns into the land of death for them. One good at preserving life does not use life for the sake of living, and this is why he stays free of the land of death.

2. There are no instruments more harmful than weapons of war. There are no beasts more harmful than the wild buffalo and the tiger. Yet if one can ensure that weapons have no way to use point or edge against him or tigers and wild buffaloes have no way to strike him with claw or horn, such a one truly does not let his person be hampered by desire, so how could any land of death exist for him? Bottom creatures deem the lowest depths shallow and burrow into them. Eagles and ospreys deem mountains low and build their nests on top of them. Because harpoon arrows cannot reach them or nets get at them, it can be said that where they locate themselves is land free of death. But, after all, there are those that for the sake of some sweet bait enter land where there is no life for them. Is this not due to placing too much emphasis on life?

3. Thus it is for people: if they neither allow craving to separate them from their roots nor let desire compromise their authenticity, even if they enter the army, they will suffer no harm, and, when traveling on land, they will be invulnerable. That one must emulate the infant and hold it in the highest esteem is perfectly true![3]

NOTES

1. Cf. Wang's commentary to section 13, second passage; and section 75.

2. Cf. section 76, first passage.

3. A somewhat different translation of this lengthy passage, together with a discussion and comparison with the Heshang Gong commentary to section 50, appears in Alan Chan, *Two Visions of the Way*, 184–88.

SECTION 51

The Dao gives life to them; virtue nurtures them, matter gives them physical form, and characteristic potential completes them.

Once things achieve life, they are nurtured. Once nurtured, they acquire physical form [xing]. *Once they have physical form, they achieve completion* [cheng]. *What is the origin from which life comes? It is the Dao. What is the source from which they are nurtured? It is virtue* [de]. *What is the cause* [yin] *of their physical form? It is matter* [wu]. *What is the agency* [shi] *that brings about completion? It is characteristic potential* [shi]. *It is this cause* [yin] *alone that makes it possible for each and every thing to have physical form. It is this characteristic potential* [shi] *alone that makes it possible for each and every thing to achieve completion. From the way all things achieve life to the way the potentiality* [gong] *of things reaches completion, all these processes have an origin. Because there has to be an origin for them, this origin without exception is the Dao. Thus, if we trace these processes back to their ultimate origin, we arrive inevitably at the Dao. It is when we follow them back to their individual causes* [yin] *that we find separate terms for these causes.*[1]

This is why the myriad things without exception must honor the Dao and esteem virtue.

The Dao is the origin of all things, and virtue is the power behind their potential [de]. *It is only after they originate that they have a potential, so this is why they must honor the Dao. Any neglect of virtue will result in harm, so this is why they must esteem it.*

This honoring of the Dao and this esteeming of virtue, none are ordered to do so, yet it always happens spontaneously.

[Ming, *"ordered (to do so), " in both cases is written* jue, *"confer noble status."]*[2]

The Dao gives them life, and virtue nurtures them, that is, grows them, rears them, ensures them their proper shapes, matures them, and protects them.

Ting *[stand up straight] means "ensure their proper shapes"* [pin qixing]. Du *[poison; cure with medicine] means "complete their physical natures"* [chengqizhi] *[thus, "matures them"].*[3] *Each obtains the protective shade it needs to ensure that no harm comes to its body.*

He gives them life yet possesses them not. He acts, yet they do not depend on him.

He provides for them but possesses them not.

They mature, yet he is not their steward. This we call mysterious virtue.[4]

> *He [the sage] has virtue, but they [the people] are unaware of his being master, for it emerges from the secret and the dark.[5]*

NOTES

1. Alan Chan discusses this passage and provides a partial and somewhat different translation in *Two Visions of the Way*, 51–52. The major difference is that Dr. Chan translates *shi* (characteristic potential) as "environment," which, though possible, is in my opinion unlikely, given other similar occurrences of *shi* in Wang's commentary, such as those at section 9, first and second passages.

2. The text in brackets is not part of Wang's commentary but an interpolation from some later commentary. "In both cases" refers to two versions of the *Laozi* that are worded *mo zhi jue er chang ziran* (none are conferred noble status [for so honoring the Dao and virtue], yet it always happens spontaneously). A sentence much like the one in brackets actually occurs in the *Daode zhenjing jizhu* (Collected commentaries on the *True Classic of the Way and Virtue*), 7:20 (17040A): "The two editions of Ming Huang [Emperor Xuanzong of the Tang] and Wang Bi in both cases write *ming* as *jue*." For scholarship on this problem, see Hatano, *Rōshi Dōtokukyō kenkyū*, 337; and Lou, *Wang Bi ji jiaoshi*, 138 n. 9. I should note that both Mawangdui texts and Fu Yi's composite edition all have *jue* instead of *ming* in the text of the *Laozi*. See *Mawangdui Hanmu boshu*, 104. The Wang Bi edition contained in the *Daozang* does have a passage of commentary for section 51, third passage: "One who is honored and esteemed only after he has been conferred noble status is not really honored and esteemed" (Wang Bi, *Laozi Daodejing zhu* [Commentary on Laozi's *Daodejing*], 3:15 [16110A]). It is unlikely, however, that this passage of commentary can actually be attributed to Wang Bi.

3. The first part of this passage, "*Ting* [stand up straight] means 'ensure their proper shapes' [*pin qixing*]. *Du* [poison; cure with medicine] . . . ," is missing from the base text but occurs in a quotation of

this passage in Li Shan's (ca. 630–89) commentary to Liu Jun's (462–521) *Bian ming lun* (Discourse on ways to approach fate), in *Wenxuan*, 54:8a, and in Xu Jian's (fl. ca. 700) *Chuxue ji* (Notes for the first steps in learning). For the latter, see Hatano, *Rōshi Dōtokukyō kenkyū*, 338. Cf. Lou, *Wang Bi ji jiaoshi*, 138 n. 10.

4. For this and the previous passage, cf. section 2, third passage; section 10, last passage; and section 77, second passage. "Mysterious virtue" is also defined in section 65, fourth passage.

5. Cf. Wang's commentary to section 10, last passage.

SECTION 52

All under Heaven has a generatrix, which we regard as the mother of all under Heaven.

> *Having been good at its [all under Heaven's] genesis, it is good at rearing and nurturing it. This is why, because "all under Heaven has a generatrix," we can regard it as the mother of all under Heaven.*

Once one has access to the mother, through it he can know the child. Once one knows the child, if he again holds on to the mother, as long as he lives, no danger shall befall him.[1]

> *The mother is the roots, and the child is the branch tips. It is by having access to the roots that one knows the branch tips, so one must not discard the roots in order to pursue the branch tips.*[2]

Block up your apertures; close your door,

> *The "apertures" [dui]*[3] *are where the desire for things arises. The "door" is where the desires for things enters.*

And to the end of your life you will never be exhausted.

> *Tending to matters without conscious purpose [wushi], one remains forever at ease. Thus "to the end of your life you will never be exhausted."*

But if you open your apertures and deal consciously with things, to the end of your life you will never have relief.

> *Such a one does not shut himself off from the source [of desire] and tries to deal consciously with things. Thus, although he might live his life to the end, he will never have relief.*

To see the small is called "perspicacious." To hold on to softness is called "strength."

> *Success in government does not consist of just dealing with the large and obvious. Seeing the large does not indicate perspicacity* [ming, *literally, "brightness"]; it is seeing the small that is perspicacious. Holding on to strength does not make one strong; it is holding on to softness that makes one strong.*

Make use of its brightness,

> *Let the Dao shine forth and thereby rid the common folk of delusion.*[4]

But always let its brightness revert.

> *Do not engage in bright scrutiny.*[5]

Never let one's person be exposed to disaster: this is a matter of practicing constancy.

> *This means the constancy of the Dao.*

NOTES

1. Cf. section 16, last passage. Despite a long running controversy over what *dui* means in the text of the *Laozi*, the context established by these two passages of Wang's commentary indicates that he seems to have understood the term as meaning something like "apertures," as the apertures of sense, that is, the eyes, ears, nose, and mouth. After weighing other possibilities, this is how Jiang Xichang interprets Wang's references to *dui* (see *Laozi jiaogu*, 321–22). Hatano Tarō agrees, though instead of citing Jiang, he cites Lao Jian's *Laozi guben kao* (Research into ancient editions of the *Laozi*, first published 1941), where *dui* is also identified with the apertures of sense (see *Rōshi Dōtokukyō kenkyū*, 342). Lou Yulie ignores all this evidence, cites other (and, in my opinion, weaker) evidence, and instead glosses *dui* as *dao* (way, path), which seems a poor fit in the context (see *Wang Bi ji jiaoshi*, 141 n. 3).

2. Cf. Wang's commentary to section 20, last passage; and section 38, paragraph 14.

3. Cf. Wang's commentary to section 65, third passage.

4. Cf. Wang's commentary to section 10, sixth passage.

5. Cf. paragraph 2 of Wang's commentary to section 49, fifth passage. The sage should let his brightness, one with the brightness of the Dao, revert to himself and not let it play upon the common folk as the searchlight of scrutiny. Cf. section 58, last passage.

SECTION 53

If, with firm resolve, I had the knowledge to travel on the great Dao [Way], I need only fear that I might try to meddle with it.

> *In other words, if I could, with firm resolve* [jieran],[1] *have the knowledge to make the great Dao prevail among all under Heaven, my only fear should be that I might try to meddle with It* [shiwei].

The great Dao [Way] might be very smooth, yet the common folk prefer byways.

> *In other words, although the great Dao [Way] endlessly stretches straight and smooth, the common folk nevertheless discard and do not follow it, preferring instead to travel the bypaths of deviancy* [xie]. *How much the more would this happen if I were to block the great Dao [Way] by meddling with it? Thus the text says: "The great Dao [Way] might be very smooth, yet the common folk prefer byways."*

The court is kept in good order,

> *"The court" refers to the palace. "In good order" means kept clean and pleasant.*

But the fields are overgrown with weeds, the granaries empty.

> *To keep the court in excessive good order will result in fields being much overgrown with weeds and granaries being terribly empty. This is to harm the lives of the many so that the one may be fulfilled.*

Garbed in patterned and colorful clothes, wearing sharp swords, satiated with food and drink, and overflowing with wealth and goods: all this is stolen extravagance and nothing to do with the Dao!

> *If anything is obtained in violation of the Dao, it is always ill-gotten, and, being ill-gotten, it means that it is stolen. Extravagance not obtained in accordance with the Dao [is stolen extravagance. Noble status not obtained in accordance with the Dao][2] is stolen status. Thus the text cites this example of anti-Dao behavior in order to clarify what being anti-Dao means: to be anti-Dao always indicates stolen extravagance.*

NOTES

1. For the argument that *jieran* should be rendered "having little," "in small measure," see Chan, *Two Visions of the Way*, 181–82, and

Henricks, *Lao-Tzu Te-Tao Ching*, 269 n. 60. This would result in: "If I had but little knowledge to travel on. . . ." Although the context does not clarify which interpretation is the more likely, I favor the one that indicates firmness of purpose. Lou Yulie, citing Lao Jian's *Laozi guben kao*, comes to the same conclusion; see *Wang Bi ji jiaoshi*, 142 n. 1.

2. The text in brackets occurs only in the *Daode zhenjing jizhu* (Collected commentaries on the *True Classic of the Way and Virtue*), 8:4 (17045A). All other editions read: "Extravagance not obtained in accordance with the Dao indicates stolen status." See Hatano, *Rōshi Dōtokukyō kenkyū*, 347–48; and Lou, *Wang Bi ji jiaoshi*, 143 n. 9.

S E C T I O N   5 4

The well-founded will not be pulled up.

> *Only after firmly establishing the roots [foundation] does one tend to the branch tips [final details]. Thus it "will not be pulled up."*

The well-embraced will not get dropped.

> *Not greedy for much, one does not carry more than he is able. Thus it "will not get dropped."*

Such a one's descendants, accordingly, will never let sacrifices to him cease.

> *Because his descendants will hand down this Dao, the sacrifices they make to him will never cease.*

If you cultivate it within your own person, your virtue will be authentic. If you cultivate it within your family, your virtue will exceed all need.

> *One extends [cultivation of virtue] to others by [first cultivating it in] one's own person. If you cultivate it within your own person, it will be authentic. If you cultivate it within your family, it will exceed all need. By cultivating it without fail, its application will become ever greater.*

If you cultivate it within your village, your virtue will endure. If you cultivate it within your state, your virtue will be abundant. If you cultivate it among all under Heaven, your virtue will reach everywhere. Look at the person from the point of view of the person. Look at the family from the point of view of the family. Look at the village from the point of view of the village. Look at the state from the point of view of the state.

These all are approached in the same way.

Look at all under Heaven from the point of view of all under Heaven.

This is to look at the Dao of all under Heaven from the point of view of the hearts/minds [xin] of all the common folk in all under Heaven. For the Dao of all under Heaven, opposition to or compliance with it results in good fortune or bad, in all cases just as the Dao operates for people.[1]

How do I know that all under Heaven is so? It is by this.[2]

"This" refers to what has just been said above. In other words: How do I get to know all under Heaven? One comes to know it by searching into oneself and not by seeking it anywhere outside. This is what is meant by the expression, "Know all under Heaven without even leaving your gate."[3]

NOTES

1. Alan Chan translates, somewhat differently, Wang's commentary to this passage and compares it to the Heshang Gong commentary. See *Two Visions of the Way*, 174.

2. Cf. section 21, last passage.

3. Section 47, first passage.

SECTION 55

One who has profoundly internalized virtue is comparable to the infant. Wasps, scorpions, adders, and vipers do not sting or bite him. Fierce animals do not attack him. Birds of prey do not seize him.

The infant is free from craving or desire and so commits no offense against the myriad things. As a result, no poisonous creature commits offense against him. It is because one who has profoundly internalized virtue does not commit offense against others that others do not try to make him lose his wholeness [quan].

His bones are soft and sinews pliant, but his grip is firm.

It is because of his softness and pliancy that his grip can be so perfectly firm.

That he is ignorant of the union of male and female yet completely erect

> Zuo *[engaged, manifest] means* zhang *[erect]. Because there is nothing to make him suffer bodily loss, he is able to stay completely erect* [quanzhang]. *In other words, when it comes to one who has profoundly internalized virtue* [de] *as such, no one can cause him to lose his virtue or dilute his authenticity* [zhen]. *The soft and pliable do not contend and so never get broken, and this always happens exactly like this.*[1]

Is because his semen is at the full. That he can cry all day long yet never grow hoarse

> *His heart/mind is free of contention and desire, thus he can sound forth all day long yet never grow hoarse.*

Is because his bodily balance is perfect. To know how to maintain balance is called "constancy."

> *People achieve constancy* [chang] *through balance* [he]. *Thus, if one knows how to maintain balance, he will achieve constancy.*

To understand constancy is called "perspicacity."

> *Neither bright nor dark, neither warm nor cold, this indicates constancy.*[2] *Such a one remains formless, so what he is cannot be seen.*[3] *Thus the text says: "To understand constancy is called 'perspicacity.'"*[4]

To extend life beyond its natural span is called "inauspicious."

> *Life must not be extended, for if one tries to extend it, he will suffer an early death.*[5]

For the heart/mind to control the vital force is called "forcing strength."

> *The heart/mind* [xin] *should consist of nothingness* [wuyou]. *If it controls the vital force* [qi], *this is called "forcing strength"* [qiang].[6]

Once a thing reaches its prime, it grows old. We say it goes against the Dao, and what is against the Dao comes to an early end.[7]

NOTES

1. Wang interprets the text metaphorically: one who has profoundly internalized virtue (*de*) is like the male infant who has erections but does not ejaculate and thus continually internalizes his semen, the *jing* of the next line. *Jing* (semen) is the essence of male virility and identified

with *de*, "virtue," in the sense of potency or power. The man of virtue similarly does not "spend" his virtue on others but harbors it within himself. The metaphor extends to the "soft and pliable" of the last sentence, which is a metaphoric reference to the male member, as the symbolic epitome of yang, male hardness and stiffness, which here, significantly, is "soft and pliable." In other words, the man of perfect virtue does not contend with others and employ hard, aggressive behavior and policies (yang and male), thus he never "gets broken" and so preserves his wholeness intact.

2. Cf. Wang's commentary to section 35, first passage.

3. Cf. Wang's commentary to section 15, second passage.

4. Cf. section 16, sixth passage.

5. "Early death" translates *yao*, which most commentators, including Lou Yulie, gloss as *buxiang* (inauspicious), but this is to miss the irony of Wang's observation: anyone who tries to live longer than he should will never feel he has lived long enough and so will always "suffer an early death." The text of the *Laozi* reads *xiang*, usually "auspicious," but ancient text attest that *xiang* sometimes means *buxiang*, "inauspicious." See Lou, *Wang Bi ji jiaoshi*, 147 n. 7.

6. "Conscious effort" means forced effort, and, while forced effort may "prime" one's strength, as the next passage tells us, once one's prime is reached aging and decline follow. Forcing one's strength just brings about early decline, because it "is against the Dao."

7. Cf. section 30, last passage.

SECTION 56

He who knows does not speak.
   Such a one acts in accordance with the Natural.
He who speaks does not know.
   Such a one forces things to happen.
Block up your apertures; close your door;[1] blunt your sharpness.
   Harbor simplicity [zhi] *within you.*[2]
Cut away the tangled;
   Eliminate the cause of contention.
Merge with the brilliant;
   If one has no particular eminence of his own, people will have no predilection to contend.
Become one with the very dust.[3]

If one has no particular baseness of his own, people will have no
predilection to feel shame.

We call this "one with mystery." Thus one can neither get close
to such a one nor get distant from him.

If one could get close to him, one could get distant from him.

One can neither benefit nor harm him.

If one could benefit him, one could harm him.

One can neither ennoble him nor debase him.

If one could ennoble him, one could debase him.

Thus such a one is esteemed by all under Heaven.

No one, accordingly, can impose on him in any way.

NOTES

1. Cf. section 52, third passage.

2. Cf. section 81, first passage.

3. For this and the previous three passages, cf. section 4.

SECTION 57

If one governs the state with governance, he will use the military
with perversity. It is by tending to matters without conscious
purpose that one takes all under Heaven as his charge.

If one governs the state with the Dao, the state will be at peace.
If one governs the state with governance [zheng], [1] *perverse* [ji]
military action will begin. But if one tends to matters without
conscious purpose, he shall be able to take all under Heaven as
his charge. As an earlier section says, "One who takes all under
Heaven as his charge always tends to matters without deliberate
action. But when it comes to one who does take conscious action,
such a one is not worthy to take all under Heaven as his charge." [2]
Thus, if one governs the state with governance, because he is
not worthy to take all under Heaven as his change, he will use
the military with perversity [ji]. *To govern the state with the*
Dao means to encourage growth at the branch tips by enhancing
the roots. [3] *To govern the state with governance is to attack the*
branch tips by establishing punishments. With the roots not firmly

established, the branch tips wither, and the common folk will
have no means to cope with life. This is why things will surely
develop to the point where one will "use the military with per-
versity."

How do I know that this is so? It is by this: The more all under
Heaven are beset with taboos and prohibitions, the poorer the
common folk grow. The more the common folk are beset with
sharp instruments, the more muddled the state becomes.

> *A "sharp instrument" [liqi] is any instrument that one can use*
> *to profit himself. If the common folk are strong, the state will be*
> *weak.*[4]

The more people have skill and cleverness, the more often perverse [*ji*] things will happen.

> *If the people increase their intelligence and knowledge, artful*
> *falsehood will arise. When artful falsehood arises, evil doings*
> *will begin.*

The more laws and ordinances are displayed, the more thieves
and robbers there will be.

> *One establishes the rule of law because of the wish to extin-*
> *guish evil, but perverse military efforts result. One increases*
> *taboos and prohibitions because of the wish to instill a sense of*
> *shame in the poor, but the common folk become increasingly*
> *poor.*[5] *"Sharp instruments" are things that one wishes to use to*
> *strengthen the state, but doing so only makes the state increas-*
> *ingly muddled. It is because one neglects the roots in order to*
> *tend to the branch tips that things all reach such a state as this.*

Thus the sage says: I engage in no conscious effort, and the common folk undergo moral transformation spontaneously.[6] I love
quietude, and the common folk govern themselves.[7] I tend to
matters without conscious purpose, and the common folk enrich
themselves. I am utterly free of desire, and the common folk
achieve pristine simplicity by themselves.

> *What the sovereign desires, the common folk are quick to pur-*
> *sue. Because all I desire is to have no desire, the common folk*
> *will also become desireless and achieve pristine simplicity by*
> *themselves. These four [engaging in no conscious effort, loving*
> *quietude, tending to matters without conscious purpose, and*
> *being desireless] are all a matter of encouraging growth at the*
> *branch tips by enhancing the roots.*[8]

NOTES

1. Cf. Wang's commentary to section 17, fourth passage.

2. Section 48, fourth through sixth passages.

3. Cf. Wang's commentary to section 38, paragraph 14.

4. In the *Laozi* weakness is self-fulfilling and good, so one must interpret "if the common folk are strong, the state will be weak" as a good thing. After all, for the *Laozi*, weakness is strength, which can be explained here in terms of how "sharp instruments" in the hands of the common folk are the means to make themselves strong and prosperous. The "sharp instruments" of the common folk thus serve to bolster rather than threaten the state. "Sharp instruments" are bad, however, when employed by the state. The *Laozi* has already warned that the state should not use sharp instruments, that is, punishment and military coercion. Cf. section 36, second passage.

5. Hatano Tarō cites Fujisawa Tōgai's (1794–1864) reading note to this passage, which asserts that *chi* (shame) is a mistake for *zhi* (stop). Hatano agrees, as does Lou Yulie when he cites Hatano's remarks (without mentioning Fujisawa). See Hatano, *Rōshi Dōtokukyō kenkyū*, 363; and Lou, *Wang Bi ji jiaoshi*, 151 n. 6. But although "one increases taboos and prohibitions because of the wish to stop poverty" is certainly possible, "instill a sense of shame [*chi*]" is still the better reading, for it is likely that Wang had the following passage from the *Lunyu* (Analects), 2:3, in mind: "If the people are led by governance [*zheng*] and kept in order by punishment [*xing*], they will evade these without shame." Cf. section 17, fourth passage.

6. Cf. section 37, first through third passages.

7. Cf. section 37, last passage.

8. Alan Chan translates, somewhat differently, this passage from Wang's commentary and discusses and compares it to the Heshang Gong commentary in *Two Visions of the Way*, 172–73.

SECTION 58

When the government is completely muddled, the common folk become pure and simple.

> *In other words, one who is good at the conduct of government has no identifiable form, name, deliberate purpose, or procedure.*

Being completely muddled, he attains great government [dazhi] *in the end. Thus the text refers to "when the government is completely muddled." The people, having nothing to contend or wrangle about, are pure and simple in their great generosity. Thus the text refers to when "the common folk become pure and simple."*

When the government conducts meticulous scrutiny, the common folk become devious and inscrutable.

It establishes punishments and names, promulgates rewards and penalties, in order to uncover treachery. Thus the text refers to when "the government conducts meticulous scrutiny." It maintains strict distinctions among different classes of people, which causes the common folk to harbor contention and wrangling in their hearts/minds. Thus the text refers to "the common folk becom[ing] devious and inscrutable."

It is on disaster that good fortune depends; it is in good fortune that disaster lurks. Who understands what the very best is? It is to have no government at all!

In other words, who understands good government at its best? It is only at its best when it is impossible to identify any act of government or to name any punishment and, though it is completely muddled, all under Heaven effects its own great moral transformation.

Correctness turns into perversion.

If one uses governance to govern the state, it easily reverts to the perverse [ji] *use of the military. Thus the text says: "Correctness turns into perversion."*

Goodness turns into deviancy.

If one establishes goodness to bring harmony to the myriad folk, it easily reverts to the disastrous advent of deviancy. Thus the text says: "Correctness turns into perversion."

The people's confusion has certainly lasted a long time.

In other words, the people in their doubt and confusion have lost the Dao for such a long time that one cannot easily make them behave responsibly by controlling them with correctness and goodness.

This is why the sage is square but does not cut,

Using his squareness [uprightness] to lead the people, he enables them to put aside their evil ways; he does not use his squareness [as a model] to cut people [into shape]. This is what is meant by "the great square has no corners."[1]

He is pointed but does not stab.

Lian [pointed] means "honest" [qinglian]. Gui [stab] means "wound." Using his honesty to lead the people, he enables them to put aside their filthy ways; he does not use his honesty to stab at and inflict wounds on them.[2]

He is straight but does not align.

Using his straightness to lead the people, he enables them to put aside their deviant ways; he does not use his straightness to dam up or strike at them.[3] *This is what is meant by "great straightness seems crooked."*[4]

He is bright but does not shine.

He uses his brightness to illuminate their way out of confusion; he does not use his brightness as a searchlight to expose what the people are trying to keep hidden. This is what is meant by "the bright Dao seems dark."[5]

NOTES

1. Section 41, eleventh passage.

2. Wang reads *lian*, "pointed" (as an arrow or sword is pointed), as a pun on *lian*, "honest"; cf. the English expression "stay on the straight and narrow."

3. Cf. *Mengzi* (Mencius), 6A:2: "To be sure, water has no propensity to flow east or west, but does it have no propensity to flow up or down? The tendency of human nature to goodness is like the tendency of water to flow downward. None lacks this tendency to goodness, just as no water fails to flow downward. Now, one may strike at water and make it leap so that it can rise higher than his forehead, and one may dam up water and force it to move so that it is sent up a hill, but what has any of this to do with the nature of water?" Both Hatano Tarō and Lou Yulie, referring to a range of Japanese and Chinese textual scholarship, suggest various emendations to the text, all of which seem superfluous in the light of this allusion to the *Mengzi*, which is not taken into account. See Hatano, *Rōshi Dōtokukyō kenkyū*, 370; and Lou, *Wang Bi ji jiaoshi*, 155 n. 19.

4. Section 45, third passage.

5. Section 41, third passage. Cf. paragraph 2 of Wang's commentary to section 49, fifth passage; and section 52, seventh and eighth passages.

SECTION 59

For ordering the people and serving Heaven, nothing is better than husbandry.

> *"Nothing is better than" is like saying "nothing surpasses." Se [husbandry] refers to the farmer. The way the farmer puts his farm in order is to bring a single uniformity to it by earnestly ridding it of weeds. He fulfills its naturalness by preventing the threat that it be damaged by neglect, that is, he eliminates that which causes damage by neglect [weeds]. For receiving the mandate of Heaven above and for keeping the people content below, nothing surpasses this.*

Only husbandry can be called the quick way to submission.

> *What there is "quick submission" to is constancy* [chang].

By "quick way to submission" we mean the repetitive accumulation of virtue.

> *Just let repetitive accumulation of virtue happen, and avoid forcing them [the people] to go faster, for only then can one have them submit to the way of constancy. Thus the text says: "By 'quick way to submission' we mean the repetitive accumulation of virtue."*[1]

If one repetitively accumulates virtue, there is nothing that he cannot conquer. As there is nothing that he cannot conquer, no one knows the limits he can reach.

> *The Dao is infinite.*

As no one knows his limits, he can, accordingly, keep his state.

> *If one attempts to rule a state while he is limited by constraints, this is not one who can keep a state.*

If one maintains the mother of the state, he can, accordingly, long endure.

> *That which keeps a state at peace is called its mother. The "repetitive accumulation of virtue" means nothing other than carefully planning the roots first and only then tending to the branch tips,*[2] *for this enables him [the ruler] to live his life to the end.*

This we refer to as having deep roots firmly established, for it is the Dao of long life and enduring oversight.

N O T E S

1. Although Wang seems to read section 59 up to this point as advice about how the ruler should rule his people—the good ruler is like the good farmer who does not try to accelerate the growth of crops but lets them gradually realize the potential (virtue) of growth—he shifts back to the ruler's own accumulation of virtue with the following passage.

2. Cf. section 54, first passage.

S E C T I O N   6 0

Ruling a large state is like cooking a small fish.

> *This means no stirring. Action results in much harm, but quietude results in the fulfillment of authenticity* [zhen]. *Thus the larger the state, the more its ruler should practice quietude, for only then can he widely obtain the hearts/minds of the mass of common folk.*[1]

If one uses the Dao to oversee all under Heaven, the malign spirits there will lose their numinous power.

> *If one governs a large state, he should do so as if he were cooking a small fish. "If one uses the Dao to oversee all under Heaven, the malign spirits there will lose their numinous powers."*

It is not that these malign spirits have no numinous power; it is just that they will do no harm to the people.

> *Numinous powers* [shen] *do not harm the Natural* [ziran]. *If people hold on to their naturalness, numinous powers will have no way to impose on them. As numinous powers have no way to impose on them, there is no way to know that numinous powers are numinous.*

It is not these numinous powers that do not harm the people but the sage, in fact, who does not harm the people.

> *If they unite with the Dao, numinous powers will not harm the people. As numinous powers do not harm the people, they are unaware that the numinous powers are numinous powers. If he*

unites with the Dao, the sage also will not harm the people. As the sage does not harm the people, they are also unaware that the sage is a sage. In other words, not only are they unaware that numinous powers are numinous powers, they are also unaware that the sage is a sage. Relying on a network of power to control the people will bring about the demise of government, but if one allows the people to become unaware of numinous powers and sageliness, it will bring about the ultimate realization of the Dao.

It is because neither of these two cause any harm that they unite their virtues and revert to it.

Numinous powers do not harm people, and the sage does not harm people either. The sage does not harm people, and numinous powers do not harm people either. Thus the text says: "neither of these two cause any harm." Because numinous powers and the sage share the same Dao, [the text says that] they unite and revert to it.

NOTES

1. Alan Chan discusses section 60 and provides a translation of it and Wang's commentary (somewhat different from mine) in *Two Visions of the Way*, 86–88.

SECTION 61

A large state is a catchment into which flow occurs.[1]

Because the river and the sea occupy large areas and are situated in low positions, all streams and tributaries flow into them. If a large state dwells in greatness and takes up a low position, all under Heaven will flow into it. Thus the text says: "A large state is a catchment into which flow occurs."

It is where all under Heaven unite.

It is that to which all under Heaven gravitate together.

It is the female for all under Heaven.

It maintains quietude [jing] and does not seek them out, so people gravitate to it of their own accord.

The female always conquers the male because of quietude. She is able to take the low position because of quietude.

It is because of her quietude that she can place herself beneath.
Pin [the female of animals] means ci *[the female of birds; thus*
pin refers to the female of species in general]. The male is aggres-
sive and active, covetous and full of desire, but because the
female always practices quietude, she is able to conquer the male.
She is also able to place herself beneath because of her quietude.
Thus the other gravitates to her.

Thus the large state, by placing itself beneath the small state,

"The large state, by placing itself beneath" in other words means
"because the large state places itself beneath the small state."

Consequently takes over the small state.

The small state attaches itself to it.

The small state, by placing itself beneath the large state, subsequently is taken over by the large state.

The large state takes in the small state.

Thus some, by taking a place beneath, take over, and some, by
taking a place beneath, are taken over.

In other words, it is only by cultivating humility that each [the
male and the female, the superior and the subordinate, the large
and the small] obtains its proper place.[2]

The large state should desire nothing more than to bring people
together and nurture them, and the small state should desire nothing
more than to join in and serve people. In order that both obtain
what they desire, it is fitting that the large one place itself beneath.

The small state cultivates lowliness, for it can do nothing more
than keep itself whole; it cannot cause all under Heaven to gravi-
tate to it. If the large state cultivates lowliness, all under Heaven
will gravitate to it. Thus the text says: "In order that both obtain
what they desire, it is fitting that the large one place itself beneath."

NOTES

1. Cf. section 28, first passage; section 32, last passage; section 66;
and section 73, seventh passage.

2. Tao Hongqing, in light of the next passage, amends the text to
read "each obtains what it desires" (*Du zhuzi zhaji* [Reading notes on
the philosophers], 17). See Hatano, *Rōshi Dōtokukyō kenkyū*, 384; and
Lou, *Wang Bi ji jiaoshi*, 161 n. 5. This seems unnecessary, however,
and the text makes good sense as it stands.

SECTION 62

The Dao is the shelter of the myriad things.

*"Shelter" [*ao, *innermost recesses of a house] is used here in the sense of* ai *[shade]; it is an expression for where shelter can be obtained.*

It is the treasure of the good man

It is a "treasure" because it is useful to him.

And the protector of the man who is not good.

It is thanks to this protection that his wholeness is kept intact [quan].

Fine words can be used to market it, and noble behavior can be used to influence others by it.

In other words, the Dao takes precedence over absolutely every-thing, and nothing could be more valuable than this. Whether it be jewels or treasures, disks of jade or horses, nothing can match it. If one were to express it in fine words, it could, accordingly, command the highest price on the market. Thus the text says: "Fine words can be used to market it." If one were to practice it in noble behavior, those even more than a thousand li *away would respond to it.[1] Thus the text says: "Noble behavior can be used to influence others by it."*

As for men who are not good, how could they ever be discarded?

Those who are not good should be protected, for they are spared rejection by the Dao.[2]

Thus the son of Heaven is established, and the three dukes are installed.

This refers to how the Dao is expressed through noble behavior.

Although one could promote it by providing them with disks of jade to hold and teams of four horses to lead, this falls short of promoting this Dao by just letting them sit quietly.

"This Dao" refers to what is said above. In other words, the reason the son of Heaven is established and the three dukes[3] installed, with these positions ennobled and high value placed on the men who fill them, is so the Dao can be carried out through them. Because nothing could be more valuable than this, "although one could promote it by providing them with disks of jade to hold and teams of four horses to lead [i.e., by enhancing their nobility and value], this falls short of promoting this Dao by just letting them sit quietly."

How did the ancients show their esteem for the Dao? Did they not say: "When beseeching it, one obtains, and, when in violation of it, one is forgiven"? Thus it was that it was esteemed by all under Heaven.

> *If one beseeches it, he will get what he wants, and, if one violates it, he will be forgiven by it. There are no circumstances under which it does not apply. Thus it was that it was esteemed by all under Heaven.*

NOTES

1. Cf. section 8 of the *Xici zhuan* (Commentary on the Appended Phrases), Part One, of the *Yijing* (Classic of changes), which reads in part: "The noble man might stay in his chambers, but if the words he speaks are about goodness, even those from more than a thousand *li* away will respond with approval to him, and how much the more will those who are nearby do so!" (Lynn, *The Classic of Changes*, 58; see *Zhouyi zhengyi* [Correct meaning of the *Changes of the Zhou*], 7:17b).

2. Cf. section 27, fifth through seventh passages.

3. For a discussion of the three dukes as the three most eminent ministers at court, see Henricks, *Lao-Tzu Te-Tao Ching*, 146; and Hucker, *A Dictionary of Official Titles in Imperial China*, 399.

SECTION 63

Act by not acting; do by not doing; find flavor in that which has no flavor.

> *To handle matters without conscious effort* [wuwei], *practice the teaching that is not expressed in words,[1] and have a taste for the utterly dispassionate* [tiandan][2] *is the ultimate of government* [zhi zhi ji].

Deal with the small as if it were the great, and deal with the few as if it were the many, but respond to resentment in terms of virtue.

> *Minor resentment is not worth responding to, but great resentment involves something for which all under Heaven desire punishment. It is virtuous* [de] *to comply with that upon which all under Heaven agree.[3]*

Plan for the difficult while it is still easy; work on the great while it is still small. Every difficult matter under Heaven surely originates in something easy, and every great matter under Heaven surely originates in something small.[4] Therefore it is because the sage never tries to be great that he fulfills his greatness. Assent lightly given surely inspires little trust. Regarding many things as easy is sure to result in many difficulties. Therefore the sage still regards them as difficulties.

> *Thus even someone with the talent of a sage still deals with the small and the easy as if they were difficulties. How much more this should hold true for someone who has not the talent of a sage and still wishes to treat such things with neglect! Thus the text says, "still regards them as difficulties."*

Thus he never has difficulties.

NOTES

1. Cf. section 2, second and third passages; and Wang's commentary to section 17, first passage.

2. Cf. section 31.

3. Cf. section 48, first passage; and Wang's commentary to section 28, last passage: " 'The great carver' [the sage] takes the heart/mind [*xin*] of all under Heaven as his heart/mind," so "virtue" here is not the conscious virtue of the inferior ruler but the "mysterious virtue" of the sage, as described in section 10, last passage.

4. These statements can be found in two different places in the *Han Fei ẓi* (Sayings of Master Han Fei), where they refer explicitly to the suppression of crime and rebellion and describe the actions of the "perspicacious sovereign" who always nips trouble in the bud. See *Han Fei ẓi*, 7:1140C (section 21) and 16:1173A (section 38).

SECTION 64

The secure is easy to maintain; the premanifest [*weiẓhao*][1] is easy to plan for.

> *When he is secure* [an], *one does not forget danger* [wei], *and, in maintaining security, one does not forget ruin* [wang] *but plans for it while its potential is still without effect.*[2] *Thus the text says that it "is easy."*

The fragile is easy to melt; the tiny is easy to dissolve.

Although it [the danger of ruin] has detached itself from noth-ingness and entered existence, because of its fragility and tiny size, it still lacks the wherewithal to initiate any large effect. Thus to deal with it is still "easy." These four [the secure, the premanifest, the fragile, and the tiny] all warn that one should be heedful of how things end. One must not fail to maintain security merely because the danger of ruin does not yet exist, and one must not fail to dissolve the danger of ruin merely be-cause it is still tiny. If one fails to maintain security while danger does not exist, danger will take root and grow into existence in that failure. If one fails to dissolve danger while it is still tiny, it will take root and grow large in that failure. Therefore, if one worried equally about disaster as it happens at the end and as it is threatened at the beginning, no endeavor would ever end in defeat.

So take action while it still does not exist

This means while it still resides in its premanifest state [weizhao].

And control it before it turns into disorder.

This means while it is still tiny and fragile.

A tree that takes both arms to clasp grows from a tiny shoot; a nine-story terrace starts from a pile of dirt; a journey of a thou-sand *li* begins under one's feet. One who takes deliberate action [*wei*] will become ruined; one who consciously administers will become lost.

It is right that one, mindful of how they end, eliminates tiny sprouts of danger and right that one, mindful of tiny sprouts of danger, eliminates disorder. However, if one attempts to bring them under control by taking conscious action and implementing procedures or tries to take administrative action against them by using punishments and names, this will, on the contrary, pro-voke the start of new troubles, and clever stealth will proliferate. Thus it is that one is "ruined" and "lost."

This is why the sage engages in no deliberate action and so never becomes ruined, does not consciously administer and so never becomes lost. People pursue matters in such a way that they always suffer ruin just when they are about to succeed.

They are not mindful about how things end.

If one is as mindful of ends as he is of beginnings, his endeavors will never end in defeat. This is why the sage desires to have no desire and does not value goods hard to get.[3]

Although likes and desires may be tiny, contentious tastes will arise out of them. Although goods hard to get might be insignificant, greedy thievery will occur because of them.

He learns not to learn and redeems the errors that the mass of common folk make.

What one is capable of without learning is the natural [ziran].[4] *To be learned in learning[5] results in error. Thus "he learns not to learn and redeems the errors that the mass of common folk make."*

Accordingly, he enhances the natural state of the myriad folk but dares not engage in deliberate action.[6]

NOTES

1. Cf. section 20, fourth passage.

2. Cf. section 5 of the *Xici zhuan* (Commentary on the Appended Phrases), Part Two, of the *Yijing* (Classic of changes), which reads in part: "To get into danger is a matter of thinking one's position secure; to become ruined is a matter of thinking one's continuance protected; to fall into disorder is a matter of thinking one's order enduring. Therefore the noble man when secure does not forget danger, when enjoying continuance does not forget ruin, when maintaining order does not forget disorder. This is the way his person is kept secure and his state remains protected" (Lynn, *The Classic of Changes*, 83; see *Zhouyi zhengyi* [Correct meaning of the *Changes of the Zhou*], 8:12a–12b).

3. Cf. section 3, first passage; section 12, second passage; section 27, fifth passage; and paragraph 1 of Wang's commentary to section 49, fifth passage.

4. Cf. Wang's commentary to section 20, first passage: "If one could stay on the mark without knowing how it is done, what should he ever seek to learn by advancing his knowledge?"

5. The interpretation of *yu yu xue* as "learned in learning" is suggested by Hatano Tarō, who notes a similar syntactic pattern in *Lunyu* (Analects), 4:16: "The noble man is learned in righteousness; the petty man is learned in profit." See Hatano, *Rōshi Dōtokukyō kenkyū*, 395.

6. Cf. Wang's commentary to section 27, fifth passage.

SECTION 65

Those in antiquity who were good at practicing the Dao did not use it to make the common folk intelligent but used it to make them stupid.

> *"Intelligent"* [ming] *means that much knowledge and clever duplicity obscure their pristine simplicity* [pu]. *"Stupid"* [yu] *means that freedom from knowledge and preservation of authenticity* [zhen] *allow them to follow the Natural* [ziran].

The reason the common folk are hard to govern is that they have too much knowledge.

> *Too much knowledge and clever duplicity make them hard to govern.*

Thus to use knowledge to govern the state is to bring about the theft of the state.[1]

> Zhi *[knowledge] is used here as if it meant "governance"* [zhi]. *The reason the term "theft" is applied to the state is that it is governed by the use of knowledge. Thus the term "knowledge" is used [instead of "governance"]. "The reason the common folk are hard to govern is that they have too much knowledge." One should ensure that he blocks up their apertures and shuts their doors[2] so that the common folk stay free of knowledge and desire. If, instead, one tries to motivate them through knowledge and methods* [zhishu], *once this incites their hearts/minds to evil, such a one will have to use ever more clever methods to try to keep their dishonest activities under check. However, because the common folk understand how these methods work, they will take protective steps and manage to avoid them.[3] The more thinking becomes secretive and clever, the more treachery will proliferate. Thus the text says: "to use knowledge to govern the state is to bring about the theft of the state."*

Not to use knowledge to govern the state is to enrich the state. One should understand these two, for they constitute a consistent rule. Constant understanding of this consistent rule is called "mysterious virtue." Mysterious virtue is indeed profound, indeed far-reaching!

> Ji *[consistent] means* tong *[same]. Because it is a rule that is the same for both ancient and modern times, it must not be abandoned. The ability to understand this consistent rule is called*

"*mysterious virtue.*"[4] "*Mysterious virtue is indeed profound, indeed far-reaching!*"

Such a one helps the people revert,

   They revert to their authenticity [zhen].

For only then will perfect compliance be attained.

NOTES

   1. Cf. section 57.
   2. Cf. section 52, third passage.
   3. This seems to criticize the *Han Fei zi*, which states: "One who uses knowledge and methods [*zhishu*] must see far and scrutinize clearly. If he cannot scrutinize clearly, he will be unable to bring clandestine behavior to light" (4:1128B [section 11]).
   4. Cf. section 51, last passage.

SECTION 66

The reason the river and the sea are able to be kings of all the river valleys is that they are good at keeping below them. Thus they are able to be kings of all the river valleys.[1] This is why, if one wishes to be above the common folk, he must use his words to place himself below them.[2] If one wishes to be at the front of the common folk, he must use his person in such a way that they think of him as behind them.[3] Therefore the sage positions himself above, yet the common folk do not regard him as heavy; he positions himself in front, yet the common folk do not regard him as an obstacle. Therefore all under Heaven happily promote him without ever tiring of it. It is because he does not contend that none among all under Heaven can contend with him.[4]

NOTES

   1. Cf. section 28, first passage; section 32, last passage; and section 61, first passage.
   2. Cf. section 68, penultimate passage.

3. Cf. section 7, second passage; and section 28, first passage.

4. Cf. section 22, last passage.

SECTION 67

All under Heaven say that my Dao is great but seems to have no likeness [*buxiao*]. The reason why it seems to have no likeness is that greatness is its only attribute. If it had a likeness, all this time it would have been insignificant!

"All this time it would have been insignificant" is like saying "it would have been insignificant all this time." If it had a likeness, it would lose the wherewithal to be great.[1] *Thus the text says: "If it had a likeness, all this time it would have been insignificant!"*

I have three treasures, which I hold tight and protect. The first is called "kindness," the second "frugality," and the third is "no presumption that I am first among all under Heaven." It is thanks to kindness that one can be brave.

"Thanks to kindness [ci], *when one takes the field, he is victorious, and, when he takes a defensive position, he holds firm." Thus "one can be brave."*

It is thanks to frugality that one can be generous.

If one is frugal and is careful with expenditures, all under Heaven will not want. Thus "one can be generous."

It is by not presuming to be first among all under Heaven that one can make one's ready device last long.

Only one who puts his person behind and aside can become someone to whom the people gravitate.[2] *Only then can such a one establish himself as a ready device* [chengqi], *be of benefit to all under Heaven, and become leader of all the people.*[3]

Now, if one abandons kindness and takes bravery,

Ju [keep intact] means something like qu *[take].*

Abandons frugality and takes generosity, and abandons the back and takes first place, such a one will die! Thanks to kindness, when one takes the field, he is victorious, and, when he takes a defensive position, he holds firm, for it is Heaven that will save him by protecting him with guards of kindness.

NOTES

1. The only attribute of the Dao is its great size; it has no other feature and resembles absolutely nothing. Cf. section 25, sixth passage. The Dao is, after all, formless (*wuxing*); *buxiao* (have no likeness) is an alternate term for *wuxing*.

2. Cf. section 7, second passage.

3. Cf. section 11 of the *Xici zhuan* (Commentary on the Appended Phrases), Part One, of the *Yijing* (Classic of changes), which reads in part: "Of those who made things available and extended their use to the utmost and who introduced ready devices [*chengqi*] and made them of benefit to all the world [all under Heaven], none are greater than the sages" (Lynn, *The Classic of Changes*, 66; see *Zhouyi zhengyi* [Correct meaning of the *Changes of the Zhou*], 7:29b). *Chengqi*, "ready device," literally means a "completed vessel," that is, the perfect man capable of assuming sovereignty over all under Heaven.

SECTION 68

One good at being a warrior is not warlike.

"Warrior" refers to a commander of troops. "Warlike" describes a fondness for aggressive action.

One good at warfare avoids anger.

Such a one holds back and does not go first, joins in but does not start the singing.[1] Thus he has nothing to do with anger.

One good at conquering the enemy does not join with him.

"Join with" means "contend with."

One good at using men places himself below them. We refer to these as the virtue in not fighting and the power in using men.

If one attempts to use men but does not place himself below them, their power will not be used.[2]

Such a one is called a companion worthy of Heaven, the ultimate attainment achieved for all time.

NOTES

1. Cf. section 10, fifth passage.

2. Cf. section 66.

SECTION 69

Military specialists have a saying: "I dare not play the host but instead play the guest. I dare not advance an inch but instead retreat a foot." In other words, campaign in such a way that there is no campaign,

> *The other side then will not stop you.*

Push up your sleeve so that no arm is exposed; wield weapons in such a way that no weapons are involved; and lead in such a way that you face no opponent.[1]

> *"Campaign" [xing] means "deploy troops." In other words, because of his humility, deference, pity, and kindness, one dares not commit his people first [to battle]. When he uses troops, it seems that he "campaign[s] in such a way that there is no campaign; push[es] up [his] sleeve so that no arm is exposed, wield[s] weapons in such a way that no weapons are involved; and leads in such a way that [he] face[s] no opponent." This means that there is no one there to grapple with.*

There is no greater disaster than having no viable opponent. If one has no viable opponent,[2] he will soon lose my [the *Laozi*'s] treasures.

> *In other words, because of pity, kindness, humility, and deference, one should not wish to seize such power that he will have no viable opponent among all under Heaven. If one cannot stop but finishes up by having no viable opponent, however, I consider this to be the greatest disaster of all. "Treasures" refers to the "three treasures."[3] Thus the text says, "he will soon lose my treasures."*

Thus, when they raise armies that are equally matched, he who feels pity will be the victor.

> *Kang [grapple with, oppose] means "raise." Ruo [like] means dang [equally matched]. The one who feels pity, sure to exercise mercy, will not pursue advantage but do everything to avoid harm. Thus he will surely be the victor.*

NOTES

1. The order of this passage has been altered to correspond to that of Wang's commentary. See Lou, *Wang Bi ji jiaoshi*, 175 n. 4; and Wagner, "The Wang Bi Recension of the *Laozi*," 52.

2. "No viable opponent" translates *wu di*. Although the base text reads *qing di*, which would result in: "There is no greater disaster than underestimating one's opponent. If one underestimates his opponent, he will soon lose my treasures," both Mawangdui texts and Fu Yi's composite edition have *wu di*. See *Mawangdui Hanmu boshu*, 110. Since Wang's commentary follows the reading *wu di*, I have altered the base text accordingly. It is likely that *qing di* (underestimate one's opponent) was, at some early time, substituted for *wu di* by a scribe who read *wu di* as the putative "think one has no opponent," but this is to misunderstand the argument involved: Once all viable opponents are eliminated by force, one would, to be sure, control all under Heaven, but such control, built entirely on force, would be the greatest possible disaster.

3. Cf. section 67, second passage. The "three treasures" are "kindness," "frugality," and "no presumption that [one] is first among all under Heaven."

SECTION 70

My words are very easy to understand, very easy to practice, yet none among all under Heaven can understand them, and none can practice them.

> *You can understand them without even leaving your gate or peering out your window.*[1] *Thus the text says they "are very easy to understand." You can fulfill them without taking any deliberate action.*[2] *Thus the text says they are "very easy to practice." But people are deluded by greed, so the text says, "none . . . can understand them," and people are befuddled by honor and reward,*[3] *so the text says, "none can practice them."*

My words have a progenitor, and my undertakings have a sovereign.

> *"Progenitor" refers to the progenitor of the myriad things, and "sovereign" refers to the master of the myriad affairs.*[4]

It is just because there is no understanding of this that they do not understand me.

> *Because his words have this progenitor and his undertakings have this sovereign, if there were people who understood how this is so, they could not help but understand him.*[5]

As long as those who understand me are rare, someone like me is precious.

*It is because I am so profound that those who understand me are
so rare. The more rare understanding of me is, the more I am
without counterparts [pi]. Thus the text says: "As long as those
who understand me are rare, someone like me is precious."*

Thus it is that the sage wears coarse woolen cloth but harbors
jade in his bosom.

*To wear woolen cloth means to be one with the very dust. To
harbor jade in his bosom means to treasure his authenticity
[zhen].⁶ The reason the sage is so hard to recognize is that he is
one with the very dust and does not stand out in any way. He
harbors jade in his bosom and does not compromise it. Thus it is
that he is hard to recognize and so becomes precious.*

NOTES

1. Cf. section 47, first passage.

2. Cf. Wang's commentary to section 47, last passage.

3. Cf. Wang's commentary to section 20, third passage.

4. The base text reads "myriad things" a second time, but, to conform to the text of the *Laozi*, it probably should read "myriad affairs"
("undertakings" and "affairs" both translate *shi*). "Progenitor" and
"master" both refer to the Dao. See section 4.

5. Both Hatano Tarō and Lou Yulie, believing that the text here is
corrupt and does not make sense, suggest various emendations, but I
think the text is perfectly clear as it stands. See Hatano, *Rōshi Dōtokukyō
kenkyū*, 414–15; and Lou, *Wang Bi ji jiaoshi*, 177 n. 5.

6. Cf. paragraph 3 of Wang's commentary to section 4.

SECTION 71

To regard not knowing as knowing is the highest; not to regard
knowing as knowing is harmful.¹

*If one does not recognize that knowledge is not worth relying
on, it will result in harm.*

It is only by regarding harm as harm that one suffers no harm.
That the sage suffers no harm is because he regards harm as
harm, and this is why he suffers no harm.

[To regard harm as harm means that one recognizes how it is harm.][2]

NOTES

1. This laconic passage has bedeviled many a commentator and translator, but Wang's commentary, considered in the context of the obvious putative verbal constructions of the next passage, indicates that the *zhi* (know) and *buzhi* (not know) of the first passage should be understood also as putative verbs: "To attribute knowing to not knowing is the highest; not to attribute knowing to knowing is harm." In other words: "To know that not to know is true knowing, this is the highest kind of knowledge; not to know that knowing is mere knowing (and false), this is the most harmful kind of knowledge." This rendering also fits with the two Mawangdui versions of the passage: "To regard not knowing as knowing is best; not to know this is harm" (*Mawangdui Hanmu boshu*, 111). For a survey of other solutions, see Hatano, *Rōshi Dōtokukyō kenkyū*, 417; and Henricks, *Lao-Tzu Te-Tao Ching*, 168.

2. The text in parentheses occurs only in the *Daode zhenjing jizhu* (Collected commentaries on the *True Classic of the Way and Virtue*), 10:8 (17078A).

SECTION 72

If the common folk do not fear force, then such great force will arrive that there will be no restricting them to the boundaries within which they should dwell, no satisfying them within the limits in which they should live.

> *Where they should dwell means in purity, quietude, and freedom from deliberate action. Where they should live means in humility, deference, and freedom from arrogance. If one [the sovereign] should abandon purity and quietude and instead practice greed, should desert humility and deference and instead rely on power, people will make trouble, and the common folk will fall into deviant behavior. This means that power is no longer able to control the common folk.*[1] *When the common folk are*

unable to bear the weight of this power any longer, they will burst forth in flood from top to bottom [from the boundaries and limits within which they should live], which means that the terrible judgment of Heaven is about to arrive. Thus the text says: "If the common folk do not fear force, then such great force will arrive that there will be no restricting them to the boundaries within which they should dwell, no satisfying them within the limits in which they should live." In other words, the power of force cannot be relied on.

It is just because one is insatiable

That is, if one does not find contentment with his own lot.

That there is no satisfying him.

It is because one does not find contentment with his own lot that nothing in all under Heaven will ever satisfy him.[2]

Therefore what the sage himself knows he does not himself reveal.

He does not himself reveal what he knows, that is, how to use the searchlight of his brightness and how to exercise his power.[3]

He cherishes himself but does not value himself.

If he valued himself, he would have to place restrictions on the boundaries within which people should dwell and enforce limits of satisfaction within which they should live.

Thus he rejects the one and keeps the other.[4]

NOTES

1. Cf. section 17, third and fourth passages.

2. Qian Zhongshu's note on this passage helped with the interpretation. Qian reads the text of the *Laozi* as if it meant: "It is just because one never has enough [*yan*] that he never gets enough [*yan*]," which brings out the different but associated meanings of *yan* as "satisfaction" and "satiation/disgust." See Qian, *Guanzhui bian*, 3:459.

3. Cf. section 58, especially the last passage.

4. That is, he does nothing to put his rulership in jeopardy, which means he cherishes himself, and places no value on his own person, which means he dwells in purity and quietude and lives in humility and deference.

SECTION 73

If one's bravery is expressed in daring, he will be killed.

Such a one will surely not get to die a natural death.[1]

If one's bravery is expressed in not daring, he will live.

Such a one will surely enjoy the full span of his years.

But both these two sometimes result in benefit, sometimes in harm.

Both involve bravery, but those who exercise bravery differ, so the same benefit or harm does not always occur. Thus the text says they might "sometimes result in benefit, sometimes in harm."

When Heaven is cruel, who understands why? Therefore even the sage finds this fraught with danger.

Shu [which one] means shei [who]. In other words, who is able to understand Heaven's intentions? It is only the sage.[2] *However, because even the sage with his perspicacity finds bravery expressed in daring to be fraught with danger, how much more true this should be for those who lack the perspicacity of the sage yet want to rush right into it! This is why the text says that "even the sage finds this fraught with danger."*

The Dao of Heaven is such that one excels at winning without contending.

It is exactly because one [the sage ruler] does not contend that none among all under Heaven can contend with him.[3]

He excels at making people respond without speaking.

Compliance means good fortune, and opposition means misfortune.[4] *This is how "he excels at making people respond without speaking."*

He spontaneously attracts without summoning.

As he takes a low position, the people gravitate to him naturally.[5]

He excels at planning while utterly at ease.

Because Heaven reveals good fortune and misfortune by hanging images [in the sky],[6] *the plans that he sets are verified before things actually happen. When secure, he does not forget danger, and he makes plans while things are still in the premanifest [weizhao] stage.*[7] *Thus the text says: "He excels at planning while utterly at ease."*

The net of Heaven spreads far and wide. Though its mesh is coarse, it never loses anything.

NOTES

1. Cf. section 42, last passage.

2. Both Hatano Tarō and Lou Yulie cite evidence that the base text of Wang's commentary is corrupt, and both suggest that the quotation of this passage in Zhang Zhan's (fl. ca. 340–400) commentary to the *Liezi* (Sayings of Master Lie) (fourth century C.E., but containing earlier material) is the reliable reading, so that is the text translated here. For the text as quoted in the *Liezi*, see *Liezi*, 6:214C. For textual scholarship on this passage, see Hatano, *Rōshi Dōtokukyō kenkyū*, 422–23; and Lou, *Wang Bi ji jiaoshi*, 183 n. 3.

3. Cf. section 22, last passage.

4. Cf. Wang's commentary to section 42, second passage.

5. Cf. section 28, first passage; section 32, last passage; section 61, first passage; and section 66.

6. Cf. section 11 of the *Xici zhuan* (Commentary on the Appended Phrases), Part One, of the *Yijing* (Classic of changes), which reads in part: "Heaven produced numinous things, and the sages regarded these as ruling principles. Heaven and Earth changed and transformed, and the sages regarded these as models. Heaven hung images in the sky and revealed good fortune and bad, and the sages regarded these as meaningful signs" (Lynn, *The Classic of Changes*, 66; see *Zhouyi zhengyi* [Correct meaning of the *Changes of the Zhou*], 7:29b).

7. Cf. section 64, first passage.

SECTION 74

If the common folk did not fear death, trying to use death to intimidate them would have no effect. If one caused the common folk always to fear death, there would still be those who behaved perversely, but these I could seize and put to death, so who would dare be perverse?

"Deviant and socially disruptive" is what is meant by "perverse" [ji].

There is the constant executioner who puts people to death. If one puts people to death instead of this executioner, this means that he is doing the hewing instead of the great carpenter.[1] It rarely happens that one who tries to do the hewing instead of the great carpenter does not injure his own hand.

Miscreants provoke hatred and anger in the compliant, and the cruel are detested by the people. Thus the text says: "there is the constant executioner."[2]

NOTES

1. Cf. section 28, last passage, where the "great carver never cuts."

2. This is in keeping with the basic idea of the *Laozi* that the best government is no government at all: Left to manage their own lives, the people will regulate themselves and get rid of troublemakers on their own. The common folk, perfectly in harmony with the Dao and with Heaven, are, in effect, the "constant executioner." If a ruler interferes with this and uses execution as a means to make people behave in conformity with his own fabricated standards, he is usurping the workings of the Dao, that is, of the "great carpenter" who never makes an unnatural cut. Such usurpation is bound to be counterproductive and most likely to bring disaster to the usurper.

SECTION 7 5

The reason the common folk starve is that the ruler eats too much grain tax. This is why they starve. The reason the common folk are hard to govern is that the ruler takes deliberate actions [*you-wei*]. This is why they are hard to govern. The reason the common folk take death lightly is that they place too much emphasis on life. This is why they take death lightly.[1] It is only by acting without regard for life that one becomes more of a worthy than one who values life.

In other words, the reasons for the common folk indulging in deviant behavior and the reasons for government ending in chaos always stem from the ruler and never stem from the subjects. The common folk model themselves on their ruler.

NOTES

1. That is, they indulge in behavior characterized by greed, arrogance, craving, and desire that leads to death; cf. section 50, second passage, and Wang's commentary there, especially paragraph 3.

SECTION 76

While alive, humans are soft and pliable, but, when dead, they are hard and stiff. While alive, plants, trees, and all the other myriad things are also soft and fragile, but, when dead, they are dried up and withered. Thus it is that the hard and stiff are adherents of death, and the soft and pliable are adherents of life.[1] This is why, if military power is stiff, it will not be victorious.

> *If one inflicts violence on all under Heaven though the use of stiff [i.e., strong]*[2] *military power, he will be despised by the people. Thus he surely will fail to enjoy victory.*[3]

If a tree is stiff, it will be attacked.

> *It will be imposed on by creatures.*[4]

The stiff [strong] and great occupy a position below.

> *This refers to the trunk of the tree.*[5]

The soft and pliant occupy a position above.

> *This refers to the branches.*[6]

NOTES

1. Cf. section 50, second passage.

2. "Stiff" translates *qiang*, whose original meaning is "stiff bow." A "stiff" bow, of course, is a "strong" bow.

3. Yi Shunding notes that for this passage the *Liezi* quotes the text of the *Laozi* and Zhang Zhan quotes Wang's commentary as follows: "'If military power is stiff, one [the ruler] will perish.' Wang Bi says of this: 'This is detested by the people. Thus such a one surely will not get to die a natural death.'" (*Liezi*, 3:202A). See Yi, *Du Lao zhaji*, B:16b. Hatano Tarō cites Hattori Nankaku's (1683–1759) note on this, made long before Yi Shunding's work, but does not come to a conclusion as which text is better. See *Rōshi Dōtokukyō kenkyū*, 430. Lou Yulie merely

cites Yi Shunding but concludes, in the light of the Mawangdui texts, both of which have "will not be victorious," that the *Lieʐi* reading of the *Laoʐi* and Zhang Zhan's quotation of Wang Bi can be disregarded. See *Wang Bi ji jiaoshi*, 186 n. 1.

4. "Attacked" translates *bing*, literally, "strike with a weapon," which seems the most likely interpretation, given Wang's comment. "Creatures" translates *wu*, which could include everything from termites, which bore into stiff (dried up, dead) trees as a source of food and lodging, to humans, who cut them down for firewood. *Bing* occurs in the base text; for a survey of other textual variants, see Hatano, *Rōshi Dōtokukyō kenkyū*, 430–31; for the Mawangdui texts, see Henricks, *Lao-Tʐu Te-Tao Ching*, 178.

5. "Trunk" seems more appropriate here for *ben*, which, as we have often seen, usually means "root" or "roots."

6. For this and the previous passage, cf. section 57, first passage; and section 59, penultimate passage. The "trunk of the tree" refers to the ruler, and the "branches" are his people. In these last two passages, the ruler, as tree trunk, stays free of the negative consequences of being "stiff" and "strong" by "occupying a position below," i.e., by humbling himself before the people.

SECTION   77

The Dao of Heaven, is it not like when a bow is pulled? As the high end gets pulled down, the low end gets pulled up: so those who have more than enough are diminished, and those who have less than enough get augmented.[1] The Dao of Heaven diminishes those who have more than enough and augments those who have less than enough, but the Dao of man is not like this,

> *Only if one makes his virtue conform to that of Heaven and Earth could he embrace them [the people] as the Dao of Heaven embraces them.[2] If one tried to embrace them with just an individual capacity for virtue, because such a one would have a stake in his own individual existence, he would be unable to establish equity among the people. Indeed, this would be possible only if one had no stake in his own individual existence and were absolutely free of self-interest! Only after attaining to the natural can one join his virtue to that of Heaven and Earth.*

For it diminishes those who have less than enough in order to give to those who have more than enough. Who can take his more than enough and give it to all under Heaven? It is only one who has the Dao. Thus it is that the sage acts, yet they [the people] do not depend on him,[3] and he achieves success yet takes no pride in it,[4] for he does not want to appear as a worthy [*xian*].

> *In other words, who is able to exist in fullness and yet be completely empty? Who is able to diminish those who have in order to augment those who have not? Who "merges with the brilliant, and becomes one with the very dust"?[5] Who can establish universal equity among the people? It is only one who has the Dao. Thus it is that the sage does not want to exhibit his worthiness* [xian],[6] *for by this [keeping it hidden] he establishes equity among all under Heaven.*

NOTES

1. Various interpretations of this passage have been attempted, some based on intricate details of the art of archery—whether the hand grip faces up or down, whether the bow is raised or lowered, whether the bowstring is relaxed or taut, and so on—but the most obvious and simple solution is to visualize the bow held vertically, the archer facing his target: when the archer pulls back on the bow, the top end is pulled down, and the bottom end is pulled up. I do not think the *Laozi* means anything more than that. The Dao, like the bow, suggests a steady-state system. Expansion in one direction results in contraction in another; thus the high are brought down, and the low raised. For other interpretations, see Jiao Hong, *Laozi yi* (Wings to *Laozi*), B4:28–29.

2. Cf. Wang's commentary to section 5, second passage; and section 16, eleventh passage.

3. Cf. section 2, third passage; section 10, last passage; and section 51, fifth passage.

4. Cf. section 2, fourth passage.

5. Section 4.

6. Cf. section 3, first passage.

SECTION   78

Of all under Heaven, nothing is more soft and pliable than water, yet for attacking the hard and stiff, nothing can beat it, so it is impossible to take its place.

> [Wu]yi *[no way] means* [wu]yong *[impossible], and* qi *[it] refers to water.*[1] *In other words, if one [the ruler] employed the softness and pliancy of water, no one could ever take his place.*

That the soft conquers the stiff and the pliable conquers the hard, none among all under Heaven fails to know, yet none can practice it. Therefore, according to what the sage says, he who sustains disgrace on behalf of the state is referred to as the master of altars dedicated to the soil and grain [its rightful ruler],[2] and he who sustains misfortune on behalf of the state is referred to as a sovereign for all under Heaven. These are true words that seem false.[3]

NOTES

1. Substituting *yong* for *yi* and *shui* for *qi* turns "it is impossible to take its place" into "water, it is impossible for anything to replace it."

2. Cf. section 28, fifth passage.

3. Qian Zhongshu cites the discourse of section 78 as exemplifying the mystic's tendency to use the rhetoric figures of paradox and oxymoron. See *Guanzhui bian*, 3:463–65.

SECTION   79

Bring harmony to great resentment, and some resentment is sure to remain.

> *If one has not arranged a tally [contract] clearly and, as such, allows things to reach the point where great resentment has already arrived before using virtue to restore harmony, the injury will not be healed. Thus the text says: "some resentment is sure to remain."*

How could this be considered good? This is why the sage holds the left half of the tally

> *It is by holding the left half of the tally that he prevents reasons for resentment from arising.*[1]

And does not place blame on the other party. A person of virtue concerns himself with his contracts,

A person of virtue considers his contracts carefully and does not allow resentment to arise and then place blame on the other party.

And the person of no virtue concerns himself with scrutinizing others.

"Scrutinizing" means correcting the mistakes of others.

The Dao of Heaven has no favorites but is always with the good man.

NOTES

1. For Wang, the left half of the tally was the debtor's half. The sage as ruler is the ostensible creditor, who, by custom, should hold the right half of the tally but here instead holds the left half, as if he were the debtor. This indicates that the sage treats his contract (relationship) with his people with the utmost care, concern, and humility, as if they were not responsible to him but he to them. This is another way of saying that the sage places himself beneath and behind the people; see, for example, section 66. It is interesting that the text of Mawangdui A reads "right half of the tally," but Mawangdui B reads "left half of the tally." See *Mawangdui Hanmu boshu*, 113. This suggests that even early readers/transcribers of the *Laozi* were sometimes uncertain how to interpret this passage. Hatano Tarō cites evidence from various ancient sources that the right half of the tally was traditionally the creditor's half and the left half was the debtor's, which leads him to conclude that the sage reverses the creditor-debtor relationship, as Wang Bi says, to prevent the occurrence of resentment and blame. See Hatano, *Rōshi Dōtokukyō kenkyū*, 437. For a brief survey of textual problems in and alternate readings and interpretations of this passage in English, see Henricks, *Lao-Tzu Te-Tao Ching*, 184.

SECTION 80

Let the state be small and the common folk few.

If the state were small and the common folk few, it would still be possible to revert to antiquity, but how much less likely this

would be if the state were large and the common folk many!
Thus the text centers its discussion around the small state.

Let there be military equipment for a company, then it would
not be used.

In other words, if one supplied the common folk with military
equipment only enough for a company but had no occasion to
use them, why need he ever worry that they [equipped common
soldiers] were not enough?[1]

Let the common folk take death seriously, then they would not
travel far.

If the common folk were not put to use [by the state for military
purposes], as it would only be their own persons that they trea-
sured, they would not covet goods.[2] *Thus, as they would find*
contentment where they dwelt, each would take death seriously
[not put life in jeopardy] and so not travel far.

Although they had boats and carriages, they would have no occasion to ride in them. Although they had shields and weapons,
they would have no occasion to array them for battle. Let the
people again knot cords, then they would use them.[3] They would
find their food so delicious, their clothes so beautiful, their dwell-
ings so satisfying, and their customs so delightful that, though
neighboring states might provide distant views of each other
and the sounds of each other's chickens and dogs might even be
heard, the common folk would reach old age without ever going
back and forth between such places.

There would be nothing that they craved.

NOTES

1. Wang's commentary clearly indicates how he thought the text
should be read. "Military equipment for a company" translates *shibai*
zhi qi, which has been interpreted differently by other commentators
and translators to refer either to "tens or hundreds of times the utensils/
tools [of material civilization]" or to those who have "tens or hundreds
of times the capacity/talents [of the mass of common folk]." See Jiao
Hong, *Laozi yi* (Wings to *Laozi*), B4:31–32; and Henricks, *Lao-Tzu*
Te-Tao Ching, 156. Neither of these two interpretations makes sense in
terms of Wang's commentary. In support of the military interpretation,

Lou Yulie quotes Yu Yue's (1821–1907) *Zhuzi pingyi* (Critical appraisal of the philosophers), which cites the entry for *bai* (company, literally, "one hundred men") in Xu Kai's (920–74) *Shuowen xizhuan* (Commentary attached to [Xu Shen's] *Explanations of simple and compound characters*): "In the *Laozi* it is said: '[If] there were military equipment for a company.' This refers to the equipment shared by the troops in a company and means types of military equipment" (*Wang Bi ji jiaoshi*, 191 n. 1).

2. Perhaps Wang understood the effects that military life often has on common soldiers in agricultural societies, both ancient and modern, which include an awareness of the possibility of upward social mobility and an expectation of rising material advantages.

3. Cf. section 2 of the *Xici zhuan* (Commentary on the Appended Phrases), Part Two, of the *Yijing* (Classic of changes), which reads in part: "In remote antiquity, people knotted cords to keep things in order. The sages of later ages had this exchanged for written tallies, and by means of these all the various officials were kept in order, and the myriad folk were supervised" (Lynn, *The Classic of Changes*, 80; see *Zhouyi zhengyi* [Correct meaning of the *Changes of the Zhou*], 8:8a). "Let the people again knot cords" symbolizes reversion to an ancient time of pristine simplicity and innocence.

SECTION 81

Sincere words are not beautiful.

> *Honesty* [shi] *consists of simplicity* [zhi].[1]

Beautiful words are not sincere.

> *Fundamentality* [ben] *consists of the uncarved block [pristine simplicity]* [pu].

Those who are good do not engage in disputation; those who engage in disputation are not good. Those who know are not broadly learned;

> *The ultimate consists of the One.*[2]

Those who are broadly learned do not know.[3] The sage is not acquisitive.

> *He keeps nothing as his own private property. Only this good one can be as giving as this, for he does nothing less than leave others entirely to themselves.*

The more he does for others, the more he himself has.

He is honored by others.

The more he gives to others, the more he himself possesses.

It is to him that others gravitate.

The Dao of Heaven is to provide benefit without doing harm.

Its action is always to beget and complete things.

The Dao of the sage is to act without causing contention.

*Because his are benefits provided in accordance with Heaven,
they do not provoke people to contend with one another.*

NOTES

1. Cf. Wang's commentary to section 56, third passage.

2. Cf. Wang's commentary to section 39, first passage: "One is the beginning of numbers as well as the ultimate number of things."

3. Cf. section 56, first and second passages.

PRIMARY SOURCES

Baizi quanshu 百子全書 (Complete works of all the ancient philosophers). Reprint (with new collations) of the Hubei: Chongwen shuju, 1875 edition. Changsha: Yuelu shushe, 1993.

Chen Shou 陳壽. *Sanguo zhi* 三國志 (Chronicles of the Three Kingdoms). With the commentary of Pei Songzhi 裴松之. Beijing: Zhonghua shuju, 1975 reprint of the 1959 edition.

Congshu jicheng chubian 叢書集成初編 (A collectanea of selections from collectanea, first series). Ed. Wang Yunwu 王雲五. Shanghai: Shangwu yinshuguan, 1935–39. Reprint. Beijing: Zonghua shuju, 1985.

Daode zhenjing jijie 道德眞經集解 (Collected exegesis on the *True Classic of the Way and Virtue*). Preface dated 1246. Edited by Dong Sijing 董思靖. *Daozang* No. 705.

Daode zhenjing jizhu 道德眞經集注 (Collected commentaries on the *True Classic of the Way and Virtue*). Preface dated 1229. With commentaries by Wang Bi 王弼, Heshang Gong 河上公, Emperor Xuanzong 玄宗 (Ming Huang 明皇) of the Tang 唐, and Wang Pang 王雱 (1042–76). *Daozang* No. 706.

Daode zhenjing jizhu 道德眞經集注 (Collected commentaries on the *True Classic of the Way and Virtue*). Ed. Peng Si 彭耜. *Daozang* No. 707.

Daode zhenjing qushanji 道德眞經取善集 (Selection of superlative remarks on the *True Classic of the Way and Virtue*). Preface dated 1172. Edited by Li Lin 李霖. *Daozang* No. 718.

Daode zhenjing zangshi zuanwei pian 道德眞經藏室纂微篇 (An edition of collected subtleties from the treasure house of the *True*

Classic of the Way and Virtue). Preface dated 1258. Edited by Chen Jingyuan 陳景元. *Daozang* No. 714.

Daozang. See *Zhengtong Daozang*.

Daozang zimu yinde 道藏子目引得 (Combined indices to the authors and titles of books in two collections of Taoist literature). Harvard-Yenching Institute Sinological Index Series No. 25. Reprint. Taibei: Chengwen, 1966.

Ershierzi 二十二子 (Twenty-two philosophers). 1874–77. Reprint. Shanghai: Guji chubanshe, 1985.

Fu Yi 傅奕 ed. *Daode jing gubenpian* 道德經古本篇 (An edition compiled from old manuscripts of the *Classic of the Way and Virtue*). *Daozang* No. 665.

Guo Xiang 郭象. *Zhuangzi zhu* 莊子注 (Commentary to Zhuangzi). In *Ershierzi*.

Han Fei zi 韓非子 (Sayings of Master Han Fei). In *Ershierzi*.

Hattori Nankaku 服部南郭. *Nankaku sensei bunshū* 南郭先生文集 (Literary collection of Mr. Nankaku). 1727–58 wood block ed. Reprint: *Kinsei juka bunshū shūsei* 近世儒家文集集成 series. Tokyo: Perikansha, 1985.

Heshang Gong. See Heshang Gong.

Heshang Gong 河上公. *Heshang Gong zhu Laozi Daodejing* 河上公注老子道德經 (The Heshang Gong commentary to Laozi's *Classic of the Way and Virtue*). *Daozang* No. 682.

HouHan shu 後漢書 (History of the Latter Han era). Ed. Fan Ye 范曄. 1965. Reprint. Beijing: Zhonghua shuju, 1973.

Huan Kuan 桓寬. *Yantie lun* 鹽鐵論 (Debates on salt and iron). In *Baizi quanshu*.

Jiao Hong 焦竑. *Laozi yi* 老子翼 (Wings to *Laozi*). In *Kanbun taikei*.

Jin shu 晉書 (History of the Jin era). Ed. Fang Xuanling 房玄靈 et al. Beijing: Zhonghua shuju, 1974.

Kanbun taikei 漢文大系 (Compendium of Chinese classics). Ed. Hattori Unokichi 服部宇之吉. Tokyo: Fuzambo, 1909–16. Reprint. 1972–87.

Kong Yingda 孔穎達. *Chunqiu Zuozhuan* 春秋佐傳正義 (Correct meaning of *Zuo's Commentary* on the *Spring and Autumn Annals*). In Ruan Yuan 阮元, ed. *Shisanjing zhushu*.

———. *Zhouyi zhengyi* 周易正義 (Correct meaning of the *Changes of the Zhou*). In Ruan Yuan 阮元, ed. *Shisanjing zhushu*.

Liezi 列子 (Sayings of Master Lie). With the commentary of Zhang Zhan 張湛. In *Ershierzi*.

Liji zhushu. See Zheng Xuan and Kong Yingda.

Liu Xie 劉勰. *Wenxin diaolong* 文心雕龍 (The literary mind carves dragons). Ed. Zhu Yingping 朱迎平. Shanghai: Guji chubanshe, 1987.

Liu Yiqing 劉義慶. *Shishuo xinyu* 世説新語校箋 (A new account of tales of the world, with collation and annotations). Ed. Yang Yong 楊侵. Hong Kong: Dazhong shuju, 1969. Reprint. Taipei: Minglun chubanshe, 1972.

Lou Yulie 樓宇烈, ed. *Wang Bi ji jiaoshi* 王弼集校釋 (Critical edition of the works of Wang Bi with explanatory notes). 2 vols. Beijing: Zhonghua shuju, 1980.

Lu Deming 陸德明. *Jingdian shiwen* 經典釋文 (Explication of the texts of the classics). In *Congshu jicheng chubian*.

Lunyu 論語 (Analects). *Lunyu yinde* 論語引得 (A concordance to the *Analects* of Confucius). Harvard-Yenching Institute Sinological Index Series Supplement No. 16. Reprint. Taibei: Chengwen, 1966.

Ma Qichang 馬其昶. *Laozi gu* 老子故 (Exegesis of the ancient meaning of *Laozi*). In Yan Lingfeng, ed., *Wuqiubeizhai Laozi jicheng xubian*.

Mawangdui Hanmu boshu [yi]: Laozi 馬王堆漢墓帛書[壹]: 老子 (Silk manuscripts from the Han tomb at Mawangdui, Vol. 1: *Laozi*). Ed. Guojia wenwuju guwenxian yanjiushi 國家文物局古文獻研究室 (National Bureau of Cultural Objects: Ancient Finds Research Unit). Beijing: Wenwu chubanshe, 1980.

Mengzi 孟子 (Mencius). *Mengzi yinde* 孟子引得 (A concordance to the *Mencius*). Harvard-Yenching Institute Sinological Index Series Supplement No. 17. Reprint. Taipei: Chengwen, 1966.

Mozi 墨子. In *Ershierzi*.

Ōta Shiryū 太田子龍. *Ō chū Rōshi kokujiben* 王注老子國字辯 (*Laozi* with *Wang's Commentary* rendered into Japanese). In Yan Lingfeng, ed., *Wuqiubeizhai Laozi jicheng xubian*.

Quan HouHan wen 全後漢文 (Complete prose of the Latter Han era). In Yan Kejun 嚴可均, ed., *Quan Shanggu Sandai Qin Han Sanguo Liuchao wen*.

Quan Sanguo wen 全三國文 (Complete prose of the Three Kingdoms era). In Yan Kejun 嚴可均, ed., *Quan Shanggu Sandai Qin Han Sanguo Liuchao wen*.

Quan Tang wen 全唐文 (Complete prose of the Tang era). Ed. Dong Gao 董誥 et al. 5 vols. 1814 wood block ed. Reprint. Shanghai: Guji chubanshe, 1990.

Ruan Yuan 阮元, ed. *Shisanjing zhushu* 十三經注疏 (Commentaries and subcommentaries on the thirteen classics). 1815 woodblock ed. Reprint. Taibei: Yiwen yinshuguan, 1955.

Sanguo zhi. See Chen Shou.

Sibu beiyao 四部備要 (Essential works from the four categories of literature [Confucian classics, philosophy, history, and belle-lettres]). Ed. Gao Yehou 高野侯 et al. Shanghai: Zhonghua shuju, 1927–31. Reprint. Taipei: Zhonghua shuju, 1965.

Sima Qian 司馬遷. Shiji 史記 (Records of the Grand Historian). 1959. Reprint. Beijing: Zhonghua shuju, 1975.

Su Che 蘇轍. *Daode zhenjing zhu* 道德眞經注 (Commentary on the *True Classic of the Way and Virtue*). *Daozang* No. 691.

Sunzi 孫子 (The sayings of Master Sun [*Sunzi bingfa* 兵法 (Master Sun's art of war)]. In *Ershierzi*.

Usami Shinsui 宇佐美灊水. *Ō chū Rōshi Dōtoku shinkyō* 王注老子道德眞經 (Wang's commentary on Laozi's *True Classic of the Way and Virtue*). In Yan Lingfeng, ed., *Wuqiubeizhai Laozi jicheng chubian*.

Wang Bi 王弼. *Laozi Daodejing zhu* 老子道德經注 (Commentary on Laozi's *Daodejing*). In vol. 1 of of Lou Yulie, ed., *Wang Bi ji jiaoshi*.

———. *Laozi Daodejing zhu* 老子道德經注 (Commentary on Laozi's *Daodejing*). *Daozang* No. 690.

———. *Laozi weizhi lilue* 老子微指例略 (General remarks on the subtle meaning of the *Laozi*). *Daozang* No. 1245.

———. *Laozi zhilue* 老子指略 (Outline Introduction to the *Laozi*). In vol. 1 of of Lou Yulie, ed., *Wang Bi ji jiaoshi*. Beijing: Zhonghua shuju, 1980.

———. *Zhouyi lueili* 周易略例 (General remarks on the Changes of the Zhou). In vol. 2 of Lou Yulie, ed., *Wang Bi ji jiaoshi*.

———. *Zhouyi zhu* 周易注 (Commentary on the *Changes of the Zhou*). In vols. 1 and 2 of Lou Yulie, ed., *Wang Bi ji jiaoshi*.

Wang Xianqian, ed., *Xunzi jijie* 荀子集解 (Collected exegesis on the *Sayings of Master Xun*). Changsha: n.p., 1891. Reprint. Taipei: Shijie shuju, 1968.

Wei Yuan 魏源. *Laozi benyi* 老子本義 (The original meaning of the *Laozi*). *Congshu jicheng chubian*.

Wenxuan. See Xiao Tong.

Xiao Tong 蕭統 ed. *Wenxuan Li Shan zhu* 文選李善注 (Selections of refined literature, with the commentary of Li Shan). *Sibu beiyao*.

Xiaojing. See Xing Bing.

Xing Bing 邢昺, et al. *Xiaojing zhushu* 孝經注疏 (Commentaries and subcommentaries on the *Cloassic of Filial Piety*). In Ruan Yuan 阮元, ed. *Shisanjing zhushu*.

Xu Shen 許慎. *Shouwen jiezi Duan zhu* 説文解字段注 (Explanations

of simple and compound characters, with the commentary of Duan [Yucai 玉裁]. *Sibu beiyao.*

Xunzi 荀子 (The sayings of Master Xun). *Ershierzi.*

Yan Lingfeng 嚴靈峰, ed. *Mawangdui boshu Laozi shitan* 馬王堆帛書老子試探 (Exploration of the silk manuscripts of the *Laozi* from Mawangdui). Taipei: Heluo tushu chubanshe, 1976.

———, ed. *Wuqiubeizhai Laozi jicheng chubian* 無求備齋老子集成初編 (Collectanea of works on the *Laozi* from the "Has Everything with Nothing to Seek Studio," first series). Taibei: Yiwen yinshuguan, 1965.

———, ed. *Wuqiubeizhai Laozi jicheng xubian* 無求備齋老子集成續編 (Collectanea of works on the *Laozi* from the "Has Everything with Nothing to Seek Studio," second series). Taibei: Yiwen yinshuguan, 1970.

Yan Kejun 嚴可均, ed. *Quan Shanggu Sandai Qin Han Sanguo Liuchao wen* 全上古三代秦漢三國六朝文 (Complete prose of remote antiquity, the three eras, Qin, Han, Three Kingdoms, and Six dynasties). 1893. Reprint. Beijing: Zhonghua shuju, 1985.

Zheng Xuan 鄭玄 and Kong Yingda 孔穎達. *Liji zhushu* 禮記注疏 (Record of rites, with commentary and sub-Commentary) In Ruan Yuan 阮元, ed., *Shisanjing zhushu.*

Zhengtong Daozang 正統道藏 (The Zhengtong era [1436–49] edition of the *Daoist Canon*). Shanghai: Shangwu yinshuguan, 1923–26. Reprint. Taipei, 1962. Reduced-size reprint Taipei: Yiwen yinshuguan, 1977.

Zhuangzi yinde 莊子引得 (A concordance to *Chuang-tzu*). Harvard-Yenching Institute Sinological Index Series Supplement No. 20. Cambridge: Harvard University Press, 1956.

SECONDARY SOURCES IN CHINESE AND JAPANESE

Fukunaga Mitsuji 福永光司, trans. *Rōshi* 老子. 2 vols. Tokyo: Asahi bunko, 1978.

Gao Lingfen 高齡芬. *Wang Bi Laoxue zhi yanjiu* 王弼老學之研究 (Research on the place of Wang Bi in *Laozi* studies). Taipei: Wenjin chubanshe, 1992.

Guo Lihua 郭梨華. *Wang Bi zhi ziran yu mingjiao* 王弼之自然與名教 (Wang Bi's relation to naturalism and ethical formalism). Taipei: Wenjin chubanshe, 1995.

Hatano Tarō 波多野太郎. *Rōshi Dōtokukyō kenkyū* 老子道德経研究 (Researches on the *Classic of the Way and Virtue* of Laozi). Tokyo: Kokusho kankōkai, 1979.

———. "*Rōshi Ō chū kōsei* 老子王注校正" (Critical edition of Wang's commentary on the *Laozi*), *Yokohama shiritsu daigaku kiyō* 横浜市立大学紀要 (Bulletin of Yokohama Municipal University), ser. A, 1, no. 8 (July 1952): 1–150; ser. A, 3, no. 15 (March 1953): 1–157; ser. A, 8, no. 27 (October 1954): 1–205.

Hou Wailu 侯外盧, Zhao Jibin 趙紀彬, Du Guoxiang, 杜國庠, and Qiu Hansheng 邱漢生. *Zhongguo sixiang tongshi* 中國思想史通史 (General history of Chinese thought). Vol. 3: *Wei Jin Nanbeichao sixiang* 魏晉南北朝思想 (Thought of the Wei, Jin, and Southern and Northern Dynasties eras). 1957. Reprint. Beijing: Renmin chubanshe, 1992.

Itano Chōhachi 板野長八. "*Ka An Ō Hitsu no shisō* 何晏王弼の思想" (The thought of He Yan and Wang Bi)," *Tōhō gakuhō* 東方学報 14:1 (1943), 43–111.

Jiang Xichang 蔣錫昌. *Laozi jiaogu* 老子校詁 (Collations and glosses to *Laozi*). Shanghai: Shangwu yinshuguan, 1937. Reprint. Taipei: Dongsheng chuban shiye gongsi.

Kitahara Mineki 北原峰樹. *Rōshi Ō Hitsu chū sakuin* 老子王弼注索引 (Concordance to Wang Bi's commentary to *Laozi*). Kitakyūshū: Kitakyūshū Chūgoku shoten, 1987.

Lu Wenhu 陸文虎. *Guanzhui bian Tanyi lu suoyin* 管錐編談藝錄索引 (Index to [Qian Zhongshu's] *The Pipe-awl Collection* and *Recorded Discussions of Literary Art*). Beijing: Zhonghua shuju, 1994.

Meng Wentong 蒙文通. *Jingxue jueyuan* 經學抉原 (Origins of Confucian classical scholarship). Taibei: Shangwu yinshuguan, 1966.

Noma Kazunori 野間和則. "*Ō Hitsu ni tsuite: Rōshi chū wo megutte* 王弼について：老子注をめぐって" (Concerning Wang Bi: Taking a turn through the *Laozi* commentary), *Tōhō shūkyō* 東方宗教 59 (May 1982): 66–83.

Ogawa Tamaki 小川環樹. *Rōshi* 老子 (*Laozi*). 1973. Reprint. Tokyo: Chūkō bunko, 1995.

Qian Mu 錢穆. *Zhuang Lao tongbian* 莊老通辨 (General insights into *Zhuangzi* and *Laozi*). 1971. Reprint. Taipei: Sanmin shuju, 1973.

Qian Zhongshu 錢鍾書. *Guanzhui bian* 管錐編 (The pipe-awl collection). 4 vols. Beijing: Zhonghua shuju, 1979.

Sawada Takio 沢田多喜男. "*Rōshi Ō Hitsu chū kōsatsu ippan* 老子王弼注考察一斑" (A cursory examination of Wang Bi's *Commentary* on the *Laozi*). *Tōyō bunka* 東洋文化 62 (March 1982): 1–28.

Shima Kunio 島邦男. *Rōshi kōsei* 老子校正 (Establishing a critical edition of the text of the *Laozi*). Tokyo: Kyūko shoin, 1973.

Tang Yongtong 湯用彤. *Wei Jin xuanxue lungao* 魏晉玄學論稿 (Preliminary discussions of the learning of the mysterious of the Wei-Jin period). Beijing: Jenmin chubanshe, 1957.

Tao Hongqing 陶鴻慶. *Du zhuzi zhaji* 讀諸子札記 (Reading notes on the philosophers). Taipei: Shijie shuju, 1962 reprint of the Shanghai: Zhonghua shuju, 1919 edition.

Wang Xiaoyi 王曉毅. *Wang Bi pingzhuan* 王弼評傳 (Critical biography of Wang Bi). Nanjing: Nanjing daxue chubanshe, 1996.

Wang Zhiming 王志銘, ed. *Laozi weizhi lilue Wang Bi zhu zongji* 老子微指例略王弼注總輯 (General introduction to the subtle profundities of the *Laozi*: A comprehensive critical edition of the Wang Bi Commentary). Taibei: Tongxing chuban shiye, 1980.

Weng Dujian 翁獨健, ed. *Daozang zimu yinde* 道藏子目引得 (Combined indices to the authors and titles in two collections of Taoist literature). Harvard-Yenching Institute Sinological Index Series No. 25. Peking: Yenching University, 1935. Reprint. Taipei: Cheng-wen, 1966.

Yi Shunding 易順鼎. *Tu Lao zhaji* 讀老札記 (Reading notes on *Laozi*). In Yan Lingfeng, ed., *Wuqiubeizhai Laozi jicheng chubian*.

Yü Yingshi 余英時. "*Mingjiao weiji yu Wei Jin shifeng di zhuanbian* 名教危機與魏晉士風的轉變" (The crisis of ethical formalism and the changing lifestyle of intellectuals of the Wei-Jin Period). In Yü Yingshi, *Zhongguo zhishi jieceng shilun* 中國知識階層史論 (Historical studies of the Chinese intellectual class), 333–37. Taibei: Lianjing chuban shiye gongsi, 1980

Zhang Chengqiu 張成秋. *Laozi Wang Bi xue* 老子王弼 (Studies on *Laozi* and Wang Bi). Taipei: Lao Zhuang Xuehui: 1992.

WORKS IN WESTERN LANGUAGES

Bergeron, Marie-Ina. *Wang Pi: Philosophe de non-avoir*. Taibei/Paris: Ricci Institute, 1986.

Boltz, William G. "The *Lao-tzu* Text that Wang Pi and Ho-shang Kung Never Saw," *Bulletin of the School of Oriental and African Studies* 48, no. 5 (1985): 493–501.

———. "The Religious and Philosophical Significance of the 'Hsiang Erh' *Lao Tzu* in the Light of the *Ma-wang-tui* Silk Manuscripts," *Bulletin of the School of Oriental and African Studies* 45, no. 1 (1982): 95–117.

————. "Review of *A Translation of Lao T̲u's Tao Te Ching and Wang Pi's Commentary* by Paul J. Lin," *Journal of the American Oriental Society* 100, no. 1 (1980): 84–86.

————. "Textual Criticism and the Ma Wang Tui *Lao-t̲u*," *Harvard Journal of Asiatic Studies* 44, no. 1 (1984): 185–224.

Chan, Alan K. L. *Two Visions of the Way: A Study of the Wang Pi and the Ho-shang Kung Commentaries on the Lao-T̲u*. Albany: State University of New York Press, 1991.

Chan, Wing-tsit. "The Evolution of the Neo-Confucian Concept *Li* as Principle," *Tsing Hua Journal* n. s. 4, no. 2 (February 1964): 123–38. Reprinted in idem, *Neo-Confuciansim, Etc.: Essays by Wing-tsit Chan*, 45–87.

————. "Review of *A Translation of Lao T̲u's Tao Te Ching and Wang Pi's Commentary* by Paul J. Lin," *Philosophy East and West* 29, no. 3 (1979): 357–60.

————, trans. *The Way of Lao T̲u*. Indianapolis: Bobbs-Merrill, 1963. Reprint. 1981.

Chang, Chung-yue. *The Metaphysics of Wang Pi (226–249)*. Ann Arbor: University Microfilms International, 1979.

Duyvendak, J. J. L., trans. *Tao Te Ching: The Book of the Way and Its Virtue*. London: John Murray, 1954.

Erkes, Eduard, trans. *Ho-shang Kung's Commentary on Lao-tse*. Ascona: Artibus Asiae, 1958.

Goodman, Howard L. *Exegetes and Exegeses of the Book of Changes in the Third Century A. D.: Historical and Scholastic Contexts for Wang Pi*. Ann Arbor: University Microfilms International, 1986.

Henricks, Robert, G. "Examining the Ma-wang-tui Silk Texts of the *Lao-t̲u*: With Special Note of their Differences from the Wang Pi Text," *T'oung Pao* 65, nos. 4–5 (1979): 166–99.

————. "On the Chapter Divisions in the *Lao-T̲u*," *Bulletin of the School of Oriental and African Studies* 44, no. 3 (1982), 166–99.

————, trans. *Lao-T̲u Te-Tao Ching: A New Translation Based on the Recently Discovered Ma-wang-tui Texts*. New York: Ballentine Books, 1989.

Hsiao, Kung-chuan. *A History of Chinese Political thought*. Vol. 1, *From the Beginnings to the Sixth Century A.D.* Translated by Frederick W. Mote. Princeton: Princeton University Press, 1979.

Hsu, Cho-yun. *Ancient China in Transition: An Analysis of Social Mobility, 722–222 B.C.* Stanford: Stanford University Press, 1965.

Hucker, Charles O. *A Dictionary of Official Titles in Imperial China*. Stanford: Stanford University Press, 1985.

Knoblock, John, trans. *Xunzi: A Translation and Study of the Complete Works*. 3 vols. Stanford: Stanford University Press, 1988–94.

Lau, D. C., trans. *Lao Tzu: Tao Te Ching*. Harmondsworth: Penguin Books, 1963.

———, trans. *Chinese Classics: Tao Te Ching*. Hong Kong: The Chinese University Press, 1982.

Legge, James, trans. *The Chinese Classics*. 5 vols. Oxford: Clarendon Press, 1893–95. Reprint. Hong Kong: Hong Kong University Press, 1970.

Lin, Paul J. *A Translation of Lao Tzu's* Tao Te Ching *and Wang Pi's* Commentary. Michigan Papers in Chinese Studies, No. 30. Ann Arbor: Center for Chinese Studies, The University of Michigan, 1977.

Lynn, Richard J. *The Classic of Changes: A New Translation of the* I Ching *As Interpreted by Wang Bi*. New York: Columbia University Press, 1994.

Mair, Victor H., trans. *Tao Te Ching: The Classic Book of Integrity and the Way*. New York: Books, 1990.

Makeham, John. *Name and Actuality in Early Chinese Thought*. Albany: State University of New York Press, 1994.

Maspero, Henri. *Le taoïsme et les religions chinoises*. Paris: Gallimard, 1971.

———. *Taoism and Chinese Religion*. Trans. Frank A. Kerman, Jr. Amherst: University of Massachusetts Press, 1981.

Mather, Richard B. "The Controversy Over Conformity and Naturalness During the Six Dynasties," *History of Religions* 9, nos. 2–3 (1969–1970): 160–80.

———, trans. *Shih-shuo Hsin-yü: A New Account of Tales of the World, by Liu I-ch'ing*. Minneapolis: University of Minnesota Press, 1976.

Miao, Ronald C. *Early Medieval Chinese Poetry, the Life and Verse of Wang Ts'an (A.D. 177–217)*. Wiesbaden: Franz Steiner, 1982.

Nienhauser, William H., ed. *The Indiana Companion to Traditional Chinese Literature*. Bloomington: Indiana University Press, 1986.

Owen, Stephen. *Readings in Chinese Literary Thought*. Cambridge: Harvard University Press, 1992.

Robinet, Isabelle. *Les Commentaires du Tao To King jusqu'au VIIe siècle*. Mémoires de l'Institut des Hautes Études Chinoises, vol. 5. Paris: Presses Universitaires de France, 1977.

———. "Review of *Commentary on the Lao Tzu by Wang Pi* by Ariane Rump and Wing-tsit Chan," *Journal of the American Oriental Society* 102, no. 3 (1982): 573.

———. *Taoism: Growth of a Religion*. Translation and adapted by

Phyllis Brooks, with the cooperation of the author. Stanford: Stanford University Press, 1997.

Rump, Ariane, and Wing-tsit Chan, trans. *Commentary on the Lao Tzu by Wang Pi*. Monographs of the Society for Asian and Comparative Philosophy, No. 6. Honolulu: University Press of Hawaii, 1979.

Schafer, Edward H. *Pacing the Void: T'ang Approaches to the Stars*. Berkeley: University of California Press, 1977.

Schipper, Kristofer. *Le corps taoïste*. Paris: Fayard, 1982.

———. *The Taoist Body*. Trans. Karen C. Duval. Berkeley: University of California Press, 1993.

T'ang, Yung-t'ung. "Wang Pi's New Interpretation of the *I Ching* and the *Lun-yü*," Trans. Walter Liebenthal, *Harvard Journal of Asiatic Studies* 10, no. 2 (1947): 124–61.

Wagner, Rudolf G. "Interlocking Parellel Style: Laozi and Wang Bi," *Asiatische Studien* 34: 1 (1980): 18–58.

———. Wang Bi: The Structure of the Laozi's Pointers (*Laozi Weizhi Lilüe*)—A Philological Study and Translation," *T'oung Pao* 72 (1986): 92–129.

———. "The Wang Bi Recension of the *Laozi*," *Early China* 14 (1989): 27–54.

Waley, Arthur, trans. *The Way and Its Power: A Study of the Tao Te Ching and Its Place in Chinese Thought*. New York: Macmillan, 1934; reprint New York: Grove Press, 1958.

Watson, Burton, trans. *The Complete Works of Chuang Tzu*. New York: Columbia University Press, 1968

Welch, Holmes. *Taoism: The Parting of the Way*. 1957. Reprint. Boston: Beacon, 1972.

Wright, A. F. "Review of A. A. Petrov, *Wang Pi: His Place in the History of Chinese Philosophy*," *Harvard Journal of Asiatic Studies* 10, no. 1 (1947): 75–88.

Yü, Ying-shih. "Individualism and the Neo-Taoist Movement in Wei-Chin China." In Donald Munro, ed., *Indivualism and Holism: Studies in Confucian and Taoist Values*, 121–55. Ann Arbor: Center for Chinese Studies, University of Michigan, 1985.

Zücher, Erik. *The Buddhist Conquest of China: The Spread and Adaptation of Buddhism in Early Medieval China*. 2 vols. Leiden: E. J. Brill, 1959.

ai.   shade 曖

an.   obscure 暗

   safety, secure; security 安

ao.   innermost recesses of a house; shelter 奧

bagua.   eight trigrams 八卦

bai.   company 伯

baoji meixing buchang.   praise arising all at once does not last long 暴疾美興不長

baoxing.   sudden arisings 暴興

baoxing buchang.   sudden arisings do not last long 暴興不長

ben.   fundamental principle; fundamentality; original substance; root, roots; trunk 本

bi.   cover 蔽

   exhausted 弊

   object 彼

   worn out; humble I (term of self-deprecation) 敝

bianhua.   change and transformation 變化

bing.   attack, strike with a weapon; weapon 兵

boai.   broad love 博愛

bu.   (negative) is not, does not 不

buci.   does not tell [them to do so] 不辭

bushi.   does not start [them to do so] 不始

buwang.   he is not destroyed 不

buwei shi. does not serve as starting point for them 不爲始

buxiang.   inauspicious 不祥

buxiao.   have no likeness 不肖

buzhi.   not know 不知

buzhi er zhong.   stay on the mark without knowing how it is done 不知而中

cai.   human talent 才

cha.   differ 差

chang.   constancy 常

changxin.   constant heart/mind 常心

chen.   minister, servitor 臣

cheng.   complete, completion; to complete; fulfill, fulfillment 成
    designate 稱

cheng qineng.   realize its potentiality 成其能

cheng xing.   complete physical existence 成形

chengqi.   completed vessel; ready device 成器

chi.   shame 恥

chu.   stay in 處

chugou.   straw dogs 芻狗

chunai.   complete love 純愛

chunpu.   pristine simplicity; uncontaminated uncarved block 純樸

chunquan.   complete; comprehensive; perfect 純全

ci.   the female of birds 雌
    kindness; kind, the kind 慈

cong.   that which is sharp (the ears) 聰

cong shi.   undertake things 從事

dachang.   great constancy 大

dazhi.   great perfection 大致

damei.   great beauty 大美

dang.   equally matched 當

Dao.   Way 道

dao jin wu ye.   it means that the Dao has been invested in things
    道進物也？

daren.   great man 大人

datong.   permeates completely 大通

daxing.   great physical form 大形

daye.   great enterprise 大業

dazhi.   great carver 大制
    great government 大治

de.   access, attain, attainment; obtain; potential; success 得
    potency; power; virtue, Virtue, virtuous 德

de qiben.   access to his roots 得其本

Di.   The Lord 帝

diben.   base text 底本

ding.   determine 定

dong jie zhi qi suowu ze wu tong yi.   If action occurs so that it always proceeds to a state of nothingness, all things will go smoothly 動皆之所無則物通矣

dou.   (ancient measure) 豆

dui.   apertures 兌

duo.   dissipated, indolent, weak 惰

　　more; much 多

e.   censure; ugliness 惡

en.   mercy 恩

fan.   flood 汎

fanai.   broad love 汎愛

fei.   disapproval 非

feiming.   against fatalism 非命

fen.   destiny; separation 分

fenbie.   distinctions 分別

fensan yuanlun.   fallacy of division 分散眢論

fu.   (ancient measure) 釜

　　father 父

　　father; origin 甫

fugai.   cover 覆蓋

fu[bu]shi.   does not give them a start 弗[不]始

gai yan.   change places with him 改焉

ge.   cut 割

gong.   efficacy; potentiality 功

gua.   the solitary 寡

gui.   high rank, status, value; esteem, honor, prestige; self-importance 貴

　　stab 劌

guo.   achievement, result 果

guo zizhi.   the state will govern itself 國自治

Gushen.   Valley Spirit 谷神

gushi.   beginning of time 古始

he.   balance; bodily balance 和

　　conform 合

hecheng.   formed by being combined together 合成

hua.   blossoms; superficial frivolity 華

huanguan.   walled hostelry 環官[館]

huangmen shilang.   director of the chancellery 黃門侍郎

huasheng.   create things 化生

hui.   kindness, mercy 惠

　　wisdom 慧

hun er wei yi.   a single amorphous unity 混而爲一

huhuang.   dim and dark 惚恍

hunpo.   ethereal spirit and earthbound soul 魂魄

hunqi.   ethereal spirits with their pneumas 魂氣

ji.   attain/extend to the utmost; ultimate extent and subtlety of things; ultimate state 極

beneficial, benefit; relief, relieve 濟

consistent 稽

perverse, perversity 奇

jian.   bind; grab; gather in, harvest 撿

establish, well established 建

strong 健

jiang.   about to 將

jiao.   border, frontier, the ends to which things revert 徼

self-denial 矯

jidu.   absolute guilelessness 極篤

jieran.   with firm resolve 介然

jiliao.   silent and empty; vague; without form or substance 寂寥

jing.   essence, the essence of things; purity; semen 精

quiet; quietude 靜

jingxiang.   embryonic essences and images 精象

jinshang.   promotions and honors; promote the worthy 進尚

jinxiang.   direction of advance 進向

jiupin zhongzheng.   nine ranks and impartial evaluation (system) 九品鍾正

ju.   keep intact 且

ju neng.   elevate/promote the resourceful/able 舉能

juan.   section 卷

jue.   confer noble status 爵

kanbun.   classical Chinese 漢文

kang.   grapple with; oppose 抗

kangakusha.   *sinologist* 漢學者

ke.   attribute 可

kong.   empty, emptiness 空

great 孔

kuai.   broken, in pieces; piece 塊

kuiran.   all muddled togther 憒然

lai wu yi wei yong.   depends on the achievement of functionality through nothingness 賴無以爲用

le.   gladly 樂

lei.   entangled, knotted; rough 纇

li.   benefit,sharpness 利

establish, established 立

govern, oversee 涖[莅]

order; principles ; moral principles; principle (equivalent to Dao) 理

li guo.   oversee, govern the state 涖 國

profit the state 利國

li tianxia.   oversee, govern the world/empire 涖 天下

li wu.   establish the people 立物

oversee, govern the people 涖物

li zhong.   oversee, govern the mass of common folk 涖 眾

lian.   pointedness 廉

liang.   capacity 量

liangyi.   two modes (the yin and yang) 兩儀

libu lang.   director of the ministry of personnel 吏部郎

libu shangshu.   president of the ministry of personnel 吏部尚書

liqi.   sharp instruments 利器

liushu.   six graphic principles of Chinese characters 六書

lü.   power of inference 慮

mao.   appearance; visible features 貌

mei.   praise 美

meixing.   praise arising 美興

meiyu.   fine reputation 美譽

mian shen.   spare oneself from harm 免身

mianmian.   on and on 緜緜

miao.   subtlety 妙

min bubi er guo zhi ye.   the people will not hide, and the state will be governed 民不辟[避]而國治也

min bubi er guo zhi zhi ye.   the people will not hide, and the state will govern them 民不辟[避]而國治之也

ming.   basic nature; destiny; individual capacity; order, ordered 命

intelligent; perspicacious, perspicacity; that which is clear (the eyes) 明

name; reputation 名

mingfen.   names and ranks 名分

mingli.   fame and wealth; reputation and material advantage 名利

mo.   mold 模

nei.   inner, inside 內

neng.   potential; resources; the resourceful 能

nengchen.   capable minister 能臣

neng wei ci hu.   can you play the female? 能爲雌乎

neng wu ci hu.   can one not be the female/can this do without the
    female? 能無雌乎

ou.   (ancient measure) 區

painang.   bellows 排囊

paituo.   bellows 排橐

paixiao.   panpipes 排簫

pao.   bottle gourd 匏

pi.   congenial; counterpart; pair, pairing 匹

pian.   bias, biased; predilection 偏

pianwei.   biased action 偏爲

pin.   the female of animals 牝

pu.   pristine simplicity; uncarved block 樸

qi.   air; vital force 氣
    composite entity; devices; physical objects of existence; tangible
    entity; vessel 器
    it 其

qi zhi ye wei / qi zhi zhi ye wei.   taking this to its logical conclusion
    we would say 其致也胃 [謂] / 其致之也胃 [謂]

qiang.   forcing strength; stiff; strong 強

qiangwu.   harmful elements 戕物

qiao.   artfulness 巧

qing.   clarity 清
    emotions; genuine; how things are in themselves; innate
    tendencies 情

qing di.   underestimate one's opponent 輕敵

qinglian.   honesty 清廉

qingtan.   pure conversation 清談

qingyi.   pure critiques 清議

qishi haohuan.   as for things in his charge, he loves to let them
    revert 其事好還

qu.   curved; (step) aside; yielding, 曲
    include; take 取
    revoke 去

quan.   fulfill, fulfillment; whole, wholeness; keep wholeness
    intact 全

quanai.   comprehensive love 全愛

quanbie.   distinctions for all 全別

quanzhang.   completely erect 全長

que. incomplete 缺

ren. benevolence 仁

trust entirely to 任

ren zhi suowei buke buwei. what people fear one cannot but fear 人之所畏不可不畏

ren zhi suowei yi buke yi wei ren. one feared by others must also fear others accordingly 人之所畏亦不可以不畏人

ren zhi suowei wu yi wei yan. feared by others, I also should be afraid of them 人之所畏吾亦畏焉

rongguan. glorious scenery 榮觀

ruo. like 若

sangong. three dukes 三公

se. husbandry 嗇 [穡]

shan. goodness 善

shangde wuwei er wu buwei. a person of superior virtue takes no conscious action and nothing remains undone 上德無爲而無不爲

shangde wuwei er wu yi wei xiade wei zhi er you yi wei. A person of superior virtue takes no conscious action and so acts out of nothing. A person of inferior virtue takes conscious action and so acts out of something 上德無爲而無以爲下德爲之而有以爲

shangshu lang. secretarial court gentleman 尚書朗

shao. less; little 少

she. contract, shrink; gather in 歙

shei. who 誰

shen. individual existence, person 身

numinous, numinous power; spirit 神

sheng. reed mouth organ 笙

sage; sagehood 聖

shengsheng. on and on 繩繩

shenming. intelligence 神明

shi. actuality; honesty; inner substantiality; really/truly; reality; solid; substantiate 實

affair; matter; undertaking 事

agency 使

approval 是

characteristic potential; characteristic property; potential; power 勢

failure 失

shi (cont.).   grab; gather in, harvest 拾

model 式

start 始

shi zhi yi wei yong.   rely on such things as reasons for action, achieve functionality through such things 恃之以爲用

shibai zhi qi.   military equipment for a company 什伯之器

shiwei.   meddle 施爲

shizhong.   palace attendant 侍中

shu.   consideration 恕

which one 孰

shuang.   err; lose; fail 爽

shui.   water 水

shun.   comply; compliance 順

shuo.   explain 説

si.   self-interest 私

si er buwangzhe shou ye.   dead yet not forgotten, this is longevity 死而不忘者壽也

sikong.   minister of works 司空

sili xiaowei.   metropolitan commandant 司隸校尉

sixiang.   four basic images 四象

sui.   despite 雖

sun.   diminish; efface; harm 損

taiji.   great ultimate 太極

tailang.   court gentleman 臺郎

taishang.   very highest 太上

taiwei.   defender-in-chief 太尉

tan.   exclamation 歎

te.   deviate 忒

ti.   power to embody 體

tiandan.   utterly dispassionate 恬淡

Tiandi.   Lord of Heaven 天帝

tianli.   natural patterns 天理

tianxia mo neng chen ye.   none under Heaven can make it his servitor 天下莫能臣也

tong.   permeate 通

same 同

tong yu dao.   becomes one with the Dao 同於道

tou.   acquiescent 偷

tou hu   (pitch [arrows] into the pot) 投壺

tu.   earth 土

tui.   meek, compliant 隤/頽

tuo.   open-ended sack 橐

tuoyue.   bellows 橐籥

wan qie bi.   doltish and rustic 頑且鄙

wan si bi.   doltish as a rustic 頑似鄙

wang.   extinction, ruin 亡

wei.   conscious effort, purposeful action 爲
   danger 危
   false, artificial 僞
   only 唯

weishun.   yield, yielding 委順

weizhao.   premanifest, premanifest state 未兆

wen.   decoration; external pattern 文

wo.   subjective 我

wu.   matter, creatures, people, things 物
   nothing; nothingness 無

wu di.   no viable opponent 無敵

wucheng zhi yan.   a term for that for which no equivalents exist
   無稱之言

wufang.   infinite 無方

wuhua.   creative transformation of things 物化

wuming.   nameless 無名

wu quan er xing de.   people will achieve their proper span of life
   and fully realize their natures 物全而性得

wushi.   disengagement from matters; tend to matters without
   conscious purpose 無事

wusi.   free of self-interest 無私

wuwei.   no conscious effort; without purposeful action; act without
   conscious purpose; nondeliberate or nonpurposeful action
   (literally, to act out of nothing) 無爲

wu yi wei.   act out of nothing 無以爲

wuwu.   nothingness 無物

wuxing.   formless 無形

wuyi.   no way 無以
   perpetuity 無[毋]已

wuyi zhi yan.   a term for that for which there is no meaning 無義
   之言

wuyong.   impossible 無用

wuyou.   nothingness; that which has no physical existence 無有

wuzhe.   as for nothingness 無者

xi.   connection 繫
   gather in, harvest 翕

xian.   worthy 賢

xiang.   auspicious; inauspicious 祥
    image 象

xiangxing.   image the form 象[像]形

xiao.   obedience; the obedient ("filial piety") 孝

xie.   deviancy 邪

xin.   heart/mind 心
    trust 信

xing.   arising 興
    character; nature 性
    external shape; phenomenal manifestation; physical form;
    physical existence 形
    to act; campaign; human behavior; to travel; 行
    punishment 刑

xinghai.   phenomenal appearance 形骸

xingpo.   physical forms with their earthbound souls 形魄

xingti.   physical form or substance 形體

xinyan.   authentication 信驗

xu.   emptiness 虛

xuan.   mystery, the dark; mysterious 玄

Xuanpin.   Mysterious Female 玄牝

xuanxue.   learning of the mysterious 玄學

xuwu.   emptiness 虛無

yan.   satisfaction; satiation/disgust 厭
    speech 言

yang.   positive, positive principle 陽

yao.   early death 夭

yaomiao.   profoundly subtle 要妙

yezhe puye.   supervisor of receptionists 謁者僕射

yi.   change 易
    concept; righteousness 義
    idea 意
    lack everything, lost all 遺
    one; integrity 一
    purpose 以

yi xing li wu.   use rules[punishment] to govern the people 以形
    [刑]立[莅]物

yin.   cause 因
    negative, negative principle 陰

ying.   correspondence 應
    fill, filled; fill up 盈

yingpo. where your earthbound soul is protected 營魄

yong. function, purpose; functionality; human resources; to function; usefulness 用

you. actuality; being; existent; something; what exists; physical existence 有

you qishi. the matters that one attends to 有其事

you xing zhi wu. tangible entities 有形之物

you yi wei. act out of something 有以爲

youwei. conscious effort, purposeful action (literally, to act out of something) 有爲

yu. carriage 輿
compromise, compromised 渝
(conscious) desire 欲
good reputation; praise 譽
stupid 愚

yu dao tong ti. is an embodiment of the Dao 與道同體

yu de tong ti. is an embodiment of success 與得同體

yu ji tong ti. is the embodiment of the [great] ultimate 與極同體

yu neng. share in these resources 與能

yu shi tong ti. is an embodiment of failure 與失同體

yu xiangwang yu jianghu zhi dao. it is when fish forget [are rendered forgetful of] the Dao of rivers and lakes 魚相忘於江湖之道

yu yu xue. learned in learning 喻於學

yue. gather; inspect, observe; convey 閱
pipe 籥

yueyue. music pipe 樂籥

zai. carry; keep, preserve; stay; uphold 載
steward 宰

zaoxing. simple ideogram 造形

ze. model 則

zhang. aggrandize; expand, stretch 張
erect 長
outer signs 彰

zhen. actuality; authenticity; authentic existence/state 眞
constancy 貞

zheng. rectification; rectitude 正
governance 政[正]

zhenglu. correct path 正路

zhenjing zhi ji. ultimate state of authentic essence 眞精之極

zhenzheng. perfect genuineness 眞正

zhi.   basic stuff; character; simplicity 質
attain, reach; become perfectly/reach perfection 致
carve 制
control; govern 治
intention 志
know, understand 知
knowledge, knowledgeable; wisdom, wise 智
perfection 至/致
proceed 之

zhi.   stop 止
zhi zhi ji.   ultimate of government 治之極
zhili.   perfect principle 至理
zhilue.   general introduction 指略
zhiren.   perfect man 至人
zhirou zhi he.   harmony characteristic of perfect softness 至柔之和
zhishi.   point to the thing 指事
zhishu.   knowledge and methods 智術
zhizhen.   perfect authenticity 至眞
simple authenticity 質眞
zhiyu wuyu.   perfect praise is no praise 至譽無譽
zhong.   centrality; the Mean 中
(ancient measure) 鍾
zhongfu.   father of everything 眾甫
zhuan.   rely exclusively on 專
zi.   asset; goods; material; make use of 資
style-name 字
zihua.   nurtured spontaneously 自化
ziran.   natural; naturalness; Nature; the Natural 自然
ziran zhi qi.   vital force endowed by nature 自然之氣
ziran zhi xing.   natural endowment 自然之性
zunbei.   superiors and inferiors 尊卑
zuo.   engaged, manifest 作

LIST OF PROPER NOUNS

Benwu lun   本無論 (On origin in nothingness)
Bian ming lun   辯命論 (Discourse on ways to approach fate)
Bian zheng lun   辨正論 (Treatise on determining what is correct)
Bowu ji   博物記 (Record of erudition)
Cai Yan   蔡琰 (b. ca. 178)

Cai Yong   蔡邕 (132–92)

Caixing   才性 (On talent and individual nature)

Cao Cao   曹操 (155–220)

Cao Pi   曹丕 (187–226)

Cao Shuang   曹爽 (d. 249)

Chen   陳 (family name)

Chen Fan   陳蕃 (d. 168)

Chen Jingyuan   陳景元 (mid 13th century)

Chung you lun   崇有論 (Treatise in praise of actuality/being)

Chuxue ji   初學記 (Notes for the first steps in learning)

Chunqiu Zuozhuan zhengyi   春秋佐傳正義 (Correct Meaning of
    Zuo's Commentary on the *Spring and Autumn Annals*)

Dao luelun   道略論 (General discussion of the Dao)

Daode jing   道德經 (Classic of the way and virtue)

Daode luegui   道德略歸 (Summary remarks on the *Way and
    Virtue*)

Daozang   道藏 (Daoist canon)

Dayan yi   大衍義 (Meaning of the Great Expansion)

Dazongshi (The great master teacher)   大宗師

Ding Mi   丁謐 (3d century)

Dong Sijing   董思靖 (mid 12th century)

Falin (7th century)   法琳

Fan Ning   范甯 (339–401)

Fan Yingyuan 范應元 (1240–69)

Fazhe.   法者 (Legalists)

Fu   复 (Return, Hexagram 24)

Fu Gu   傅嘏 (209–55)

Fu Yi   傅奕 (554–639)

Fujisawa Tōgai   藤沢東畡 (1794–1864)

Gaoping   高平 (county in Shanyang commandery during Han era)

Guo Xiang   郭象 (d. 312)

Han Fei zi   韓非子 (Sayings of Master Han Fei)

Han Kangbo   韓康伯 (d. ca. 385)

Hattori Nankaku   服部南郭 (1683–1759)

He Jin   何進 (d. 189)

He Shao   何劭 (late 3d/early 4th century)

He Yan   何晏 (190–249)

He Zeng   何曾 (199–278)

Hong Yixuan   洪頤 (1765–1837)

Huang Xian   黃憲 (75–122)

Ji Kang   稽康 (223–62)

Jia Chong　賈充 (217–82)

Jiang　姜 (family name)

Jiao Hong　焦竑 (1541–1620)

Jingdian shiwen　經典釋文 (Explication of the texts of the classics)

Jingji zhi　經籍志 (Treatise on bibliography)

Jingzhou　荊州

Jingzhou wenxue ji guan zhi　荊州文學記官志 (Record of classical learning in Jingzhou: an official account)

Jining　濟寧 (city in southwest Shandong)

Jiu Tang shu　舊唐書 (Old history of the Tang era)

Jundao　君道 (The Dao of the sovereign)

Kong Anguo　孔安國 (2d century B.C.E.)

Kong Yingda　孔穎達 (574–648)

Lao Jian　勞健

Laozi benyi　老子本義 (Original meaning of the *Laozi*)

Laozi gu　老子故 (Exegesis of the ancient meaning of the *Laozi*)

Laozi guben kao　老子古本考 (Rearches into ancient editions of the *Laozi*)

Laozi yinyi　老子音義 (Prounciation and meaning of terms in the *Laozi*)

Li Er　李耳, style-name (*zi*) Dan　聃

Li Lin　李霖 (mid-late 12th century)

Li Shan　李善 (ca. 630–89)

Liezi　列子 (Sayings of Master Lie)

Liji zhushu　禮記注疏 (*Record of Rites*, with commentary and subcommentary)

Liu Biao　劉表 (144–208)

Liu Cong　劉琮 (late second–early 3d century)

Liu Jun　劉峻 (462–521)

Liu Tao　劉陶 (3d century)

Liu Xie　劉勰 (ca. 465–522)

Liu Yiqing　劉義慶 (403–44)

Lu Ji　陸機 (261–303)

Lu Deming　陸德明 (556–627)

Lü Huiqing　呂惠卿 (1031–110)

Lunyu shiyi　論語釋疑 (Resolving problems in interpreting the *Analects*)

Ma Guohan　馬國翰 (1794–1857)

Mao Heng　毛亨 (2d century B.C.E.)

Mawangdui　馬王堆

Mingyi   明夷 (Suppression of the Light, Hexagram 36)

Mingzhe   名者 (Nominalists)

Momoi Hakuroku   桃井白鹿 (1722–1801)

Mozhe   墨者 (Mohists)

Ōtsuki Joden   大槻如電 (1845–1931)

Pao Ding (Cook Ding)   庖丁

Pei Hui   裴徽 (late second–early 3d century)

Pei Kai   裴楷 (237–91)

Pei Songzhi   裴松之 (372–451)

Pei Wei   裴頠 (267–300)

Pei Xiu   裴秀 (224–71)

Peng Si   彭耜 (first half 13th century)

Qi   齊 (ancient state)

Qian   乾 (Pure Yang, Hexgram 1); also one of the eight trigrams

Qian Mu   錢穆

Qin Gong   秦恭 (1st century B.C.E.)

Qu dai   去代 (On ridding oneself of boastfulness)

Que Zhi   卻至 (6th century B.C.E.)

Ruan Ji   阮籍 (210–63)

Ruzhe.   儒者 (Confucians)

Sanguozhi   三國志 (Chronicles of the Three Kingdoms)

Shanyang   山陽 (commandery during Han era in Shandong)

Shen Yue   沈約 (441–513)

Sheng wu aile lun   聲無哀樂論 (On the nonemotional character of music)

Shuowen xizhuan   説文繫傳 (Commentary attached to [Xu Shen's,] *Explanations of simple and compound characters*)

Siben lun   四本論 (Treatise on the four basic relations between talent [*cai* 才] and human nature [*xing* 性])

Sima Guang   司馬光 (1019–86)

Sima Shi   司馬師 (208–55)

Sima Yan   司馬炎 (236–90)

Sima Yi   司馬懿 (179–251)

Su Che   蘇轍 (1039–112)

Suishu   隋書 (History of the Sui era)

Sun Chuo   孫綽 (314–71)

Sun Fang   孫放 style-name (*zi*)   齊莊 (b. ca. 327)

Sun Sheng   孫盛 (ca. 302–73)

Sunzi bingfa   兵法 (Master Sun's art of war)

Tiantaishan fu   天台山賦 (Rhapsody on roaming the Celestial Terrace Mountains)

Tan shi fu　歎逝賦 (Lamentation on death)

Tōjō Ichidō　東条一堂 (1776–1857)

Tong Lao lun　通老論 (General discussion of the *Laozi*)

Toutuo si beiwen　頭陀寺碑文 (Dhūta Temple stele inscription),

Tuanzhuan　彖傳 (Commentary on the Judgments)

Wang Anshi　王安石 (1021–86)

Wang Bi　王弼, style-name (*zi*) Fusi 輔嗣

Wang Bi ji　王弼集 (Collected works of Wang Bi).

Wang Can　王粲 (177–217)

Wang Chang　王暢 (mid-later 2d century)

Wang Chen　王沈 (3d century)

Wang Hong　王宏, style-name (*zi*) Zhengzong 正宗

Wang Ji　王濟 (ca. 240–ca. 285)

Wang Jin　王巾 (d. 505)

Wang Kai　王凱 (late 2d century)

Wang Li　王黎 (3d century)

Wang Qian　王謙 (late 2d–early 3d century)

Wang Yan　王衍 (256–311)

Wang Ye　王業 (late 2d–early 3d century)

Wei Feng　魏諷 (d. 219)

Wei Yuan　魏源 (1794–1856)

Weishi chunqiu　魏氏春秋 (Spring and autumn annals of the Wei)

Weishu　魏書 (History of the Wei era)

Weitong　通 (未 Impasse)

Weizhi　魏志 (Chronicle of the Wei era)

Wenxin diaolong　文心雕龍 (The literary mind carves dragons)

Wenxuan　文選 (Selections of refined literature)

Wenyan　文言 (Commentary on the words of the text)

Wenzhang zhi　文章志 (Treatise on letters)

Wuming lun　無名論 (On the nameless)

Wuwei lun　無爲論 (On nonpurposeful action)

Xiahou Xuan　夏候玄 (209–54)

Xiao Tong　蕭統 (501–31)

Xiaojing　孝經 (Classic of filial piety)

Xiang zhuan　象傳 (Commentary on the Images)

Xiangyang　襄陽

Xici zhuan　繫辭傳 (Commentary on the Appended Phrases)

Xin Tang shu　新唐書 (New history of the Tang era)

Xu Gan　徐幹 (170–217)

Xu Kai　徐鍇 (920–74)

Xu Jian　徐堅 (fl. ca. 700)

Xu Shen   許慎 (fl. ca. 100 A.D.)

Xun Rong   荀融 (3d century)

Xunzi (Master Xun)   荀子 (ca. 310–ca. 200 B.C.)

Yanzi (Master Yan)   晏子

Yi Shunding   易順鼎 (1858–1920)

Yiwen zhi   藝文志 (Treatise on bibliography)

Yu Liang   庾亮 (289–340)

Yu Yue   俞樾 (1821–1907)

Yuhan shan fang jiishu   玉函山房輯佚書 (Reconstruction of lost works done in the Mountain Retreat Where Jade is Harbored).

Zazhe.   雜者 (Eclectics)

Zhang Hua   張華 (232–300)

Zhang Zhan   張湛 (fl. ca. 340–400)

Zhi Yu   摯虞 (late 3d century)

Zhong Hui   鍾會 (225–64)

Zhongshan shi ying Xiyang wang jiao   鍾山詩應西陽王教 (Poems on Mount Zhong written in response to instructions received from the prince of Xiyang)

Yibian   易辨 (The *Changes* explained)

Zhouyi   周易 (*Changes* of the Zhou)

Zhouyi dayan lun   周易大衍論 (Discussion of the Great Expansion in the *Changes of Zhou*)

Zhouyi qiongwei lun   周易窮微 (On disclosing all the subtle meaning of the *Changes of the Zhou*)

Zhouyi zhengyi   周易正義 (Correct meaning of the *Changes of the Zhou*)

Zhu Pu   朱普 (1st century B.C.E.)

Zhu Zheng   朱整 (3d century)

Zhuang Zhou   莊周 (369–286 B.C.E.)

Zhuangzi   莊子 (Sayings of Master Zhuang)

Zhuzi pingyi   諸子評議 (Critical appraisal of the philosophers)

TRANSLATIONS FROM THE ASIAN CLASSICS

The Pillow Book of Sei Shōnagon, tr. Ivan Morris, 2 vols.   1967
Two Plays of Ancient India: The Little Clay Cart and the
  Minister's Seal, tr. J. A. B. van Buitenen   1968
The Complete Works of Chuang Tₜu, tr. Burton Watson   1968
The Romance of the Western Chamber (Hsi Hsiang chi), tr.
  S. I. Hsiung. Also in paperback ed.   1968
The Manyōshū, Nippon Gakujutsu Shinkōkai edition. Paper-
  back ed. only.   1969
Records of the Historian: Chapters from the Shih chi of Ssu-ma
  Ch'ien, tr. Burton Watson. Paperback ed. only.   1969
Cold Mountain: 100 Poems by the T'ang Poet Han-shan, tr.
  Burton Watson. Also in paperback ed.   1970
Twenty Plays of the Nō Theatre, ed. Donald Keene. Also in
  paperback ed.   1970
Chūshingura: The Treasury of Loyal Retainers, tr. Donald
  Keene. Also in paperback ed. 1971;   rev. ed. 1997
The Zen Master Hakuin: Selected Writings, tr. Philip B.
  Yampolsky   1971
Chinese Rhyme-Prose: Poems in the Fu Form from the Han
  and Six Dynasties Periods, tr. Burton Watson. Also in
  paperback ed.   1971
Kūkai: Major Works, tr. Yoshito S. Hakeda. Also in paper-
  back ed.   1972
The Old Man Who Does as He Pleases: Selections from the
  Poetry and Prose of Lu Yu, tr. Burton Watson   1973
The Lion's Roar of Queen Śrīmālā, tr. Alex and Hideko
  Wayman   1974
Courtier and Commoner in Ancient China: Selections from the
  History of the Former Han by Pan Ku, tr. Burton Watson.
  Also in paperback ed.   1974
Japanese Literature in Chinese, vol. 1: *Poetry and Prose in*
  Chinese by Japanese Writers of the Early Period, tr. Burton
  Watson   1975
Japanese Literature in Chinese, vol. 2: *Poetry and Prose in*
  Chinese by Japanese Writers of the Later Period, tr. Burton
  Watson   1976
Scripture of the Lotus Blossom of the Fine Dharma, tr. Leon
  Hurvitz. Also in paperback ed.   1976
Love Song of the Dark Lord: Jayadeva's Gītagovinda, tr. Barbara
  Stoler Miller. Also in paperback ed. Cloth ed. includes
  critical text of the Sanskrit. 1977; rev. ed.   1997
Ryōkan: Zen Monk-Poet of Japan, tr. Burton Watson   1977

MODERN ASIAN LITERATURE SERIES

STUDIES IN ASIAN CULTURE

COMPANIONS TO ASIAN STUDIES

INTRODUCTION TO ASIAN CIVILIZATIONS
Wm. Theodore de Bary, General Editor

NEO-CONFUCIAN STUDIES